THE OARSOME ADVENTURES OF A FAT BOY ROWER

Kevin Biggar

THE OARSOME ADVENTURES OF A FAT BOY ROWER

HOW I WENT FROM COUCH POTATO TO ATLANTIC ROWING RACE WINNER

KEVIN BIGGAR

RANDOM HOUSE
NEW ZEALAND

For more information about our titles go to www.randomhouse.co.nz

A catalogue record for this book is available from
the National Library of New Zealand

A RANDOM HOUSE BOOK
published by
Random House New Zealand
18 Poland Road, Glenfield, Auckland, New Zealand

Random House International
Random House
20 Vauxhall Bridge Road
London, SW1V 2SA
United Kingdom

Random House Australia Pty Ltd
Level 3, 100 Pacific Highway
North Sydney 2060, Australia

Random House South Africa Pty Ltd
Isle of Houghton
Corner Boundary Road and Carse O'Gowrie
Houghton 2198, South Africa

Random House Publishers India Private Ltd
301 World Trade Tower, Hotel Intercontinental Grand Complex
Barakhamba Lane, New Delhi 110 001, India

First published 2008

© 2008 Kevin Biggar

The moral rights of the author have been asserted

ISBN 978 1 86979 021 9

Random House New Zealand uses non chlorine-bleached papers
from sustainably managed plantation forests

Layout: IslandBridge
Cover photograph: Dinesh Parmar, Parmar Photography
Cover design: Anna Seabrook
Printed in Australia by Griffin Press

CONTENTS

To Mum — you told me so

PROLOGUE

This is a story about trying to find happiness. There is a strange trick to being happy. You have to think certain things, believe certain things, and hold your tongue the right way. This is the story of how I lost the trick and found it again. There's quite a bit about rowing as well.

If you are in a hurry, here are the contents of this book in around 150 words or less:

> I stop being immortal. I have a traumatic pizza-ordering experience and life becomes meaningless. I quit my job, girlfriend and house, and go live with my mother. I watch a lot of daytime TV. The *How's Life* show tells me to row the Atlantic. I team up with the original Naked Rower, we struggle to raise money, start building a boat, start training insanely. I go to the desert and come back loopy. Find a rowing partner, lose a rowing partner, find another rowing partner. Meet Hot Polish Girl with cold hands. Start the race (badly). Row into a storm. Take the lead. Lose the lead. Row. Row harder. Nothing happens. More

rowing. Hallucinations. Slowly catch up. Another storm. Neck and neck, with a week to the finish. Capsize and get thrown out of the boat. Get back in. Get to Barbados first! Protested against. Win at the protest hearing. Still living with Mum. Still mortal. Now happy.

The events described in this book actually happened, and are based on paper, video and audio diaries I kept at the time, as well as my own, inevitably faulty recollections. Some licence has been taken with the timing of minor events, to accommodate the demands of storytelling.

All the people in the book are real, although some names have been changed. The exception is the Don, who is complete fiction but represents the more robust advice and colourful views I received from several real-life characters who are best left nameless.

CHAPTER ONE

An unexpected swim

18:00, November 26, 2003
Atlantic Ocean — approximately 120nm ENE of Barbados

I have been pulling at the oars for most of the last three and a half hours. The digital clock on the bulkhead tells me that I have another ten minutes to go. This has been a long shift but not a boring one.

Behind the boat enormous waves are advancing in ranks, their crests a football field apart. Any one of them is large enough to topple a slab of Atlantic onto our little boat and drive us under. They never do, of course.

I need a wave that is a bit steeper than the rest. Here comes one now, a blue-green, undulating, watery hillock with a foot of grumpy white water on its crest. Just as it seems it is going to dump onto the boat, we start to rise up and surge forward. I give six quick strokes and then lean back with the oars out of the water and tucked in to the side of the boat. The boat starts to accelerate and I twitch the foot-steering mechanism to keep us square onto the wave. The GPS says 6 . . . 7

knots, the boat careers down the tumbling, rushing wave, and water starts to hose in through the scuppers.

After a few thrilling seconds the boat slows as the swell passes underneath. There is a brief pause, then a second powerful surge as the boil of passing white water sucks the boat along. Now the wave is gone and the boat, like large cow slapped into an uncharacteristic gallop, gratefully slows back to a plod. I start prodding the water again and wait for my heart-rate to return to normal, while around me the white water fizzes and hisses like a freshly poured Coke.

For most of the day the clear sky has been a great blue lens, taking the light and heat of the tropical sun and magnifying it to a laser. Now the sizzling red disc finally starts to quench itself into the western horizon. The air cools, the glare fades and I can take off my sunglasses and hat, wipe my forehead with the back of my wrinkled hand and enjoy the view, at least for a few minutes, while the brief tropical twilight still lingers. The relief of being out of the furnace of the day has not yet been outweighed by the fear of spending another long inky-black night in a small boat in these big seas.

As the boat rises up on the shoulders of another wave, I am treated to a brief glimpse of the vast, heaving seascape lit up green by the setting sun. There is a flash of white on the horizon. Is it a whitecap or the hull of a rowboat? The next boat in the race, *CRC*, is somewhere behind us, but we can't be sure exactly where. After chasing them for most of the last five weeks we finally muscled our noses in front only a couple of days ago. They aren't likely to be happy about that. They will be throwing everything they have at us. We have to get to the finish line in Barbados, two days away, before they catch us.

With just a few minutes left on my shift, my arms feel like over-cooked spaghetti. My head bobbles on my neck like those toy dogs in the back windows of cars. My brain, tired of being alternately rinsed in adrenaline and lactic acid, decides to abandon ship, and I start to feel a warm, disembodied floating. I don't know what it means but it is very pleasant to disconnect from the aches from my poor battered body. I probably need some sugar, and I definitely need some sleep. I haven't had my eyes closed for longer than two hours at a time in more than five weeks.

Six and a half minutes before the end of my shift I call out 'Six minutes!' to the cabin hatch in front of me. Half a minute later I call out 'Still six minutes!' The hatch springs open an inch, Jamie's signal that he is awake and that I can stop yelling. A few minutes later it opens a bit more and I can see inside. Jamie is taking a break from getting ready, pausing with his bum in the air and his face down on the mattress, trying to get a last few seconds of sleep.

'Two minutes!'

Jamie sighs and levers himself out of the hatch.

'How's it been?' he asks.

'Yeah, not too bad. Mostly above 3 knots. There's 30 seconds to go, by the way.'

A few days ago the steering broke on the other rowing position in the bow, so now we must swap places. I pull my feet out of the shoes bolted onto the foot-stretcher and roll away while Jamie quickly sits down in my seat and picks up the oars.

I step into the footwell in front of the hatch, the only place in our little rowboat that you can stand upright. I straighten up slowly, because . . . here it comes . . . ow! A strange, wrenching ache in my gut as some cramped muscles get pulled back into position and blood flows into long-compressed internal organs. Now I can stretch properly, arching my back to coax the synovial fluid back into my spinal discs.

I look out over the nodding bow to the rapidly darkening horizon. Somewhere out there lies the finish line at Barbados. Early in the morning of the day after tomorrow, that piece of horizon, which for the last six weeks has been nothing but ocean, should start to sprout solid hills, green leafy trees and white sand beaches. There, under a palm tree, I will wallow in a spa pool filled with clean, cold rum punch and chunks of fresh, crisp watermelon, while calypso music wafts from the nearby bar.

Until then I open one of the deck hatches and slop some white powder into a special large cup to make a warm, gooey, fatty milkshake. Then I pull out one of our last remaining freeze-dried meals and empty it into the thin aluminium pot. Only 'Thai chicken curry' left — not the mushy delights of 'fish pie' or the Willy Wonka extravaganza of 'roast lamb and vegetables' but it's still remarkably tasty. Now I add some water from the hand pump. Very carefully. Too much water and it turns into soup. I put the pot on the gas burner on the bulkhead.

I can't afford to muck around — I have to be back on the oars in half an hour — but this is such a pleasant time of day, and it is such a treat to be not rowing.

I reach into the cabin to pull out one of the head-lamps. The previous night it had stopped working. In my last break I had spent a few seconds scraping off the weeks of corrosion on the switch contacts. I show it to Jamie.

'See! It's working again.'

'Oh, good one.'

Then he looks past me and scowls. The bow starts to tilt down again, then more and more until we are plunging downwards like the front car on a roller coaster. But we aren't square on to the wave. As we drop and accelerate the boat begins carving to the right. The port rail gets lower and lower as the boat starts to roll. Where the starboard horizon should be is now the upturned deck of the boat, and where the deck was is now the Atlantic. It is like being in a chair that has been suddenly been twisted and tipped up. There is no time to brace.

The port rail digs in near the bow and a great slab of the Atlantic surges into the boat towards me. As I'm swept away, my outstretched, flailing hand tries to connect with the hatch to try to slap it shut the last inch. We are going over, and if enough water gets into the back cabin the boat won't right itself.

The rushing water rips the boat from my grasp and I tumble backwards. As I fall away I see the deck perpendicular to the water and continuing to roll. It looks as if it is going to land on top of me. I can't see Jamie. Then I'm thrust under the warm, dark water and I can't see anything at all.

CHAPTER TWO

The fall

When all think alike no one is thinking
— Walt Lippmann

July 2001

I am young. I have always been young. I will always be young. In fact, there is nothing the least bit mortal about me.

I have a steady relationship with a wonderful woman. I live near the centre of Auckland in a funky apartment with an enormous balcony that has views from the Harbour Bridge around to the Waitakere Ranges. I brunch at cafes where I drink decaf soy mochaccinos. Sometimes I go surfing on the weekend, at least I do when I have time — which is rarely. But there will be time for other things later. I am still young.

I work in an office in the city. The hours are long. I nearly always work until late at night, either at home or in hotels out of town during the week, and often on weekends. When I am not working I am worrying about work. Fridays I go out and drink. Partying is done at a frenetic pace in snatches between periods of stressful work assignments.

It is an exhausting, demanding lifestyle, but fortunately I am young.

I am only about 25, which I suppose is curious because I have been 25 for a while, for some years anyway, and I have no reason to expect that I won't be 25 for some years to come.

Then one day as I look in the mirror I find a grey hair. I pull it out and forget about it. A few days later there is another. Then another. I start to have strange dreams about going bald.

I go to a new gym. The trainer, a young woman, tells me that I will be doing a fitness test in which I'll run on a treadmill and they will wire me up to an ECG.

'Oh, you mean like Steve Austin at the start of *The Six Million Dollar Man*?' I suggest.

She looks at me blankly: 'Like who?'

I am chatting with a taxi driver. The radio is playing the latest boy-band hit. But it is a remake of a song that was playing just a few years ago when I was at school. 'It's a bit early for a remake, isn't it?' I say. 'That song has only just been a hit!'

The driver half glances at me through the rear-view mirror. 'Man, that song is from the mid-eighties. Anyone who's at school now wasn't even born when it first came out.'

I ring the dentist to make an appointment to get a tooth looked at. The receptionist asks me how long it has been since I was in. I guess about six months. She comes back a few seconds later: 'We changed software two years ago, Mr Biggar; it must have been before that.'

Two years ago? Is that possible? Where did the time go?

'And how old are you, Mr Biggar?'

'Let me see . . . I was born in 1969 . . . that makes me . . . thirty-two.'

Thirty-two? How did that happen?

I take a flight, and as I get on the plane I see that I am considerably older than the pilot. I am watching the All Blacks and I realise that I am older than all the players. I cannot deny it any longer. I am mortal. I am getting older. In fact, I am almost halfway through my allotted time on Earth.

But then things get much worse.

It's late one night and I have been at the pub. It's drizzling, and as I walk down the rain-slicked streets I pass a glass-fronted pizza place. The name is painted in an arc on the glass in ye olde style heavily serifed fonts. I push open the door and go in.

There is a small crowd of customers inside, all talking animatedly, their cheeks flushed from booze and sprinkled with raindrops. Behind the counter and taking up most of the wall is a blackboard that stretches up to the overheight ceiling. The blackboard lists the range of pizzas, dozens and dozens of them — maybe a hundred in all. There are all the usual — Italian, Hawaiian, Meatlovers, Chicken — and then some with more exotic ingredients — yoghurt, kiwifruit, chili, fish, banana, kangaroo, broccoli and even chocolate bars.

Fine, I'll play the game. I weigh up my options carefully. I want something a little spicy, not too rich, lots of cheese, not too weird. OK, maybe a little weird — I hate being one of those people who only order safe food when they eat out. I love tomato, so plenty of that. I don't often eat mozzarella, so maybe one with that. Hmmm, so that narrows it down to the Margherita or the Americana. Margherita or Americana?

Now I am at the front of the line. I am looking across the counter at a short, wizened man with a flamboyant moustache. He is scowling indifferently, tapping his pencil on the order pad.

'Waddya want?'

'I'll have the Pizza Americana thanks.'

'What size?'

'Regular.'

The old man snorts and shakes his head as he writes down the order, muttering to himself in a lilting Italian accent.

'Everybody orders the Americana.'

He's kidding me. How could that be? It's an absolute fluke. I want to shout at him, 'I could have chosen any of the five hundred stupid pizzas that you have up there!' But I say nothing, take my pizza and go out into the rain to think.

Look, maybe he says that to everyone just to mess up their heads. Even the people who order the Kangaroo Sweetbread and Parsley Pizza. Maybe he shakes his head and says, 'Everybody orders the Roo Guts.' Maybe.

But then it happens again. My girlfriend wants to look at houses. So I go off to look with her. I doubt whether I will be much help, as I haven't thought about houses much at all. One of the first places we see is a restored 1920s villa. I haven't thought much about villas as opposed to a more modern house or an apartment, but I have to admit that the little white picket fence does have some quaint retro appeal, and the postage stamp-sized lawn certainly sets off the bay windows. The front door opens onto a hallway with smartly polished wooden floors. I am aware that there is something of a debate over carpet vs polished floors, but I haven't thought much of it. But now I have seen polished wooden floors I think I prefer them.

Walking down the hallway I pass the children's bedrooms. Their names are on raised wooden letters on the doors: 'Benjamin' and 'Joshua'. I haven't thought about boys' names before, but if you had forced me to come up with something I would probably have chosen those two. How strange. Then I go into the dining room. There on the table is an Alessi kettle. Just like the one we have at home. I wonder idly where they got theirs. They are quite hard to find. I wander over to the bookshelf to have a nosy glance. That's funny — they have most of the same books that I have, right down to *Captain Corelli's Mandolin*. I walk out blinking into the sun. This is all a little weird. I feel like I am walking out of a house that has been designed for me.

Then we go to another place, and it's exactly the same. Except they have the red Alessi kettle, and the hard-cover *Captain Corelli's Mandolin*. How did they know what I wanted before I had chosen it myself? And what is it that is making us all spend a lot of money on the same ridiculously impractical kitchen appliances and interior design?

OK, so maybe it's a oncer. Maybe yuppies tend to have the same tastes in interior design. But as much as I try to shrug it off I can't. I start to see predetermination everywhere.

Did I really have a choice about what career I was going to have when I was growing up? Aren't we the generation that was told we could be anything? But in reality most people I know fall into one of about five occupations. It appears I have real choices, but in reality the choices have been made for me. Someone who met me at the age of five could have guessed my future and got it pretty much right.

What about that OE I did after leaving university? I could have gone anywhere in the world, right? So where did I go? Paraguay? Tashkent? Turkmenistan? Benin? No. Instead I went to the places that 99% of young New Zealanders go to — the countries that were once part of the Roman Empire. I could have saved myself the time of looking at travel guides — my decision about where to go was made two thousand years ago by Emperor Augustus.

What is worse, I realise now, much much worse, is that, with the whole world to go to, I *wanted* to go to Western Europe. It's bad enough being told what to do, but it adds another degree of horror to realise that I wanted this fate that some other people had picked out for me. This is pure frigging Matrix meets George Orwell.

The more I look the more I see that I don't really have genuine choice at all. The invisible hand of Culture is not only nudging my elbow. It has reached into my pocket, nicked my wallet and stolen my pin number. It is what I buy. It is what I wear. It is my name. It is what I had for lunch. It is what I am thinking and not thinking. It is my little bourgeois goals and dreams.

It is even my rebellion to it, because even those people rebelling against culture aren't really rebelling. Why is it that all those people who have consciously dropped out of the mainstream look self-consciously like all the other 'alternative' people. How does that happen? Do they have Alternative Lifestyle Fashion Police? Dreadlocks and beads, gang patches and tattoos — they are all just subtribes, defining themselves by where they stand in relation to the mainstream.

For months I have been stumbling on these clues and they have been spinning around in my head. Finally all the individual radioactive pieces coalesce, reach critical mass, and explode. Now I can see things as they really are. As surely as if I had taken the Red Pill, I have become detached from my world, and for the first time I can see a 10,000-foot view of my life and the forces that shape it.

I won't run away and join the circus. I won't become a witch doctor or a wizard, an All Black or an astronaut. A jewel thief or a Jedi knight. I am never going to start a rock band, or win an Olympic gold medal. The outline of my life has already been chosen for me. All that is left for me to do is fill in the colours, literally — the hue of the woodstain on the floor of the house, the shade of that damn kettle I'm going to have. But the suburb I will live in, the house I will buy, the job I will have, these are all as good as banked.

If I didn't really choose this career, do I really want it? When will the hard work and sacrifice end? Wasting a decade or two building a career when I am immortal is one thing, it's quite another when I realise that the precious seconds of my life are draining away, have already drained away.

What is my plan? What am I working for? To be a spectator of life as it goes past my office window? A few brief days of vacation each year?

When did I last think about options for my future, not in terms of sterile practicalities, but by how much they excited me? Somehow that part of my life where I get to live out my dreams has nearly ended and I haven't even noticed. I desperately want and need something more but I don't know what. I don't even know what I have the right to want. Shouldn't I be happy with what I've got?

No, there has to be more than this. I have to start again. I have to take control and live my life deliberately, make my own decisions. If such a thing is possible.

But I have no right to want any more than what I have. Only a colossal dickhead would leave his well-paying job, sell his apartment with the beautiful panoramic views, and leave his lovely girlfriend to chase after some half-arsed, unthought-out, inarticulable, immature, vague childish ambitions.

I am a dickhead. I pull the cord on the Bus of Predetermination. It jerks to a halt. I get off and watch it shake and rattle down the highway until it disappears into a cloud of its own dust. Then I am left in the eerie quiet, standing by the side of the road with my baggage and the occasional windblown clump of tumbleweed. I am in Howick.

CHAPTER THREE

'Awaken the rower within'

The top rowing self-help titles never written:
Awaken the Rower Within
Feel the Fear and Row Anyway
Think and Row Rich
The Seven Habits of Highly Effective Rowers
What Colour Is Your Rowboat?
The Rowed Less Travelled
Your E-Row-neous Zones

Imagine that you are an alien with a powerful spacecraft capable of travelling anywhere in the galaxy. Imagine that you are also in trouble with your local law-enforcement agency and need a place to lie low for a while.

You want a place that is a long way away from anywhere. Nothing as glamorous as the actual end of the galaxy, that's the first place the Space Cops will look. Your hiding place must not even be remarkable in its unremarkableness. It must be dull, without redemption. So you look at your map of the galaxy and choose an area somewhere about two-thirds of the way out along one of the spiral arms. Where the star systems have long since left the excitement of the core and have for some time been rolling on with desperate monotony.

Some hours later when you finally cut the hyperspace drives you find yourself next to a bland little solar system, just nine or so planets, including a couple of big gassy ones and one with quite pretty discs. You could hide forever in the suffocating gas giants, or in the howling winds of the red planet. But that is too exotic, too exciting — you want somewhere a bit quieter. Ahh, there it is! The third planet from the sun. It looks very quiet indeed.

Soon you are circling above it in high orbit, scanning for the most suitable spot to land. Your sensors detect high concentrations of life in the northern hemisphere, so you head for the southern, toward a cluster of three islands tucked away at the bottom of the world on the edge of a vast, desolate ocean. You choose to land in a small city near the top of the northern island, but not near the city centre. Instead you touch down in one of the quieter areas far to the southeast, in one of the rambling dormitory suburbs that carpet all sides of the city for hundreds of square kilometres.

The place you have chosen is called Pakuranga. Pakuranga is a sleepy place where the schools are good, the people are pleasant, and for the most part they spend their lives commuting, breeding, watching the soaps on wide-screen TVs, selling Amway to each other and twitching curtains.

Surely now you can relax? Surely now you are safe? Aren't you lost in oblivion, in the most suburban of suburbs in a city of suburbs, in a country that is in the suburbs of the world in a planet that is in the suburbs of the galaxy?

No. Not quite.

For two suburbs and eight sets of traffic lights away from Pakuranga lies Howick.

Howick must be the only suburban centre of Auckland where it is possible (even desirable) to do a U-turn on the main street on a Friday night. Howick makes Pakuranga look exciting. Pakuranga is where people from Howick go to party. This is where I have returned.

I have moved to my mother's house in a dead-end street in a quiet corner of Howick. It is, for all intents and purposes, the End of the Universe.

I lie on a bed as if I have just fallen backwards from a ladder. My eyes are glazed and unfocused, my mouth is open. My hands are pressed down into a worn pink duvet with frilly tassels. I am pinned down by a combination of despair and lethargy.

I am in what used to be my sister's room, but she has long since grown up and moved overseas. The room has been kept like a time capsule of early-nineties teenager. There is even a poster of George Michael sniffing the inside of his leather jacket. On the top shelf, above the books on ponies, are dozens of garishly coloured soft toys staring down at me with lidless eyes, grinning ghoulishly.

But I am staring at the ceiling, the better to concentrate while I try to count my miseries. I think it is seven or eight, though I suspect I might be doing some double counting:

1   I am living in Howick.

2   I am living with my mother in Howick.

3   I am 32 years old and therefore only have my middle age and a long, doddering descent into decrepitude and senility in front of me.

4   I am 32 years old, living in Howick with my mother and her obscenely fluffy white cat called Chantelle who is incontinent and has deep personality problems.

5   I do not have a girlfriend, though I just left a good one.

6   I do not have a job, though ditto.

7   Life is Empty and Meaningless.

Superman and I have at least one thing in common. We are allergic to our birthplaces. Superman was born on Krypton, but in the presence of green glowing Kryptonite he would lose his powers and become weak and feeble. Similarly Howick, the place where I was raised, has become toxic to me. I cannot stand its sinister quiet. I cannot stand its suffocating sameness. Nothing ever happens here. It is a place of frustration and isolation. A man could die trying to find a decent cappuccino here.

Nor is it helpful being in the place where I was a child, because I feel just like a child again, and that is the last thing I want to feel. I don't know what to do with myself. I don't know what to do each day. At least when I was on the Bus I had a purpose. It is very strange not having the work imperative to drive your life. I hadn't realised how much I relied on its routine.

I have trouble sleeping. I lie awake on the bed and stare at the ceiling wondering what I have done. I have made a terrible mistake. I feel ashamed and foolish. This is all wrong. At 4am I wake to the sound of sinister cackling laughter. Is it Fate tormenting me? No, it is the Tickle Me Elmo that has fallen off the shelf. I have to get out of here.

An email arrives inviting me to a wedding in Boston. I leave a trail of flaming footprints all the way to the airport.

I spend the next few months travelling in the US and Europe. Everywhere I go I am looking for insight and inspiration. I want to know the answers to the big questions — What is life about? What are we here for? How do I make myself happy?

I go to modern art galleries in London and search for answers in a white painting on a white background called 'White on White'. In smoky cafes in Amsterdam and Madrid I drink tiny cups of dark coffee and read *The Complete Idiot's Guide to Nietzsche*, and *Existentialism for Dummies*. I begin to fill pages in my notebook with scribblings. Slowly, with great reluctance, and mostly as a result of time and distance rather than any great revelation, my issues become clearer and less painful.

It is true that if you look at human life down the wrong end of a telescope we are all just ants scurrying around. From this perspective the narrative arc of our lives is predetermined — we are born, we wriggle and twitch a little, we swap DNA, and then we die. I may *be* a meat puppet, but down at my level it doesn't *feel* like I am. That has to be enough.

Yes, the particular culture that I happened to be born into predisposes me towards certain types of behaviour. But this is just a role I am playing. If push came to shove, in 48 hours I could fly to the Kamchatka Peninsula, burn my passport, and live out my life as a bear trapper.

And maybe most people order the Pizza Americana because it is the best choice. If the price of being unique is having to eat Kangaroo Sweetbread Pizza, then maybe it isn't that bad being with the crowd.

One thing that is certain is that I'm not immortal anymore. But if the end of my life is clear, then how I get there is still largely up to me. In fact, more than ever I realise now that my life is a completely blank landscape. Now I have to get on and fill it.

One day in Madrid the money machine stops giving me cash. I fly back to Howick to sit on the sofa and get fat.

How to tell that your standards are slipping:

1 You put your clothes on back to front.

2 It takes you until 11am to discover 1.

3 After discovering 1 you don't do anything about it.

4 You watch daytime TV shows.

5 You don't know what day of the week it is.

6 You work out what day of the week it is by what TV show it is.

7 The show in 6 is a reality TV show.

I return to Howick intending to get my life back together, to find a place to live, to get a job. But the weather isn't helping. After the cold and grey northern-hemisphere winter the New Zealand summer is intoxicating. Each night I write 'Find a job' on my list of things to do tomorrow, and each morning I throw open the curtains to another fine summer's day. If it's windy I jump in my sister's old, cranky Toyota Starlet and drive north to go windsurfing at Lake Pupuke. If it's slightly less windy I drive south of Auckland and out to the west coast and go parapenting.

If it is wet there is the TV. You would have heard that 99.7% of our genes are the same as those of the chimpanzee. Which perhaps explains why we like bananas and swings. It is less well known that 50% of our genes are the same as the lettuce's, which is my excuse for spending a lot of time on the couch in front of the TV.

I am particularly enjoying watching infomercials. I love Infomercial World. Everyone looks like they are having so much fun. The products are such good value, and storage is no problem. And they throw in lots of other stuff as well. I'm enthralled. Wow! It can do that to my abs? And I am going to look like him? No way! And it rolls under the bed! Look at those bonus gifts! And easy payments! I buy an Abdominiser. It gathers dust under the bed.

I also seem to have a slight food-intake problem. Mum is still cooking for four children, yet I seem to have no trouble clearing the table. It's still just debatable whether or not I'm actually clinically obese. The charts at the GP's office say so, but they have a particularly anorexic view of the world. They must have been calibrated during some dark period of history when highly processed carbohydrate was not freely and cheaply available. According to the charts I should be about 20 kg lighter or 15 cm taller. If I were 20 kg lighter I would only weigh 90 kg — I would look like an x-ray.

With my lack of motivation and self-discipline I am appalling myself, but not enough to do anything different. So rather than fight the inevitable I decide to give in to it. I will gorge myself on Mum's cooking, watch daytime TV until it's night-time, immerse myself in the full horror of deep suburban living until I finally touch the hard bottom of the Pit of Self-Loathing. Then I will have no choice but to bounce back, bigger, faster and stronger than ever.

So on Friday and Saturday nights I force myself to listen to a radio show on one of the stations that play nostalgic hits from the 'Golden Age of Radio'. On nights when I should be giving myself inner-ear damage at a nightclub, I instead listen to an elderly DJ croak into the mike, 'Here's one you won't have heard for a while! Max Jaffa and his Palm Court Orchestra with the Palmerston North Pipe Band playing Rod Stewart's "Sailing"!'

It's revolting. It's nauseating muzak. It's audio Valium. I struggle but I can't escape. My foot starts tapping, I start to hum along.

What big-band sounds can't do maybe partner dancing can. I take rock and roll dancing lessons with my mother at the Buckland's Beach community hall. Sometimes at the end of the class they throw in a bit of line-dancing just for fun.

I walk out to the letterbox every day to check the mail. Once I look down and find myself wearing socks and sandals. 'Whoops!' I chuckle to myself. 'That would have been a fashion faux pas!' I go and put on some Ug boots instead.

Occasionally I go for a jog, dragging myself to the top of a small hill nearby. Red-faced and puffing, from here I can look out upon an endless wasteland of houses stretching into the distance. But there is no time to linger. I have to get back for Oprah.

I'm coming to an uneasy truce with Chantelle the Cat. As a kitten

Chantelle was a cute, playful little snow-white ball of fur — now she's a fat, neurotic, beachball-sized blizzard. The Cat produces so much white fluff that it is difficult to tell exactly where she ends. Snowdrift-like clumps of hair can be found everywhere. Long white strands cover clothes. Food fresh from the oven is lightly garnished with hair. A few days living with Chantelle and you have fur-lined lungs. Spend a week and you will have passively digested most of a cat.

Mum indulges and mollycoddles the Cat, and finds excuses for all her misbehaviour. 'Oh the poor thing, she eats her biscuits too fast!' says Mum as she fetches the mop.

Chantelle has a habit of sneaking up on me while I'm at the dinner table, and injecting a tetanus-laden claw in my thigh.

'Kevin, be gentle — she's just asking for a pat!' exclaims Mum. Looking at Chantelle smirk from the safety of Mum's lap, I am not so sure. I think she just likes seeing how high she can make the plates jump.

The other inhabitant of the house is Carlos, Mum's lodger, who is living downstairs in my old room. Carlos is originally from Portugal, but that is a stint in the army, the merchant marine, four languages, three wives and two children ago. Carlos works in the same hotel as Mum, as a conference manager, where he can put his passionate Latino temper to good organisational effect. When he isn't working he sits in the La-Z-Boy in his room downstairs watching SKY Sport and smoking little cigars. Every hour or so he brings his coffee cup upstairs to the kitchen for a refill.

''ey Boy, 'ow's it going?' he asks. 'Why are you seeting around? Why don't you come work at the 'otel?'

At night, lying in my sister's pink frilly bed, watched by cuddly toys, while listening to eruptions of Portuguese throat-clearing rumbling below and Chantelle patiently scratching her way through the door, I wait for the bottom to hit and my apathy to be replaced by energising ambition.

Still nothing.

Perhaps it is because I am secretly starting to enjoy it. I have discovered the library again. Without work ruling my schedule I can make dinner dates with friends and keep them. I have picked up some hobbies. I am remembering people's birthdays. I'm seeing friends I haven't seen since they got married. I'm not getting their children's names mixed up. I'm taking singing lessons, ceroc lessons and drama classes. My line-dancing is really coming along.

You know there are some countries with highly regarded cultures, such as Italy, where it is quite acceptable for grown men to live with their mothers, at least until they get married. Really, it is nothing to be ashamed of.

At some point, though — and it is going to be within weeks rather than months — I'm going to have to get some paid employment, if only to fix the Starlet, which is now producing white smoke at a quantity normally associated with D-day landings. I have played too long. Now I have to get a job. Yes really.

⤬

I flick listlessly through the classifieds section of the newspaper. Why do I find it so hard to get a job? It's because I don't want a 'job'. That's the kind of old-school thinking that got me in this mess in the first place. I want to have fun. I want to have fun and get paid money. And save the world.

The self-help books I have been reading are unanimous. They all say that I should do something I enjoy doing. Something I enjoy doing? When was the last time I could think about this without being practical? Let me see . . . when I was twelve. What did I want to be when I was twelve? Maybe a movie-maker like Steve Spielberg and George Lucas, or a Jedi knight slashing my way through ranks of stormtroopers. If not a Jedi knight, then an inventor. In the movies inventors are always making cool jet-packs or time-machines. My favourite is the professor in *Chitty Chitty Bang Bang* who invented a gadget where you put a chicken in one end and an omelette comes out the other. Or maybe an explorer, driving huskies across the Antarctic and flying helicopters over the jungle. Or someone like Jacques Cousteau.

But there is a reason why I never pursued any of these 'career' paths. They are ridiculous. I'm not going to move to a galaxy far far away, play with poultry, or even wear a red beret. But as I turn to the situations vacant section of the paper, and its rows of grey type offering such listless, lifeless, soul-destroying roles as Assistant Inventory Planner, I keep being haunted by those schoolboy daydreams. They are strangely difficult to kill. They are like the Undead — even if I stab them with the Sword of Practicality and turn away, I inevitably feel a decomposing finger tapping me on the shoulder.

Somehow I have to revisit those childhood fantasies, or at least their adult variations, and put them to rest. I will get out there and talk to people doing the dream jobs that I thought I wanted. I will find that they aren't all that great and then, disappointed but grounded in reality, I will at last go and work for the Man again.

So I make another list. Once I have crossed off the fictional jobs this is what is left:

- Video editor

- Explorer

- Astronaut

- Industrial designer.

Now it is time to find people with these occupations and interview them.

Surprisingly, it isn't difficult. Just a few days later I am in a dark, windowless room in the bowels of Television New Zealand watching a documentary being edited. It is interesting, and very similar to what I do with my PC at home, and it's close to glamorous people in a glamorous industry, but it isn't glamorous. I'm cured. Excellent, that's one I don't have to worry about ever again.

For me, being an explorer means going to a Pole, and I've been a fan of Antarctic adventures since I don't know how long. I've read all about the original legends — Scott, Amundsen, Shackleton — and the latter-day elite superhuman explorers — Hillary, Swan and Fiennes. I have been thrilled by their encounters with crevasses, frostbite and endless icy wastes. But where can I find a patient polar explorer who doesn't mind talking and will give me the real lowdown?

A few days later, I'm reading an article in the newspaper about extreme holidays. There's mention of a company based in the UK that is offering treks to the South Pole. But isn't polar exploration for super-fit and highly experienced mountaineers? How is it that pudgy tourists are able to waddle their way there?

That night I call up the trekking company and get put through to one of their guides. I am a little in awe. This guy has actually been to the South Pole! Twice! After a little small talk we cut to the chase.

'But isn't it tremendously difficult to trek to the South Pole?'

'Well, actually it's not too bad.'

'But what about the cold?'

'You know it's going to be cold. You take extra mittens.'

'But what about the crevasses?'

'You know where they are. You walk around them.'

'So what's the hardest bit?'

'I guess it's dealing with the boredom really. Most of the time it's just a long, boring slog.'

I thank him for his time and put down the phone. I'm stunned. All of the polar exploration books I have read emphasised the terrible deprivation and suffering and risks they faced. Could it be possible that they were, ever so slightly, turning up the volume on the adjectives? The guide's words come back to me: 'You know it's going to be cold. You take extra mittens.'

Does this mean that a Muppet like me could do it? Does this mean that walking to the Pole doesn't have to be all about endless suffering and frozen blackened stumps? These are weighty questions that need to be digested on the sofa, along with some nice steak and kidney pie. I turn on the TV and catch the end of the sports news. There are shots of a woman rowing alone in an enormous rowboat. It looks a bit like the semi-covered lifeboats that you see on the side of cruise ships.

The commentator says that this English woman called Debra Veal has just that day arrived in Barbados as the last person to complete the second trans-Atlantic rowing race. Is that the same race that Rob Hamill and Phil Stubbs won a few years ago? It has taken this woman four months. Wow, that's a long time to be at sea in a little boat. The commentator concludes by saying that two New Zealanders, Steve Westlake and Matt Goodman, had won the race some months earlier, with a New Zealand women's team of Steph Brown and Jude Ellis coming fourth.

Strange, I haven't heard anything about that. I guess it must have happened when I was overseas. Here's another adventure that's out of my reach. I don't know how to navigate a boat, or survive a storm. Or row, for that matter.

But the phrase keeps coming back to me: *'You know it's going to be cold. You take extra mittens.'* This woman, for all her pluck, is no Captain Cook, yet she had managed it. Could I do the same?

The next day I'm on the couch again, but this time with a dog-eared copy of *The Naked Rower*, Rob Hamill's book about winning the first trans-Atlantic rowing race. I'm intrigued by the photo on the front cover. It shows the two rowers at the end of the race, oars held aloft, their physiques showing the results of six weeks' hard labour under the tropical sun. Man, these guys are buffed! This race would be great for getting me into shape! I bet they get the ladies.

I expect the photo is going to be the best thing about the book. I mean, six weeks rowing non-stop at sea — how interesting can it be? Quite interesting, in fact. I don't so much read it as inhale it. I'm flicking through the pages as fast as possible looking for the juicy bits. Ah, there they are! I thought so, loads of girls.

But also, wouldn't it be cool to be sitting out there in the middle of the ocean? I wonder what it's like to be at sea at night with the full moon on the water? And look, quite frankly, how hard can it be? There was a mother-and-son crew in the first race. They stopped every night to have a gin and tonic as the sun went down, and they got to the end, no problem.

What is clear is that you don't have to be an old salt to take part. Judging by the backgrounds of the participants in the race, complete novices seem to be able to handle it almost as well as seasoned mariners. Maybe the Atlantic, the place that gives us liner-sinking icebergs, perfect storms and the Bermuda Triangle, can be managed by an overweight, Mummy's boy, ex-office worker like me.

Except there's no point in getting too enthusiastic. Putting together an international rowing campaign isn't exactly practical for someone who doesn't have a job, or money, and is living with their mother and driving their sister's car. It would probably help if you knew how to row as well, had spent some time in the open ocean, and weighed less than a tenth of a tonne.

But wouldn't it be cool? And what about the girls? I do a search on the internet and find that the next race is less than two years away, starting in October 2003.

This strange emerging desire needs to be squashed quickly. I need to get hold of this Rob Hamill and find out the true story behind the hype. The real story. That the race really is excruciatingly long and boring. How he had to bankrupt himself, how the picture for the front cover had been airbrushed, how his butt was never the same again, that sort of thing. Then I can put a line through explorer on my list and move on to astronaut.

Mum walks past.

'Kevin, what are you reading?'

'*The Naked Rower*.'

'Why are you reading that?'

'Because I'm thinking of rowing across the ocean.'

'Oh Kevin, that's your most ridiculous idea yet! You're not a rower!'

The email to Rob Hamill is tricky to write. I don't want to come across like a gushing groupie. I don't know much about him. Only that he is the kind of sport celebrity who does game shows on TV, and every so often appears with a baby in the *Woman's Weekly*. He probably gets thousands of these emails. He'll probably be too busy eating possum brains on some *Battle of the Champions* show to respond.

Rob

I have just finished reading *The Naked Rower* and couldn't put it down. In some ways I am in a position similar to your own at the start of the book. At 32, and having just left a corporate job I am incredibly motivated to take on a challenge like the trans-Atlantic race.

I see that the next race is going to be held next year. I'm thinking of putting together a challenge but I don't have a rowing or particularly marine background and would like to know a little more about what I would be getting into! Could we spend an hour discussing the type of effort required to mount a credible challenge, ie budget requirements, time commitments, training etc?

Thanks very much!
Kevin Biggar

Well, how about that. He does respond. He even suggests that we meet, at the BP service station in Newmarket of all places. There must be fifty cafes in Newmarket, and he wants to meet in a petrol station? Maybe he's worried about the paparazzi.

I get to the service station early and wait at the cafe area. I'm not quite sure what to expect. He's meant to be quite tall, isn't he? Or am I getting him mixed up with Rob Waddell, the Olympic sculler? When he comes in he's smaller than I expected, and has fewer shoes. Are you allowed to go barefoot in petrol stations? He doesn't seem like a big star or athlete. In fact he looks a lot like everyone else, just shorter.

'Can I get you something?' he offers. 'They do fantastic pies here — have you tried the Thai chicken?' He buys two pies and comes back to the table.

'So, what can I do for you?'

'Umm, well, like I said in the email, I'm thinking of taking part in the next trans-Atlantic rowing race, but I have a lot of doubts about whether or not I can do it and whether it will be worthwhile, and I'd rather know now than after I've wasted two years working towards it. In fact, I would be quite happy if you could just tell me now that it's not a very good idea.'

'I think it's a great idea,' he says. 'If you really want to, and you're passionate about it, then you should definitely give it a crack.'

Well, he would say that, wouldn't he? I decide to try another tack. 'Okay, so what's the hardest part?'

'Getting to the start line. That's 90% of the race. Getting sponsorship . . . and getting a boat built . . . it just takes forever. There's a thousand and one things you have to plan and coordinate. Then all you have to do is row your guts out.'

'OK, great. What are some of the worst parts of the race?'

'You mean how your bum takes a beating?'

I nod vigorously. Now he's getting it!

'Yeah, it is awful, but it soon comes right again after the race. Maybe you're worried about your hands getting cut up?'

'Yup!'

'That gets sorted out in training. We didn't have too many problems.'

Bugger. OK, let me try again.

'How about the fact that I don't have any international rowing experience like you did, so no one's going to sponsor me? How about the fact that it's going to be really expensive, and I'll spend the rest of my life paying off the debt?'

'Yep, that might happen.' He thinks for a moment. 'Tell you what — how about the chance of death?'

'Exactly!'

'Well, that's got to interest you.'

I'll be damned. It does.

'Next time you're down in Hamilton give me a call and I'll show you the boat.'

I walk out feeling strangely nauseous. It's not the pie. It's the thought that just maybe I could do this. Or maybe it's the thought that I won't.

CHAPTER FOUR

Dealing with the doubts

The nightmares start almost immediately. I am lying in the back cabin of a rowboat when I somehow perceive a house-sized wave rearing, whitecapped, out of the darkness. It's so big it's blocking out the stars. Then it tumbles onto the boat and I wake up gasping for air.

I need to speak to some more people about this rowing thing. Apparently Rob had been going to do the race again in 2001, but he had broken his hand or something just before the start and couldn't do it. So maybe he had forgotten how painful the race was.

With Rob's help I get hold of one of the rowers who won the 2001 race — Steve Westlake, a policeman. I arrange to meet him at Vivace, an Italian restaurant on High Street in the city. I thought he was going to come in his police blues. He didn't, but when a tall, solidly built guy with bulging forearms, calloused hands and red-mirror Ray-Bans walks in I figure it must be him.

When our food arrives I start with the most important question.

'So what's the hardest part?'

'Getting to the start line. That's 90% of the race.'

'Where did it hurt the most?'

'Your backside — the fat burns off the bum until you are left rocking on just the sciatic nerve.'

'That sounds painful.'

'Agonising,' he says matter-of-factly, tucking into his risotto. 'But you can't eliminate all pain.'

Apparently they had problems with boils and rashes too. This is better. Now we are warming up.

'How's the sleep deprivation?'

'It's not that bad. You're still sleeping six times a day for about one and a half hours. There aren't really any bad effects. I still had my fingernails and hair growing.'

'How about the boredom?'

He smiles. 'It wasn't a problem. I guess there isn't a lot up top to get bored. You get a bit philosophical, look out at the waves, think about things, see a fish jumping. That kind of thing.'

Steve mentions that in the last race their seats had not worked well. They had used foam-topped seats, and in the latter stages of the race they had been forced to give up sleep while they whittled away at the foam, trying to alleviate the pressure points and compensate for the changing shape of their backsides over the course of the race.

The training also sounded brutal. According to Steve, most days he would get up very early to row for at least 20 km, which would take about three hours. Then he would have a short nap and go to work. Steve comes from a strong rowing background — he has done quite a bit of surf-boat rowing, he was a reserve for the Olympics in 2000, and when I meet him he is training for the 2004 Olympics. Man, this guy is a machine.

It's clear Steve spent an enormous amount of time preparing for the Atlantic race — sourcing the right equipment, doing the physical preparation, getting the right nutrition. He and his rowing partner consulted a nutritionist called Rachel Brown who he rated very highly. They were burning up between 9000 and 12,000 calories a day, and obviously needed a very special diet. For the six months leading up to the race they ate the same food that they would have on the boat.

During the race, Steve says, persistence is vital — he's convinced that one of the keys to their speed advantage was that they kept rowing when bad weather caused everyone else to stop. He reckons that if the weather is right it should be possible to beat the record by ten days! But near the end of their race they had struck some bad headwinds — he says they were stuck thirteen days out from the finish for four days.

Steve suggests that if I want to take part in the next race I should talk to the Australian crew who came second in 2001. One of them might be keen to be involved again, and they had a pretty good boat. As for Steve, he's going to focus on the upcoming Olympic trials.

I ask him — purely hypothetically, because I certainly haven't made any decisions — if I were to try to put together a campaign, would he be available to help out? He says yes, but with three provisos. First, he wouldn't want to get involved in the time-intensive jobs like finishing the boat; second, he would like to be paid for his time; and third, Rob Hamill isn't to be involved. On this last point he is very clear.

'If you have anything to do with Rob Hamill, then I will have nothing to do with you,' he says firmly.

OK, sounds like they aren't getting on.

Time's up. I pay for the meal and we walk out to the street, where I shake Steve's hand enthusiastically. 'It's not every day you met a real sporting hero,' I gush.

But I walk away feeling disheartened. I wanted a cold dose of reality and that's exactly what I got. Now I feel like a complete fraud for even thinking about taking part in the next race. I simply don't have the right sporting background. Compared with Steve Westlake I am a frigging powder-puff. When he asked me what sporting events I had been in I'd love to have been able to say, 'Oh, I just defended my title at the Northern Territories Crocodile-Wrestling Competition, and last year I was runner-up at the Grizzly Bear Tossing Nationals in Alaska.'

And where would I fit training in with all my singing and dancing lessons? Oh sure, Steve Westlake might be able to row an ocean, but can he do a left-handed swizzle with shoulder drop while holding an A above middle C? He might be all right on the deck of the *Telecom Challenge*, but what's he like on the deck of HMS *Pinafore*?

And that stuff about what happens to your bum! Ouch! And that sleep deprivation! I just can't see how sleeping for only one and a half hours at a time can be sustainable. I know I asked him what he enjoyed about the race, but I forgot to listen to the answer. I was still thinking about those oozing saltwater boils.

I decide to talk to Steph Brown. She and Jude Ellis had crewed the other boat in the New Zealand challenge last year, and had finished in 50 days, coming a very creditable fourth and beating 30 men's crews. She is also Steve's fiancée.

A few days later, I knock on the door of a flat in Orakei. It's Steve who answers the door. He introduces me to Steph, who has a ruddy, cheerful face, and is as bubbly as Steve is reserved. Originally from the north of England, she came to New Zealand for its outdoor lifestyle, and was working as a drug rep for a pharmaceutical company when she decided to take part in the rowing race.

I chat with Steph while Steve does his own thing on the couch. We talk about her experience of the race, and all goes well until Rob Hamill is mentioned. At that point her eyes flash and her face darkens. She looks me straight in the eye as she repeats the words Steve had used a few days earlier: 'If you have anything to do with Rob Hamill, we will have nothing to do with you.'

Then the storm passes and the smiles are back again. They both come down the stairs to wave me goodbye.

As I drive away all I can think about is that strange statement that stopped just short of being a threat. It was such an odd thing to say. How would my having anything to do with Rob Hamill affect them? Why are they trying to isolate the guy? I need to find out.

So I go to the library to look for any articles about the last trans-Atlantic rowing race. There are plenty.

As I scroll through the internet websites and the microfiche machine my eyes widen. Punch-ups! Allegations of cheating! Mutiny! I had no idea what drama I missed out on while I was overseas.

Rob Hamill goes for two in a row

28 July 2001

After winning the inaugural trans-Atlantic rowing race, Rob Hamill just can't help sticking his oar in again, as ROBIN BAILEY writes.

Why are you doing it again? That's the question Rob Hamill has been asked dozens of times since he announced his campaign to defend his title in the Atlantic Rowing Race 2001.

His answer is simple: 'It's a race. We set the record in 1997 and we want to win it for Phil Stubbs.'

Hamill is referring to the first 2900 nautical mile (5000km) race from Tenerife in the Canary Islands to Barbados that he and Stubbs won by almost eight days.

Hamill and Stubbs had planned a two-boat challenge for 2001. Then, in December 1998, Stubbs died in a plane crash at Karekare Beach.

Phil's prospective partner for the race is sports all-rounder Steve Westlake, aged 30, who subsequently joined Hamill for the title defence.

This time things are different. They have secured naming rights sponsorship from Telecom and a second-tier commitment from TV3, which will be their host broadcaster. Then come those who are on board for the first campaign, including Mainfreight and the Lion Foundation.

Now aged 37, Hamill admits he is almost too old for what is billed as the ultimate test of strength and human endurance. In his book, The Naked Rower, he described the challenges he and Stubbs faced: storms with mountainous seas, physical and psychological exhaustion, sunburn, headaches, hallucinations, blistered hands, feet and buttocks and sleep deprivation. It's the sleep deprivation that worries him most.

'Last time we were not aware of what we were letting ourselves in for. This time I know exactly what it will be like and I have been doing a course of self-hypnosis, a form of relaxation therapy that helps you relax even if sleep is impossible.'

Hamill believes the first week of the race is the toughest.

Consequently, he and Westlake have embarked on a series of two- and three-day rows between now and the time the contingent heads for the start line at Los Gigantes marina in Tenerife on October 7. They are determined to be as well-prepared as is possible to ensure a successful defence.

— New Zealand Herald

Gallantry injury dims hope for Hamill

September 28 2001

Kiwi rowing hero Rob Hamill's hopes of completing a unique double have been dashed by his breaking his right hand saving a woman from a bashing.

Hamill won the 1997 Trans-Atlantic Rowing Challenge with the late Phil Stubbs. He has been in Tenerife, in Spain's Canary Islands, preparing for the latest challenge next month partnering Auckland policeman Steve Westlake.

But the hand injury, suffered when Hamill helped a Tenerife woman being beaten by her husband, means he is now a doubtful starter for the 4667km race from Tenerife to Barbados starting on October 7.

'I'm just devastated,' Hamill said last night. X-rays have revealed that he has a broken knuckle which will require surgery. He has only a small chance of being able to compete.

Hamill has spearheaded the two-boat Telecom Challenge campaign this year. He is to have rowed with Westlake; the other entrants are women Jude Ellis and Steph Brown.

National rowing representative Matt Goodman is heading off to Tenerife to replace Hamill if he is finally ruled out.

— NZPA

Kiwi worried rivals will use hatches as sails

October 2, 2001

LONDON: New Zealand rowers in the Trans-Atlantic Challenge fear some of their rivals have the potential to cheat by using boat hatches as a type of sail.

They voiced concerns to organisers of the 4667km race,

which starts from the Canary Islands on Sunday, requesting design changes to prevent unfair wind assistance on the journey to Barbados.

In the 1997 race, won by New Zealanders Rob Hamill and the late Phil Stubbs, the two-crew boats were able to have hatches that slid open only.

This time hatches that can be lifted up are allowed.

The concerned New Zealanders, already worried by a hand injury to Hamill that may keep him out of the race, noted that some crews had the ability to latch hatches vertically open.

Steph Brown, of the Telecom Challenge women's crew, said that made her uncomfortable, as a sail that size could generate power equivalent to having an additional rower.

'Some teams have made their hatches much larger, like twice the size, in order to get into their cabins easier,' she said.

'If they opened horizontally it would not be a problem, but they open vertically. They have then cut off part of the cabin roof, which is illegal, so that they can open them right up.

'What you get is two very effective sails, one on the front cabin and one on the back. Some teams have even used ties to secure them in that upright position.

'The whole thing makes us very uncomfortable. We are not saying they will use them but how do we know they won't.'

— NZPA

Hamill injury not as bad as feared
October 2, 2001

LONDON: Orthopaedic specialists have advised New Zealand rower Rob Hamill he may yet be able to row in the Trans-Atlantic Challenge, even with a broken hand.

. . . Yesterday the Telecom Challenge team said two orthopaedic specialists, one in New Zealand the other in England, felt there was a possibility that Hamill would be able to row.

He would be in pain for two to three weeks as the bone would be only 50 percent healed at the start of the race.

'While both specialists acknowledged that some other sports

people have been able to compete with such an injury they were unable to relate it to an endurance event of this magnitude,' team spokesman Rob Nichol said . . .

'Rob will have to start rowing on Wednesday morning and complete three continuous days of training.

'He will have to prove to himself and (rowing partner Steve Westlake) that he can attend to all the necessary duties around the boat including key safety procedures such as getting in and out of the boat at sea, throwing safety lines and pulling up the sea anchor.'

. . . Westlake said the target remained to win the race and break the record Hamill and the late Phil Stubbs set in 1997. The team could not afford to be less than 100 percent.

'We need to give Rob every opportunity while also remembering what we are here for,' he said.

'Either way it will be one of the hardest calls either of us have ever been involved in.'

Auckland policeman Goodman arrived in Tenerife on Friday night after receiving the call-up two days earlier.

Goodman has been Westlake's partner in double sculls rowing events, in which they are past holders of the national pairs title.

— NZPA

Fit Hamill ditched by team-mate

October 8, 2001

New Zealand rower Rob Hamill's quest to start the Trans-Atlantic Rowing Challenge is dashed by his team-mate just hours before last night's start.

After a race against time to recover from a broken hand suffered 10 days ago, Hamill was confident he was fit enough to tackle the demands of the 4667km trek across the Atlantic to Barbados. But he was overruled by his partner in the two-man boat, Steve Westlake.

'I've done a series of rowing tests so far — four and two-hour rows — and my hand's come up very well,' Hamill said hours before the start from Tenerife, in the Canary Islands.

But Westlake is not convinced.

'Even though I've done these tests that isn't enough to change Steve's impression of my ability to do the job, so he isn't prepared to row with me.'

Hamill, who won the race by a huge margin with the late Phil Stubbs in 1997, is left with the options of rowing alone or finding another partner. Neither prospect appealed.

Westlake opted to row with Matt Goodman, who flew from New Zealand several days ago as an alternative when Hamill injured his hand after intervening in a domestic dispute in Tenerife.

Hamill said he is still '100 per cent behind the guys'.

— NZPA

Mum sees me packing the car.

'Where are you going?'

'Down to see Rob Hamill in Hamilton.'

'Whatever for?'

'He's going to show me the trans-Atlantic rowboat.'

'Oh Kevin, you might as well go to sea in a coffin!'

The view of the Waikato from the top of the Bombay Hills on a cold sunny morning pumps helium into your heart. Drifts of white fog nestle in the folds of the hills like clumps of Chantelle's fur in a rucked carpet.

Rob lives in a pleasant little wooden house in a quiet street in Hamilton East. I arrive a little late as I have stopped to buy some baby shoes for his new son, Finn. I knock but there is no answer. I hear someone talking and the door is open, so I push it and go in. 'Come in! Come in!' I hear Rob shout. 'I'm just on the phone!' I follow the voice into a small room off the hallway. Every surface is covered with books, magazines and bank statements in tall, precarious piles. There's a desk that has only enough room for a fax machine and a laptop and a phone. Rob is in a swivel chair talking on the phone.

'Yeah yeah, no no, fair enough, OK . . . I've got someone here, can I call you back later?'

Then a cellphone rings.

Rob looks confused. 'Is that yours?'

I shake my head.

'Shit, it must be mine — where is it?'

He rummages briefly through paper under the desk before pulling out a new-looking phone. 'I only just got this one after I lost my old one.' He pushes the answer button then holds the phone two feet away from his head. 'Hello!' he shouts. Throughout the brief conversation he alternates between shouting at the handset and waving it at arm's length in the rough vicinity of his ear.

'It's the radiation,' he explains when the call is over. 'Brain tumours. It affects your memory.'

'Where did you hear that?'

'I can't remember,' he says. 'Here, let me get my laptop going — I want to show you something.'

It's a video of two guys in a rowboat struggling in the surf at Muriwai Beach. I had heard about these guys on the news — they were planning to row to Australia. The surf is large, and it is remarkable how well they manage for the first few waves. But then they are pushed broadside, the next wave rolls them over, and they are thrown out spectacularly into the surf.

'Ouch! So what are they going to do now?'

'They're going to try again, but this time they're going to start from Australia.'

Rob offers to buy lunch, so we go to a cafe nearby to talk over braised lamb shanks. We talk about details, about the rowing shifts. I ask him why they chose to row two hours on and two hours off.

'Because three hours is too long to row and one hour is too short to sleep. We didn't know any better and neither will you, and that will be your strength.'

Weird — he's talking to me like I'm going to do it.

A short drive from the cafe is a storage yard. Inside a small shed is the rowboat. It looks bigger up close. I look at it in awe. This is the boat Rob and Phil used in the 1997 race. Every line and scratch tells a story.

'Why don't you try getting into the cabin,' Rob suggests.

It isn't that easy. The hatch isn't very big. I try going in one leg at a time — it doesn't work.

'Try ducking your head.'

Now I am lying on my back in the cabin on the foam flooring. It feels very snug. It is about as snug as . . . well, as the coffin Mum said it would be. Without too much trouble my feet could touch one end and my head the other.

What if I am in the cabin when it capsizes? How would I get out? The plywood walls are covered with a kind of aluminium foil that gives it a pleasant space-capsule kind of feel. But it stinks like a dead llama from the litres of sweat that have soaked into the discoloured yellow foam.

I get out of the cabin and try sitting on the rowing seat. It is a piece of wood slightly shaped with two scoops to take a bum. I can't believe how painful it looks. It reminds me of when I visited the dungeons of medieval castles and some of the more unsavoury bits of hardware were pointed out. I sit there daydreaming until Rob says it's time to go.

Back at the house, he shows me a little shrub in his front yard that has a number of monarch butterfly pupae on it. He talks about the amazing way caterpillars turn into green pulp and then into butterflies.

I drive back to Auckland thinking so hard that I am indicating at bends in the road rather than at intersections. I keep thinking of the end of our conversation.

'Do you think I can do it?' I had asked.

'I wouldn't be talking to you if I didn't think you could do it.'

'Well then. What should I do first?'

'Learn how to row!'

><

Mum: 'Kevin, if you are going to take two years out of your life, why don't you do something that is going to help people? Why don't you go and work in an orphanage in China? Or why not do something that hasn't been done before? Rowing the ocean has been done!'

She's right, but only to a degree. The statistics show that rowing the ocean has been done far less often than you might think. About

1300 people have climbed Mt Everest. Only about 180 people have ever rowed an ocean.

Back in Auckland, two hours after leaving Rob, it's time to make a decision about whether or not to do this thing. Let's look at this rationally. I get out a pen and paper and make a list of all the problems I have with the race.

1   *I could die.*
    People die doing these things. I'm not sure how many or how. But there have to be a few. Small boat, big ocean.

2   *I don't know how to row.*
    Hard to ignore this one.

3   *I'm not into pain, and this race is all about pain.*
    I like my bottom. I don't want to lose it, certainly not by spending three months having it sanded off.

4   *I hate being bored, and three months of rowing 24 hours a day is going to be excruciatingly boring.*
    This is a real problem. I am totally boredophobic. Losing my Walkman is grounds for not going for a half-hour run. I have eight books by my bed which I'm reading at the same time. When I travel, half my luggage is books.

5   *I hate getting out of bed, and I will have to get out of bed six times a day during the race.*

6   *Putting together a campaign is going to cost hundreds of thousands of dollars, and I don't know anything about fundraising.*

7   *Why not do something original? Rowing the ocean has been well and truly done.*
    Who was the third person on the moon? Exactly.

OK, there you are. That looks pretty conclusive. There doesn't seem to be much point in going on. I look at the list and am amazed at how effectively an idea can be killed. This is how to deal with those fantasies.

You don't have to be negative, you just have to be reasonable.

Look. If I want to get fit and tanned there are much better ways of doing it. If I want to see the Atlantic there are much more pleasant and cheaper alternatives. In fact, for what it would cost me to enter the race I could rent out a suite on the *QE2* and fill it full of roses. Time to kill this silly dream. Now I can start looking at being an astronaut.

But there is no sense of relief. Damn it. I really want to go. I want to sit in a small boat out on the Atlantic with a full moon above. I want to take on a challenge that is mind-bogglingly big and beat it. I want consequence. I want to take my life into my own hands, to face risk and use my judgement and skill to prevail. I want to pack my own parachute. Maybe then I'll start taking myself seriously.

I want to do something difficult. Really difficult. Right now getting through all the little day-to-day hassles in my life seems difficult, and I want to do something that is going to blow those snivelling gripes back into proportion. I want to do something so big that, as Shackleton said to inspire his men, 'Nothing will ever be difficult again.'

So I get out the list again, and this time I take a different stance.

1 *I could die.*
   The most important thing is clearly understanding what the risk of death is. I know that nobody has died in the previous two races, so that has got to be a good sign. I go onto the www.oceanrowing.com website to look at their statistics. It turns out that only six people have died rowing oceans. Four of these people rowed solo. The interesting thing is that in all these cases the boat was found intact later. There seems to be a clear lesson here — provided you are clipped onto your boat at all times you have an excellent chance of surviving. Particularly on this route, on this type of boat, and at this time of year.

2 *I don't know how to row.*
   It doesn't matter how bad I am at the start, I'm going to be an expert by the end!

3 *I'm not really into pain, and this race is all about pain.*
   'You know it's going to be cold. You take extra mittens!' If there is any part of the race that is painful I have

47

eighteen months to sort it out and find a solution. In fact, if I've done my preparation properly, there shouldn't be any pain in this race at all except the pain of effort.

4   *I hate being bored.*
Same as the above. If there is going to be anything uncomfortable about this race I have time to fix it.

5   *I hate getting out of bed, and I will have to get out of bed six times a day during the race.*
I get to *go* to bed six times a day!

6   *I don't know anything about fundraising and putting together a campaign.*
But I am pretty sure that I know some people I could ask! At the end of the day it is just suits talking to suits, and I am pretty sure I can manage that.

7   *Why not do something original?*
I would prefer to be doing something unique —
I mean, I'm sure there are some mountains in Outer Mongolia that haven't been climbed. But I'm also sure that it would take me some months to find them. There will always be something better I could be doing, but if I try to find the best possible thing I will very likely end up doing nothing. Mum is right in a way — this generation has too many choices. If I want to move away from paralysis I have to stop trying to find the best and settle for good enough. It would be wonderful to do something original, but most of all I need to do something.

That's that then. The world's newest and most reluctant ocean-rower crawls into his bed.

June 2002

Tonight, as usual, Mum and I are on the sofa at 5:30pm to watch *How's Life*, a daily show where viewers send in their relationship questions and get advice from a panel. But tonight it is different; there is tension in the air. Tonight is a showdown, and my fate is in the balance.

Ever since Mum realised that my hypothetical idea had become actual she has become increasingly vitriolic in her opposition. This has led to some major rows and an unpleasantly tense atmosphere in the house. Two weeks ago I suggested a simple solution: we would present our case to a third party and let them decide. Something as important as this had to go to the highest court in the land. So we agreed that she should write to *How's Life* and we would let the panel decide. Whatever they come up with, that's what we will stick to.

The show starts. Mum takes an early knock. Tonight the show is going to be dealing with men's problems, and it has an all-male panel. There are radio personalities Marcus Lush and Martin Crump, writer and reviewer Colin Hogg, and actor Pio Terei. The show is fronted by 'it' girl and former model Charlotte Dawson.

Charlotte begins. 'Our next letter is from a mother who's worried because her son is determined to paddle his own canoe! God bless him!'

Dear *How's Life*, my 33-year-old son has a Masters degree and a successful business career. He threw it in to go travelling and now wants to compete in the trans-Atlantic rowing race next year. This will take up all his time and savings and when it's over he will be 35, broke, jobless and probably still living at home with me. I think he should be building his career — how can I make him see reason? Concerned Mother (by email)

Charlotte turns to the panel: 'Marcus! What does he do? Fulfil his ambitions?'

Marcus Lush: 'Just imagine if we were on this show 50 years ago on the radiogram, you know? "Dear *How's Life*, my son wants to throw in his bee-keeping practice to go and climb Mt Everest!" Can anyone here see any problem at all?'

Charlotte: 'OK Marcus, we've got a gay issue coming up soon so you might want to belt up until that one's on! Pio?'

Marcus: 'Goodness gracious!'

Pio: 'Yeah . . . well . . . I . . . She should be celebrating that this guy's busting free. I mean, how boring would life be if he just keeps going the way he is. Thirty-five! I don't know about your fellas' culture but in mine that's young! Life's not over at thirty-five — OK? You're just starting to learn anything worthwhile!'

Martin Crump: 'You're looking good, Pio!'

Pio: 'Kia ora, brother!'

Martin: 'Of course he's seeing reason — he's seeing it, all right. He's following his heart. He's following his passion . . .'

Marcus: '. . . his spirit!'

Martin: 'Yeah! The adventurous spirit of it all, you're dead right Marcus. Yeah, and I think that, uh . . . she's got the problem with this. He's right on track as far as I'm concerned!'

Colin Hogg: 'I'm concerned about "Concerned Mother", quite frankly. She's got a son here who can take her on a row of an afternoon. Yeah, you know? The guy's only thirty-three — he's got his whole life ahead of him!'

Charlotte: 'Even though it's "Go the rowing!" Go for it! Do what you want, you've still got to talk to your mum!'

Back in the living room pandemonium breaks out. The phone's ringing, I'm screaming and jumping up and down like a wild Indian shouting, 'I am concerned about "Concerned Mum"!'

Mum exits, muttering something about not wording the question right.

Next day I call up the race organisers, Challenge Business, and register to get an information pack. While I'm waiting for it to arrive I do some more research about what I am up against — the legendary Atlantic Ocean.

CHAPTER FIVE

A brief history of the Atlantic

If you had to choose the features of the ideal ocean to row across, there would be a few obvious things high on your list. First, to keep the monotony to a minimum, you would like the gap between the continents to be slim. Then you would like the height of any waves to be modest. Ideally, the ocean would also be shallow so that if you sprang a leak, or just got tired of the whole business, you could simply hop out and slosh home.

The weather would be sunny but also refreshingly cool. And in the evenings a playful school of cheerfully squeaking dolphins would turn up to provide some entertaining aerobatics and toss freshly filleted fish and cans of cold beer into your boat.

It goes without saying that you would choose an ocean free of swarms of wriggling eel larvae, ferocious currents, hoovering water spouts, island-sized icebergs, yawning bottomless abysses, prehistoric fish well past their extinction date, and aliens in mysterious spacecraft seeking a quiet spot from which to pluck up hapless Earthlings for scientific experiments.

The Atlantic fails dismally in all respects.

There was a time when it was possible to travel from Africa to the Caribbean without getting your feet wet. Just 200 million years ago South America was snuggled deep into the notch in the southwest coast of Africa, while the eastern seaboard of North America was mashed up against the northwest of Africa.

Even if you had been able to find a piece of water wide enough to put a boat in, you would have had a difficult job finding a crew. At that time our small, mouse-like ancestors were busy twitching their whiskers and wringing their paws as they tried to avoid being devoured by slavering allosauruses or squished by the hooves of a giant brachiosaurus.

But then the Earth's magma gave a small burp and the plates that carry the continents began to move apart. Perhaps a pair of stegosauruses were walking along and one of them jumped across the gap. By the time he looked back he would have seen that the gap was getting wider. His partner may have hesitated, and then the moment was gone, the gap was too wide, the water was rushing in, and all they could do was flap their trunks mournfully as South America whirled away across the Proto-Pacific, sending up a bow wave as it hit a top speed of 2 cm a year. An inch a year is not much, but over aeons of time it adds up, so that now we have an ocean that covers 20% of the Earth's surface — an immense 2800 km at its narrowest point, between Brazil and Liberia, and a heartbreakingly vast 4800 km between the US and Morocco.

Nor does the Atlantic lend itself to being traversed in a pair of waders. Whole continents could be dropped into the vast undersea abyssal plains with hardly any but the highest peaks remaining above water. The average depth of the Atlantic is 3900 metres. But just off the coast of Puerto Rico there is a trench that plummets down to more than twice that depth.

There is a colossal amount of water in the Atlantic. If you took all the water out of the Atlantic Ocean it would cover the entire surface of the moon to a depth of 9 kilometres. Since you've gone to the trouble of removing the water you really should take a look around at the sea floor. It has been estimated that 99% of the sea bed remains unexplored and unknown to science. It is a strange fact that we know quite a bit more about the surfaces of the moons of Jupiter than the bottom of our own oceans. Even the moon has been visited far more times than the deepest part of the ocean — the 10,916-metre-deep Mariana Trench in the Pacific. This was first seen in 1960 by Jacques Picard and Donald Walsh through the tiny six-inch-thick Plexiglas portholes of the bathyscaphe *Trieste*. No one has been back since, and no one has ever been to the bottom of the Puerto Rico trench!

Imagine for a moment that you have been unlucky enough to become separated from your boat out in mid-ocean. For a while you try to swim, but eventually you are exhausted and find yourself sinking. What happens next?

For the first part of your fall you are still in sunlit waters. This thin layer is where most of the life in the ocean lives, or at least feeds — mostly on each other. If you are lucky you might see a shark. If you are unlucky you might meet a school of the ferocious bluefish. This fish makes the more famous piranha look like a grumpy guppy. The *Ocean Almanac* reports bluntly that 'there is no more aggressive creature in the sea than the bluefish'. In the late nineteenth century the US Commissioner of Fisheries, Spencer F Baird, called the bluefish an 'unmitigated butcher' and recommended that it be eradicated 'lest it destroy all fishes'.

There have been many reports and several documented cases of schools of bluefish attacking and injuring human bathers. In 1976 a marauding school attacked a dozen swimmers in Florida and forced authorities to close 24 km of beach. 'The fish are all acting crazy,' said a lifeguard who was bitten by one of the bluefish. 'We were just standing on the sand and they came flopping onto the beach, biting people who aren't even in the water! I've never seen anything like it.'

But better you meet an entire school of salivating bluefish than suffer a single prick from the deadly weever fish, reportedly the most dangerous of all cool-water poisonous fish. Despite only growing up to 45 cm long they inflict one of the most painful stings of any animal — and they are aggressive. According to the *Ocean Almanac* 'the weever will . . . swim out, fins vibrating, and take on a diver if even slightly disturbed'.

Victims report that the pain of a weever sting is at a level well beyond excruciating. One diver actually cut off his affected finger, while another plunged his hand into fire. The pain is followed by fever, nausea, convulsions and sometimes death. Weevers are reportedly good to eat if properly cleaned.

But by now you have sunk past 150 metres and are safe, for almost all the surface sunlight has been filtered out. For the rest of the descent, the remaining 98%, it will be completely dark. Now any fish that you meet have been grotesquely transformed by the difficulties of life in the depths. Down here their eyes have become disproportionately enlarged. Many fish have little or no pigment, and some are completely transparent.

You may, as you descend, imagine that you see a faint blob of green light. Perhaps it is the hideous humpbacked angler fish, which lures creatures towards it with a blob of bioluminescence dangling in front of its grotesquely enlarged jaws, which are filled with rows of needle-like teeth.

As you pass through a depth of 2000 metres you will notice that it is getting very cold. In the deep ocean the temperature seldom rises above a very chilly 4°C.

At this point you are on your own. There could be just about anything down there. For example, in late 1938 a strange fish was netted by a South African trawler off the coast of Africa. It was a metre and a half long and weighed around 55 kg, was steel-blue in colour, and had large scales and stumpy fins. It was a coelacanth — a fish that was around when the Atlantic was a muddy ditch. It was supposed to have died out with the rest of the dinosaurs. This is the marine equivalent of going for a walk in the woods and coming across a brontosaurus munching quietly. It was fourteen years before another coelacanth was caught, and altogether only ten have ever been found.

By now you have passed 7000 metres and your ocean plunge is nearly at an end. If you are very lucky you will come to rest near a rare hydrothermal vent. Here you will see raw magma squeezing like toothpaste through the Earth's crust. Superheated water, at up to 300ºC, squirts from the floor. Anywhere else it would be steam, but the intense pressure at this depth keeps it fluid. Only a few metres from the vent the water can be near freezing, yet in that few metres, in some of the most hostile environment anywhere in the solar system, there exists abundant life.

In the dim red volcanic glare you will see waving gardens of giant tube-worms. These are classified as animals but they have no mouth or anus — they survive through their symbiotic relationship with bizarre bacteria that convert the hot, toxic hydrogen sulphide gushing from the vents into energy. Scuttling in the edges of the light you will also dimly glimpse the clicking pincers of thousands of bone-white galatheid crabs. They normally feed on molluscs, but for you they may be prepared to make an exception.

But the hydrothermal vents are relatively rare — it is much more likely that you will land somewhere on the vast undersea plains. Here your plunge will be gently arrested as you are enveloped in a sticky ooze. This has been created over millions of years by the gentle shower of tiny sea creatures that have lived and died in the sunlit layers miles above. In some places this goo is only 60 metres thick; in others it can be up to several kilometres thick. If you don't manage to stay relatively near the surface you are likely to meet (and be digested by) a sea pig, a slug-like creature that very successfully inhabits the very bottom of the ocean, grazing on the carcasses of unfortunate creatures that tumble out of the cold, dark, wet 'sky' above.

But you don't even have to go very deep to experience some very strange phenomena in the Atlantic. The sun and the Earth's spin have turned the North Atlantic into one giant whirlpool. Water heated in the tropics is spiralled clockwise up to the Arctic to be cooled before making its way down again to the equator.

The most famous of these currents is the Gulf Stream. This is the name given to the enormous river of warm water that sweeps up the eastern seaboard of the US before heading across the top of the North Atlantic to Europe. The amount of water travelling in the Gulf Stream is colossal — 50 times more than all the rivers flowing into the Atlantic combined. The amount of heat it delivers to Europe is as much as 100 times the entire world energy demand, which gives Great Britain its balmy climate (which it is, if you consider that London is more or less the same latitude as Warsaw).

The returning arm of the Gulf Stream is the North Equatorial Current, which travels from Africa to the Caribbean. From June through to November, this current helps to create storms almost unimaginable in their intensity — a tropical hurricane releases energy at the rate of a 10-megaton nuclear bomb every 20 minutes.

Close to Bermuda lies an area of the Atlantic called the Sargasso Sea. This patch of the ocean is almost completely still and devoid of current. It takes its name from the large concentration of sargassum weed that floats in this area. It is also said to be the birthplace of every eel in Europe and North America.

In summertime some internal instinct sends eels of breeding age downstream and out into the ocean on a one-way trip back to their ancestral breeding grounds. During this migration their bodies undergo a strange metamorphosis. By the time they leave the continental shelf their gut has dissolved and they must survive on stored energy alone. Their eyes start to grow larger, so they can see in the dim ocean light, and their bodies turn silver to better escape detection by predators.

What happens next, and where the eels go, no one knows for sure. Presumably they meet at some point in the ocean, mate and spawn. But despite extensive research none of this has been observed. What scientists have done is to catch and measure the wriggling eel larvae making the trip back to Europe. The smallest larvae are found in the Sargasso Sea, confirming that they start their journey there.

Some romantics like to argue that the Sargasso Sea is the location of the mythical island of Atlantis, in whose flowing rivers the ancestors of all eels once frolicked. When the island sank the eels had to leave and find new lands, but their descendants still return to the site of their lost homeland year after year to breed.

Without a doubt the most famous part of the North Atlantic is the Bermuda Triangle. This area of water, between Bermuda, Puerto Rico and Miami, is notorious for the large numbers of aircraft and ships that have disappeared here — occasionally very big ships, often in fine weather, and often without a single clue to help explain the tragedy. No distress calls, no oil slicks, no life jackets. Nothing. It is as if the craft and crew have been plucked from the air and sea.

In 1918, in what has been described as the US Navy's greatest mystery of the sea, the USS *Cyclops* disappeared with 309 people on board. Despite a massive naval investigation no survivors or any trace of the ship were ever found. In the words of President Woodrow Wilson, 'Only God and the Sea know where the great ship has gone.'

Sightings of unusual lights have occurred in this area since the very first voyage of Columbus. Some modern theorists say these are the lights of professional hijackers, others say they are drug runners.

Some people say that giant bubbles of gas being released from the sea floor swallow up ships. Still others say that the missing crews have been abducted by aliens, and even that aliens have established a base there under the sea. Others (who tend to arrive in pairs unannounced at your house wearing black suits and dark sunglasses) will tell you that it can all be explained by a combination of weather balloons reflecting off marsh gas under lenticular clouds and you are to desist further investigation.

But whether I am to be snuffed by a Colombian drug cartel, hoovered up by a writhing waterspout or whisked away to become part of a scientific project in Alpha Centauri, no one disputes that very weird and very dangerous things happen in this part of the ocean.

CHAPTER SIX

Swallowing the elephant

I go to bed tired, I wake up tired,
I'm tired all the time and I'm tired of it.
— Anon

Finally the information pack arrives from Challenge Business. It's in so many pieces that after the Post Office had finished playing soccer with it they had poured it into a plastic bag. I spread it out on the dining-room table and turn the pages with eager, pudgy fingers.

There is one photo in the brochure that immediately catches my eye. It's a picture of two army guys who had a boat in the first race. The boat is on the side of a wave, heeled over hard. One guy is standing in the footwell squinting at the horizon through his Ray-Bans, one hand on his Rolex Oyster Perpetual. The other guy is in his seat, scanning the ocean, probably looking for a shark he can wrestle into the boat for dinner or something. Oh yeah, this is for me!

But when it becomes clear what I would have to do to put together a campaign, I feel overwhelmed with tiredness and just want to go to bed. Not the least is raising the race entry fee of £13,800, about NZ$35,000. But let's worry about that later. What can I do now? Learn how to row. Sounds good. I can lose a few kilos and start looking the part.

So today at 4:38pm training begins. I go to the gym and up to the rowing machines on the mezzanine floor. I sit down on the hard little plastic seat of one of the ergos and reach out for the wooden handle that is chained to the fan thing. I put my feet into the foot-straps and give a hesitant pull. A little clock on the LCD screen springs to life. It gets to 2 minutes before the pain in my bum goes from uncomfortable to really excruciating. I'd thought my plump, juicy buttocks were my secret weapon, good for at least a quarter of a million k's each!

The problem is the ridiculous rowing seat. If you sit on a normal chair you are supported by your glutes and your thighs. If you then bring your heels up and put them on the edge of a seat in front of you, you will notice that the whole weight of your body is being pressed through the bones of your pelvis into an area of the seat about the size of a 50-cent piece. It's about as daft as doing a handstand on your elbows.

As well as that I am feeling nauseous, like I had chugged a bucket of custard. The problem is my stroke. Right at the end of the stroke the power is coming off so quickly that the oar handle is punching me in the guts, 20 times a minute. I take some comfort from the fact that I am going faster than the people next to me. And I don't care if the guy on my left is an octogenarian with an old whaling boat style, and the guy on the right is just going through the motions while he flirts with the blonde next to him.

By the time the clock shows 15 minutes (and I am having my first break) I'm desperately trying to redesign the whole seat system in my head. It sucks. I can't believe rowers put up with it. I try to distract myself from the pain by imagining large seas and capsizing. It is not a jolly time.

Other people come and go, but not me. I make myself stay for an hour: I go 12,350 metres. According to the LCD screen I am going 2:25 — 2 minutes 25 seconds — per 500-metre split. And my bum! Ow! I waddle away discouraged.

May 2002

The alarm goes off at 6:10am. I flick the curtains — it's cold and overcast, the trees are whipping in the wind and the street is being strafed by rain. I had been planning to go to the Auckland Rowing Club. It had seemed a good idea last night and I had made an earnest promise to myself to get up. But I am unused to such early starts. It really hurts. I need to stop thinking about it and just do it.

I drive down to a strange industrial part of Mt Wellington, and after only getting lost once I find the clubrooms. Despite the early hour there is quite a lot going on. A steady stream of people are emerging from the boathouse with long, gleaming boats over their shoulders. They place them on the water and skim off like insects.

I meet Barry, the coach, who was going to let me take out a single scull, a very narrow and tippy racing rowboat, but he changes his mind when I tell him I have never sculled before. He thinks it's better if I come back tomorrow when there might be some more people around and I could crew in a four or an eight.

So I take my tea down to the waterline to watch the crews. I see Steve Westlake coming down to the water. He gives me a big smile and asks me what I am doing here. 'Thought I'd better learn how to row,' I suggest, to which he gives a little grin.

'What are you doing here?' I ask in return. 'Oh, a bit of recovery,' he says. Isn't recovery when you are in a spa pool with a beer? Why would you do more exercise for recovery?

Steve tells me to keep an eye out for Matt Goodman: 'He's the big hairy bastard.'

I find a guy of that description down by the water and introduce myself. I tell him that I am planning to take part in the next trans-Atlantic race, and ask if he'd like to meet for a chat. He asks right away if I have met with Rob Hamill. I feel flustered for a moment. The hostility towards Rob is so palpable. I have to remind myself that whatever is going on between them it's nothing to do with me.

Matt doesn't say very much, but what he does say is to the point. He mentions that it would have been good if the race had been a bit shorter, as the last couple of weeks dragged a bit.

The next day I am back at the rowing club at 7am. Bruce Lodder, a straight-talking middle-aged Dutchman who lives at the club as a caretaker, offers to take me out in a double scull. We go into the boathouse, where racks and racks of sleek, gleaming boats are stacked to the ceiling, and take down a double scull, carrying it on our shoulders down to the water. I am surprised how light it is.

Bruce holds the boat while I get in. I'm glad he does, as the boat is incredibly unstable. He motions for me to tie my feet into a pair of one-size-fits-all shoes that are bolted into the boat. This seems a bit reckless.

Bruce sticks his oars out flat on the water to act as trainer-wheels while I prod the boat away from the shore. You'd think rowing would be a relatively simple motion — and in fact it's not hard to do it badly (after all, we are moving through the water) — but it turns out there is a lot to it. Bruce, sitting behind me, has plenty of advice as we head gently down the Tamaki River.

Soon the warehouses on the banks of the river are replaced by farmland. The weather is grey and overcast, but for once it isn't windy or raining. It turns out that gliding along the smooth water is an incredibly pleasant experience.

It's my fourth time at the rowing club before they let me go out by myself. Bruce decides that rather than a scull I will be better off in a 'Rowbug', a lump of brightly coloured fibreglass that any respectable rower would not be seen dead in. But it is stable, and self-draining, so I could take it out on the Hauraki Gulf — if I could get that far.

'Ha ha! The Rowbug!' one of the gun 20-year-olds says in the changing rooms. 'You won't be able to fall out of that! It's this wide!' He holds up his hands to indicate a width that doesn't seem that generous — in fact, it seems considerably less than the dimensions of my arse.

So, very self-conscious, I carefully get my boat down off the racks, carry it to the water and put it in. I then pause, hoping that anyone watching me is thinking that I'm summoning my strength, when in fact I'm wondering which is the back and which is the front. I get in carefully and screw in the oars the wrong way round. Finally I get myself sorted out, then I start stabbing at the water until eventually the current and my uncoordinated thrashings take me out of sight of the clubhouse and I can prod the estuary in peace.

The little boat is not stable at all. I feel like I'm trying to sit on a log with a flounder tied to my bum. The smallest amount of movement sends me hurtling off to one side or the other. It's beyond the power of my twitching buttocks to get the damn thing stable in the water.

But the weather is perfect as the golden glow on the horizon eventually parts to reveal the morning sun. I coast around the bend and find water as still as glass. I have plenty of time to appreciate the view as I only seem to manage a few strokes before I need to take a rest. It's wonderful to see a side of Auckland that so few people see, and it's entirely pleasant, with the bank gliding past and the blades making a fizzing sound as they skim back along the water. I have the whole river to myself.

The thing with going backwards is that you can't see where you are going. A couple of times I'm surprised by a moored boat flashing two feet past my blade, and I shudder at the thought of what might have happened if I had hit it at full speed. At my full speed, probably nothing.

Eventually I make it back to the clubhouse, full of goodwill for my new sport. I'm entirely chuffed.

Two days later, I'm wobbling down the river when Barry, who is in a metal dinghy with a little outboard chasing one of the crews, zooms over to give me some advice. 'You're throwing too much water up at your release,' he shouts. 'Pull the handle in up to your tits!'

I try this advice, and for two of the next three strokes it works beautifully; another gentle pull and I am neatly popped over the side as if I had just stomped on the 'Incompetent Rower Ejection' button. The rowboat doesn't even seem to slow down — it sails along serenely like the *Mary Celeste* while I explore the Tamaki River's muddy bottom. I eventually surface, spluttering, and have to decide if I should make a lunge for the oar that is floating away downstream, or for the boat that is floating upstream.

I come back after an hour. I'm exhausted, but at least it means that now I can do half of one two-hour rowing shift. Now I just need to do six of these in one day in a boat that's 20 times heavier. I return to the clubhouse to see Matt and Steve getting ready to go out. They ask innocently why I am wet and how the preparations are going. Steve tells me about two guys who were attempting to row across the Indian Ocean. They'd been rescued off the coast of Australia a few days ago

— just three days out, during a storm, the boat had capsized, probably after hitting a whale. Both rowers were trapped upside down in the back cockpit, and the boat (the same design as the one used in the trans-Atlantic race) refused to right itself. With water trickling in they had no choice but to open the hatch, flood the cabin, and swim out. They managed to activate a rescue beacon, but they still spent fourteen hours on top of the slippery upturned hull, with sharks circling about in the water trying to give them a pedicure.

They just thought I should know.

June 2002

Now every other morning I strap myself into the Rowbug and make worm tracks up and down the Tamaki River, gradually going further and further afield.

One of my big concerns is crashing into other boats. It's so dark, and the boats move so fast, with such a low profile. A rowing eight might be a ripple in the distance one minute and a Viking longboat the next.

I seem to be suffering from Heavy Liver. Even when I sit dead in the middle and pull symmetrically, the boat veers off to the left. At least now my technique has improved to the point where I can start to put some power into the water. I have started to give names to the faces I find myself making when I am training. I start off my row with a little gentle cheek-puffing Louis Armstrong, then after 20 minutes I work into Hannibal Lecter before turning around and coming back to the clubrooms with the full 'Midnight at the Playboy Mansion'.

Mum and I are watching a documentary on TV about a woman who has anorexia. I find it very strange that she just can't see the consequences of her actions, despite their being obvious to everyone else.

I turn to Mum. 'How could someone embark on a path that is going to kill them, and not see it?'

Mum arches an eyebrow.

'You mean like your rowing plans?'

July 2002

Today I am on my way to Performance Lab to meet an exercise physiologist called Jon Ackland. It's a pearler of a day, and as I drive over the Panmure Bridge I wish I was rowing — there's not a breath of wind, and the Tamaki River is as full and inviting as a cup of shiny blue milk.

My training has been a little chaotic, and several people have recommended I go and see Jon, and ask him to write me a training programme. He is in hot demand with marathoners and triathletes, and it has taken me several weeks to get an appointment.

Jon is in his forties, a slight figure, and fully caffeinated. He's friendly enough at first, but when I go into his room and shut the door he questions me for a full three-quarters of an hour about my plans for the race. Only after he is convinced that I'm not a complete dreamer does he start talking, and even then not about training programmes.

'Sure I can write you a training programme — that will take ten minutes. What I want to talk to you about is your PERFORMANCE.

'I was watching the last British Masters,' he continues, 'the one where Tiger Woods beat everyone by a mile, and they were interviewing the guy who came second and he said, "Tiger's out there trying to play the perfect game of golf and we're just trying to beat Tiger," AND THAT IS WHY THEY WERE LOSING!

'Look at Michael Johnson in the 1996 Olympics — he ran faster then the 100-metres guys for his 200-metre time. In 1968 Bob Beamon long-jumped 50 cm past the world record. Do you think these people are just trying to beat the opposition? NO! They are trying to PLAY THE PERFECT GAME!

'You need to be focused on the race sixteen hours a day and dreaming about it the other eight — and surrounding yourself WITH PEOPLE WHO ARE WINNERS.

'When you are sitting around in a bar in the Canaries talking shit, there should be NOTHING you don't know about the Atlantic, there should be NOTHING that you can be tripped up on, AND, *AND*, you should show an innovation that is a step change different from what has gone before. You HAVE TO OWN THE RACE! OWN IT! OWN IT!'

Wow! OK!

Finally we start talking about an exercise programme.

'So how hard do I have to train? Two hours a day? Five hours? Or as much as I can, right?'

Jon shakes his head emphatically.

'Kevin, if it was simply a matter of the person who trains hardest getting the gold then there would be some nutcases out there training 25 hours a day. You don't get fit when you are working out your muscles. You only improve when you are NOT training. Your rest periods are as important as your training periods.

'In fact,' he says, 'overtraining early on is one of your biggest risks. It's to do with your central nervous system. If you train it too much you can cook it, and it can take months to recover. If you wake up in the morning and don't really feel like training, you shouldn't.'

When I leave the office I feel like I have plugged my fingers into a power socket. I am totally infected with Jon's energy.

I have to know everything possible about the race, know it so that it is automatic. I have to be completely comfortable in the boat in all conditions. Surround myself by people who are athletes? I wonder if that means Mum and Chantelle?

I take Jon's training programme home and stick it to the wall above my desk. I know that at 5:30am when the alarm goes off there will be no end to my mind's creativity as it tries to get out of training. I will have to follow Jon's training programme to the letter or not at all.

I don't know about central nervous system fatigue, but I am definitely getting Exercise-Induced Alzheimer's. Today I'm late going to the gym and I leave the house in a rush. Before I walk out the front door I pat my jeans pocket to make sure my car keys are there. Then I go out and lock the door, carefully pushing the Car Key Teleport button. Sure enough, the car and house keys that only a moment ago were in my pocket are now inside the house, and since I am now locked outside I have to climb in through a window to get them.

I have driven about two miles from home when I realise that I have left my heart-rate monitor behind. When I finally get to the gym I realise that I also left my workout shirt at home, so I borrow one from lost property. I have just reached the ergo when there is an announcement over the PA that the gym is closing in half an hour's time. I work out for 22 minutes before the lights go out, then I go downstairs to have a shower. As I'm getting dressed I chat to the guy next to me. Later at the supermarket I bump into the same guy, who tells me that I left my toilet bag in the gym. I thank him, and go to pay at the checkout, but I can't find my wallet — it's in the car.

Jon's exercise programme starts off very gently. A bit too gently for me. After two 'rest' days, I am fizzing full of energy. It's a relief to go to the gym and thrash myself with a 20-km row on the ergo, at a pretty reasonable pace, and my reasonable pace is getting more and more reasonable all the time. I even have a couple of strokes that are fluid and graceful.

Today I treated myself to a massage from Martina the German masseuse. Martina is very solidly built in the best Bavarian beerhall tradition. She has extremely strong fingers. The jar has not been made that she couldn't get the top off. Martina seems to think that my internal organs would be better off neatly packed into my skull. I try to stay relaxed as Martina industriously works my pancreas towards my neck. I feel like a used toothpaste tube when she is finished with me.

The next morning I wake up at 4am with my back throbbing and my heart pounding. It feels like I have been hit with sticks. I turn on the electric blanket to try and warm the aches out. I take some aspirin and lie awake until breakfast thinking about what 5000 kilometres is going to feel like.

I am definitely getting larger. I am growing and metamorphosing like the Hulk getting angry. My arms in particular have inflated like I am wearing waterwings. I also seem to be expanding around the abdominal region, although I am checking less regularly after a bursting button nearly hit me in the eye. I am eating a lot. As my level of exercise increases so does my appetite. I am eating in a kind of unconscious way — perfectly good food disintegrates into crumbs around me. I pop chocolate biscuits into my mouth like they are Smarties.

Rob kindly lends me his ergo, an indoor rowing machine, which when installed in the basement downstairs makes training a lot more convenient. To try and increase the resistance and make it more like rowing the heavy Atlantic rowing boats, I have taken off the cage that surrounds the fan. It works well but it does create quite a breeze. Unfortunately the basement is also where, among all the boxes, old clothes, worn-out sofas and books, Chantelle hides and moults. The first time I wind up the ergo the air becomes a blizzard of white hair. I feel like I am inside one of those water-filled paperweights that you shake to create a festive snow scene. I work out that I can avoid choking if I row with the vacuum cleaner running and my shirt pulled over my mouth.

I went and saw the nutritionist at the gym today. He told me that because of all the exercise I am doing I can pretty much eat what I want, including pies!

Jon's plan has me doing another rest day, so I am back watching TV on the couch, with a plate of steaming steak and kidney pie. It occurs to me that I am doing exactly the same thing that I have been doing a lot of in the last few months, only now it's called training to row the Atlantic!

CHAPTER SEVEN

Show me the money

The training is the easy bit. I need money. I need great steaming wads of it — to build a boat, to put equipment in it, to freight it to the start of the race, to pay airfares and the entry fee.

The training I can do by myself, but getting the money together requires calling in some expertise — not to mention that as an ocean rower I completely lack credibility. Companies are only going to give me money if they think I am going to make it to the end of the race — since I can scarcely believe I can do it, why should they?

I could also really do with some expertise to put the boat together. I have already come up with dozens of questions that I need to get answers for, and teaming up with someone who has already put an Atlantic rowboat together would save me weeks of work. So I really need to work with Rob and Steve. In fact, given Steve and Steph's ultimatum, Rob *or* Steve.

Rob is a great guy, who seems easy to get along with and has the experience of putting together two trans-Atlantic campaigns. And, most importantly, he seems to genuinely believe in my ability to pull it off — whereas I don't believe my campaign would last long under Steve's cool, rational assessment of my ability. But Steve clearly had issues working with Rob; would I, too? I really need to find out what is going on between them.

I call up Rob and he suggests I come down and discuss it with him over dinner.

I drive over the Bombays through a storm the TV news later describes as a 'weather bomb'. I can only go as fast as the limply flailing windscreen wipers on the Starlet will slosh away the bucketing rain. When I finally reach Rob's house I go through the picket fence and knock on the door. A tall, attractive woman holding a very young baby answers the door and introduces herself. 'Hi, I'm Rachel, Rob's wife. Come in. Rob's in the kitchen.'

Rob comes out wiping his eyes with the backs of his hands.

'I hope you like garlic.'

'Sure. Why's that?'

'I've just put twelve cloves into the spag bol.'

We go back into the kitchen, Rob opens a bottle of shiraz, and we chat while the rain lashes the windows and hits the roof in a way that sounds uncannily like someone peeing on it. When dinner's ready we move to the living room, where the heat from the open fire seems to be causing rapid evaporation of my wine. Another bottle of red is opened, and then another.

I get to the point.

'So what's got Steve Westlake and Steph Brown so upset?'

'I think they're telling people I took money I wasn't entitled to from the trust account. In reality, I think they are really disputing the timing of when I got paid.'

'What's the story?'

'It's pretty straightforward. Before the race we agreed that I was going to be responsible for putting the campaign together, including getting sponsorship, and that I would be paid a certain amount for doing it.'

'So how did the fundraising go?'

'Very ordinary at the start — it was bloody hard going. We had some big bills coming in that had to be paid, and I was paying them out of my own pocket. No one else was going to. I paid a huge amount

upfront for things like the kitset, air freight, and building the kit —
stuff like that. It was pretty stressful for a while. It was only a few
months before the race that Telecom came on board and it all came
right.'

'Did you get paid?'

'Yeah, when the fundraising proved successful all the contractors
were paid, including me. I don't think the amount's the issue, but they
seem to have a problem with me being paid before the campaign had
finished.'

'So is there enough left to pay them too?'

'They already have some money. When Telecom came on board the
trust was able to pay them when they took time off work. But we do
still need to work out how the surplus is split up.'

'So it's probably going to get resolved eventually?'

'Oh yeah, I'm sure it will eventually.'

From the piles of videotapes Rob finds some of the original footage
shot during the '97 race. There they are out in the middle of the ocean.
The sun is beaming down. There is a wiry Phil Stubbs pulling at the
oars and laughing into the camera. At last I get a chance to glimpse the
horror that I have been seeing in my nightmares. It doesn't look so bad
— the indigo waves are muddled and small. The bright sunshine even
looks inviting, and they are *rowing the Atlantic*!

I wake up on the sofa the next day, barely able to wriggle my toes
without causing calamity in my head. Official business is conducted
very quickly. I draft a little agreement setting out how we could work
together: we would share all the work and we would each underwrite
the costs equally. Rob's new family commitments have ruled him out
of being the other rower that I need, but he would help find someone,
and would be the reserve.

The phone rings — it's Rob. 'Why did I just call you?'

'You wanted to tell me you had just raised half a million dollars?'

'No, it's something else. Never mind, I'll call you back.'

Ring ring.

'I know what it is now. I think you should take a cat on board the
boat.'

'[Long pause] . . . I don't need any more cats in my life.'

'Think of the media coverage — the cat could have its own blog site!'

'You're nuts! What if it falls overboard? . . . Wait! Great idea! I know just the cat to practise on.'

><

The first company we target for sponsorship is Telecom. They had sponsored the 2001 campaign, and by all accounts it had worked out very well for them. In fact, they had been nominated for some sponsorship award for the way the partnership worked.

Rob and I arrange to fly to Wellington for a meeting, and I drive down to Hamilton the night before. It's always cold in Hamilton — either cold or raining. I wake up at Rob's at 5:45am. Our flight leaves at 6:30. Overnight the windscreen has iced up, so I drive with my head out the window. We miss the airport turn-off, so I have to do a U-turn on the motorway. We finally make it to the airport and I drop Rob off to start the check-in while I park the car. As I run into the terminal the plane waiting on the tarmac has already started its engines. Rob can't find our boarding passes, but somehow manages to convince the airline staff to let us on anyway. It is the only time in my life that I have literally run onto a plane after having nothing to do with the check-in or boarding process. It feels like it's my private jet. I love New Zealand.

I'm wearing a suit, a new gold 'winner's' tie and matching cufflinks. Rob is dressed in casual, but insists it's 'smart casual'. His concession to formality is to wear shoes — at least until we get into the plane. He looks at me.

'What's with the tie? You look like a poof.'

It's still early when we arrive at Wellington airport, so we get a coffee. Rob goes to the bathroom and a few minutes later slips back into his seat looking guilty. He looks from side to side before whispering, 'I've just done something that might be perceived as odd.'

'Stolen all the soaps?'

'No.'

'Squatted on the seat?'

'No, I hovered — who squats these days?'

'Opened the door with your pinky?'

'Of course, but that's not it.'

'Well what then?'

'I turned all the mixer handles around to cold. It saves power. Can you believe how many wusses there are out there who have to wash their hands in warm water?'

We take a taxi to Rob's sister's place and borrow her car to go into the city. We are still early for the meeting, so we have another coffee. Rob buys us both a fortune cookie. Mine says, 'A great day for communicating.' Rob's says, 'Hold on tight to the reins.'

The meeting goes well. The head of sponsorship compliments me on my tie and cufflinks. They thank us for our presentation and say they will get back to us in a couple of weeks.

So then we are off to Serco, another sponsor of the previous campaign.

'Rob, do you know where you're going?'

'Uhh, not exactly.'

'So how are we going to get there?'

'I'm going to steer by the stars.'

The CEO is all business. At the end of our presentation he tells us he will need to discuss the proposal with his colleagues. At the door he shakes our hands and we thank him for taking the time to see us.

'Not at all,' he says. 'I figured you were coming. I've just received a proposal from Steve Westlake and Matt Goodman.'

We walk back to the car, both trying to come to terms with this new information.

I can't really understand their motivation for returning to the race. They have already proven to themselves that they can get a boat in the water, row the Atlantic, and beat all the opposition. Surely that is 99% of the point of taking the challenge on? The only thing they don't have is Rob's world record. Is that worth all the months of preparation, and the effort and discomfort of doing the race again?

On the positive side, if the experience had been really terrible they wouldn't want to do it again would they? But it also means that there are two New Zealand teams trying to access the same limited amount of sponsorship money. And they will be a much better bet than us, I would have thought.

'So I guess Steve changed his mind about the Olympics?' I suggest to Rob at last.

'Yeah, Matt too. He was pretty keen to be in the Olympics. It looks like they realised they weren't going to make the team.'

><

The phone rings. It's Rob.

'Gidday. I've just spoken to Mount Gay Rum. I'm trying to convince them that we should get the old Atlantic boat painted up in Mount Gay colours and have you rowing around the harbour giving out rum samples.'

'You mean like the Jagermeister Girls?'

'Exactly!'

'Except we would be the Gay Rum Boys?'

'You got it. What do you reckon?'

><

Telecom politely turn us down, so we start knocking on other doors.

A few days later I am invited into a large boardroom where the CEO is sitting, flanked by po-faced advisers. He looks up.

'I'm sorry. We are running a little short on time to hear your presentation. Why don't I just get out my cheque book?'

He is joking.

We get an appointment with Bell Tea; they sound very positive on the phone. Rob and I are brought into the boardroom. A few minutes later the CEO comes in and offers us something to drink.

'Coffee thanks,' says Rob.

We have an appointment to speak to a manager at Sanitarium. I am quite excited about this because we are a good fit with the sporting image they use to promote their Weet-Bix brand. Once again we find ourselves waiting nervously in a large boardroom.

'Rob, you know Sanitarium are owned and operated by the Seventh Day Adventists?'

'Yeah?'

'So we should probably watch our p's and q's.'

One of the Sanitarium marketing team arrives. He is young, polite, and conservatively dressed. After a few moments of small talk, during which some hot drinks are brought in, the presentation gets under way. I am just explaining the race when suddenly there is a loud exclamation from the other side of the table.

'Jesus!'

The Sanitarium man and I look around to see Rob pushing his chair away from the table and flailing at his crotch.

'I just spilt my coffee all over me. Bugger!'

The search for sponsorship isn't helped by the fact that the race takes place overseas, nor that it coincides exactly with New Zealand's most eagerly awaited event of the last four years — no, not the Olympics, the Rugby World Cup. Many of the sponsors we talk to have also been approached by Matt and Steve, and having to decide which New Zealand campaign to back is just another complicating factor, and another reason to defer and eventually decline sponsoring us.

Both Rob and I are keen to use the campaign to support a charity. Rob's new baby Finn has been diagnosed with a rare eye condition, and my nephews suffer from cystic fibrosis. It's the CEO of Hewlett-Packard who suggests working with the organisation Cure Kids. A few days later we meet with their boss, Kaye Parker.

The thing that makes Cure Kids different from most other child-focused charities is that they use the money they raise to support researchers who are working on finding solutions to child-related illnesses. It turns out that there is a lot of great work being done right here in New Zealand. Kaye is an inspirational and dynamic leader, and it's clear they are doing phenomenal work with their fundraising. We agree to work together to help boost their profile and raise funds for them where we can.

While we are pitching to the ANZ they ask if we have had any word about the progress of the latest trans-Tasman attempt by the New

Zealand rowers — these are the guys who had tried to launch from Muriwai, then decided to go the other way and leave from Australia. We hadn't. No one had.

Then news comes through.

Dramatic sea rescue of Kiwi duo

October 26, 2002

Two Kiwis trying to row the Tasman have been rescued off the Australian coast after spending two days clinging to the upturned hull of their boat.

Nick Barbara, 26, of Gisborne, and Cathal Dickens, 31, were pulled off their 7.7m upturned boat by a passing fishing vessel late last night about 450km east of Sydney.

Mr Barbara's wife, Glenis Philip-Barbara, is hoping to fly to Sydney today to see her husband and his rowing partner when they arrive.

Australian search and rescue officials were quoted by Reuters today as saying the pair were in good condition.

They left Australia 11 days ago on the planned 2600km voyage to Auckland.

The voyage is to raise money for a children's hospital ward in South Auckland.

This week they were fighting to stay on course in very rough seas and winds of more than 50 knots.

In 15-metre waves they lost their sea anchor, a parachute-like device to help steady the boat. They also lost their VHF radio in the storm.

Two days ago the authorities lost contact with the pair and aerial patrols searched for the rowers on Thursday and yesterday.

Mrs Philip-Barbara told the Waikato Times today she got a message at 11.30 last night from the skipper of the rescuing fishing boat to say the pair had been found.

She said, although details were sketchy, both men 'were fine and well'.

— Independent Newspapers

CHAPTER EIGHT

1% inspiration

'I don't know,' I say hesitantly, but I suspect I don't really understand the question. I am back in Jon Ackland's office to pick up the next instalment of my training programme — or that's what I thought I was there for. But now, out of the blue, Jon has come out with this strange question. Seeing the uncertain look on my face, he repeats himself.

'Kevin, you need to make up your mind NOW if you are going to win or not. I'm happy either way, but we need to know now. What's the plan?'

'I guess I'm going to try my best and just see what happens when we get out on the water. You know, there are lots of things that can go wrong . . . we might get some bad weather, or the watermaker might break down . . . I mean it would be nice to win, but you can't really hang your hat on it, there are a lot of factors . . .'

'WRONG! WRONG! WRONG! You've got to decide NOW! If you decide that you are going to win it will change everything about the campaign — the way you prepare, the way you train, the equipment you buy, the funds you need, the type of person you row with, EVERYTHING!

'When you get to the start line most of the crews will just be there to take part. But there will be a handful of teams, just a handful, that have made up their minds to win, and one of them *will* win. If you don't make your mind up now you won't even be in the same race as them.'

He sits back in his chair and regards me coolly.

'So, what is it going to be? Are you taking part or are you going to win?'

'Ummm . . .'

He cuts me off. 'Look, have you seen *The Empire Strikes Back*?'

'Sure.'

'Remember when Yoda is teaching Luke Skywalker about how to use The Force, and Luke is messing up and trying to justify it by saying that he's trying? You know what Yoda said? He said, "Do or do not. There is no try." So what's it going to be — are you there to take part, or are you there to win?'

'OK. I'm going to win.'

His expression doesn't change.

'Good, now let's talk about how you are going to do it.'

Later that day, back at home, I think about what I said. Could I really win? Winning means beating Steve and Matt. How possible is that?

Steve has already been involved in a campaign that won the race. In psychological terms, whatever method they had used had been strongly reinforced; it would be very hard for them to make a significant departure from it. Unless things had obviously failed they are likely to use the same food, the same route, the same equipment.

On the other hand, I have no preconceptions about how to win the race, so I'm going to start with a blank slate. That just might mean that I come up with some better answers. Also, unlike them, I haven't come from a flatwater rowing background. I strongly suspect that up to this point ocean rowing has borrowed equipment and techniques from flatwater rowing without necessarily considering whether they are the best for the job. There are many differences between flatwater rowing and ocean rowing. For one thing, the weight of the boat is hugely different — a single scull only weighs about 15 kg, whereas the weight of an ocean rowboat is around 700 to 800 kg. Flatwater rowers have their bums only a few centimetres above the water. We are going to sit 60 cm above the water. A flatwater rowing boat, and the rowing technique, and the training methods, are all about maximising speed in short bursts, whereas we are about maximising speed over weeks.

By living with Mum and doing a bit of part-time work I could make the campaign my full-time job. I could spend 40 to 50 hours a week more working on a campaign than somebody who had a full-time job. That would add up to thousands of extra hours of effort that I could put into planning and preparation. There is no doubt that they have more experience, they know what it is like to be out in the open ocean, and they know what worked and what didn't. But the race doesn't start for almost a year, which gives me plenty of time to get similar sorts of experience, and to talk to people who have done the race before.

The question is whether innovation is going to be able to trump experience. Since this is only going to be the third time the race has been held, there is a good chance that some new ideas and many little improvements could add up to an extra few per cent of boat speed. And every 1% I can find will take at least ten hours off the race.

OK, Mr Blank Slate. How are you going to start?

What if this wasn't a boat race? What if it was a mad cross-country rally race where you could take any route to get from the start to the end? Then what would I need to win? It would be something like:

- lightest, most aerodynamic chassis
- best fuel
- most skilful driver
- biggest engine
- shortest route

Each of these has a direct parallel to the boat race:

- lightest and slipperiest boat
- best nutrition
- best boat-handling skills

- fittest possible rowers (and an efficient rowing set-up)
- shortest route

Of course I need all of these things to be as good as possible, but where am I going to get the biggest bang for my buck?

In the first race the winning strategy was to build a boat that was as light as possible, but the race organisers quickly saw that there was an alarming incentive for boat-builders to be very vigorous on the sanding and skimpy on the glue. The way things were heading, the boats were going to be just a few paint molecules hanging off the gunnels. So they wisely decided that there should now be a minimum weight of 410 kg for the basic empty boat. Before turning up at the start of the race each team now has to send in an official weighing certificate to show that their boat is above the minimum amount. We'll still have to be careful about the equipment we bolt onto the boat, but just going light isn't going to be enough.

Maybe there is something we can do to make the boat a bit more slippery, but that isn't likely to make a significant difference. Nor is nutrition, nor boat-handling skills. We could get very good, but so could other crews.

Nor do I think there's going to be much of a speed advantage from how fit I and my team-mate are. To make a rowboat go twice as fast takes far more than twice the energy — it takes eight times! In fact, if you only row twice as hard, for example by having two people rowing at once, you will only go about 25% faster. Which means that you could train until you looked like the Incredible Hulk had swallowed Arnold Schwarzenegger and you wouldn't go *that* much faster. Of course, I do have to get as monster as possible — it's just that the other crews will too, at least the ones that are trying to win, so by itself getting super-fit is unlikely to be enough to win the race.

There is more to rowing fast then just getting gorilla about it. There is all the physics and physiology of the rowing action — the height of the seat in relation to the water, the gearing of the oars, the size of the blades, the width of the oar handles, the position of the rowlocks in relation to the sliding seat, the angle of the footplate, and a range of other things. Maybe there is something that could be tweaked here. It is going to take something like 1.3 million oar strokes to get across the Atlantic, so if I can find just a 0.0001% advantage it would be significant.

But surely the easiest way to shave time off the journey across the ocean would be to take a shorter or faster course? I know from Rob's book that there is a wide divergence of views about the fastest route to Barbados. Some people think it is the shortest possible path, while others argue for a more sou'westerly route to take advantage of the trade winds and the equatorial current. I could sweat blood in training, swallow exotic supplements until I turned yellow and spend thousands of dollars on carbon fibre, all to get an extra fraction of a knot of speed — wouldn't it be easier just to find a route that was 50 miles shorter?

The other easy way to go faster is by not going slow — eliminating any dead time on the boat. Rob had mentioned how much time they had wasted between shifts when they should have been sleeping and recovering, and instead were trying to chip away at their foam seats to improve the shape and slow down the deterioration of their raw skin.

And talking about my backside, do I really have to sacrifice it, layer by layer? Is all that pain absolutely necessary?

'You can't eliminate all pain,' Steve had said at that first lunch. But with months to prepare there is no reason why the seat can't be made comfortable. I want my hands to be in good shape too, and my back, and my head. If I am going to be spending days doing a boring repetitive exercise then at least I can listen to music or something while I am doing it. I want the only pain to be from effort.

I had better get started. There is a lot to do just to get up to speed — let alone go faster!

Using the internet at first, and the library, I read and read about exercise physiology and sports nutrition and the physics of rowing. I dig through shelves of journals, looking for articles with titles like 'Effect of high-intensity versus moderate-intensity exercise on lymphocyte subpopulations and proliferative response' (DC Nieman et al., *Int J Sp Med* 15:199, 1994). Most are unhelpful, but occasionally I find a nugget I can use.

I find out about when you should exhale during the stroke, about how the position of the hands affects the strength of the pull, about the optimal angle of the foot-stretcher. I read books on anatomy and find out about the curve of the ischial tuberosities and the path of the sciatic nerve.

I read about the advantages of high-altitude training, and find there is a New Zealand company that has invented a device which simulates the same effect at sea level. Every other day for weeks at a time I sit at a table in their Mt Eden clinic and breathe in oxygen-depleted air. It's strangely relaxing.

I read about the physics of rowing. I start corresponding with a professor at Oxford, and I talk to a Russian researcher who works for the Australian Institute of Sport about the ideal size of our oar blades. I find out how to increase the effective blade size without increasing the size of the spoon.

Rob encourages me to chase down every path. Every so often I call him up about a new idea.

'That's a great idea!' he'll respond enthusiastically.

'But do you think it will work?'

'Ah, no.'

'Why?'

'Because we tried it in '97.'

There is something of a debate about the best nutrition for ultra-endurance. Some researchers say carbohydrates, others say fats. We would much prefer to take more fat, because for the same weight fat has twice the energy of carbohydrate. And that would translate into a huge weight-saving. But what do ultra-distance athletes actually eat? That's when I read about the people who are the epitome of ultra-endurance runners — not the Kenyans or the Moroccans — the very weird Tarahumara Indians of Mexico.

The Tarahumara Indians are a small group of people who live in the rugged Sierra Madre region of northwestern Mexico. The area is one of the coldest in Mexico and soil conditions are very poor. This is why the Tarahumara are semi-nomadic, and are cave-dwellers for part of the year. The Tarahumara are not really into cleaning — clothes washing is usually done once or twice a year. Nor do they have regular sleeping habits — they simply go to sleep whenever and wherever they are tired and feel that they need rest. If this sounds like one of your old flatmates, there is a reason — the Tarahumarans put enormous amounts of energy into drinking and running.

In the Tarahumara culture it is considered a matter of pride to be intoxicated. It has been estimated that the Tarahumara Indians are either participating in or recovering from parties that involve drinking large amounts of fermented corn liquor for approximately one hundred days of the year. The only thing they love more than partying is running. It's a way of life, the result of their isolation and the incredibly rugged terrain. It is not uncommon for a Tarahumaran to travel between 80 and 130 kilometres every day.

Their favourite sport is a race run between two teams where each team kicks along a wooden, baseball-shaped ball as they run to the next village — which may be up to 250 km away. The Tarahumara continue drinking and smoking until just before each race starts — including imbibing a combination of tobacco and dried bats' blood to help them run faster and keep away the other team's evil spirits.

So what do they eat? Their diet is practically meatless, and consists mostly of complex carbohydrates (and a little dried bats' blood).

If the world's greatest ultra-endurance athletes eat mostly carbo-hydrates, then why shouldn't we? The problem is weight. Can we get the same performance from a lighter, high-fat diet?

Unfortunately the body of research into fat metabolism for endu-rance athletes is slim, and for ultra-endurance athletes it's even slimmer. There are very few experts anywhere in the world who have studied fat metabolism for sport. But one of them is in New Zealand — Dr Rachel Brown, from the University of Otago, the nutritionist Steve had mentioned and rated highly. By happy coincidence she has just moved up to Auckland.

I meet Rachel Brown at her house in South Auckland. We discuss Auckland house prices over a cup of tea. She is very friendly and approachable, and in a very unassuming way, extremely knowledgeable about nutrition. She is also a fan of Matt and Steve, having worked with them for the 2001 event, and she lets me know that she checked with them before talking to me.

I listen eagerly while she lays out the basic framework for the diet that's necessary on the boat. It's very simple: 40 MJ of food a day, 50% of energy from fat (more if possible) and 2 grams of protein per kilogram of bodyweight. We also talk about the make-up of the 'recovery' drink, a kind of sweet, fatty milkshake that we need to have at the end of most shifts. Taking a slug of sugar at the end of a workout is supposed to increase insulin levels, shut down fat metabolism and trigger recovery.

The body needs to adapt to digesting this amount of fat, but apparently with little effort I could train my gut to become the equivalent of an oil refinery.

'So I can eat anything I want?' I ask eagerly.

'Anything. With cream on top.'

'Including pies?'

'Make them cheese-top pies, and put on extra mayonnaise.'

'So I shouldn't feel bad about that donut I had this morning?'

'Best thing you've had all day.'

My prototype tilting rowing seat just exploded underneath me. With a loud crack of overstressed fibreboard I am dumped six inches to the ground, narrowly avoiding doing a serious injury to my, uh . . . lower abdominal area.

The idea for a tilting seat came from noticing that my normal rowing seat produces maximum pain when my knees are brought in to my chest. I had gone to the library and rented out a CD that showed on the computer screen a 3-D representation of the body, which could be tilted and observed from any angle. It seemed to me that if the rowing seat could be made to tilt back a little at the front of the slide, then my bodyweight would be spread more across the backs of my legs. This would also be a much more effective position for the legs to start their drive from.

After several false starts I completed a prototype of a tilting seat. A wooden platform was raised and balanced on an axle, allowing it to rock back and forth. To give it some tension, I attached a spring to one end of a steel bar bolted onto the front of the platform. When I tried it out the bar bent ominously as I rocked back, and the wooden board creaked as the screws struggled to hold it in place. When it was finished it looked very strange and slightly sinister — like a see-saw for midgets, or a medieval device for spectacularly removing testicles. Now it's broken I am relieved, and I never rebuild it.

'Rob, I think it's time you taught me how to row in one of the Atlantic boats.'

'I guess we better,' says Rob.

The Starlet splutters up over the Bombay Hills and lurches towards Hamilton. It gets most of the way, gliding to a halt on the shoulder outside Ngaruawahia. Rob comes and gets me and tows me to a service station.

'Your alternator's buggered,' says the mechanic. 'Didn't you see the warning light on the dashboard?'

I don't like to tell him that at some point every warning light flickered on and off — it's quite a pretty effect in a 'bridge of the Starship Enterprise' kind of way.

'What will it cost to fix?'

'Well, to replace the alternator might cost a couple hundred bucks, or you could tap it with a hammer every time it plays up and you'll be right for a while.'

We pick up the boat from Rob's place and head on to Lake Karapiro. On the boat ramp we undo the straps that hold the boat in place on the trailer, and Rob suggests I hop on board while he backs the last few feet into the water.

'Hold on!' he shouts.

The car accelerates backwards and as the trailer hits the water he jams on the brakes and skids to a splashy halt. The untethered boat rockets off and hits the water like the end of an amusement park log-flume ride. Rob gets out of the car and laughs as he watches me helplessly heading backwards out into the lake. Then he looks concerned. 'Hey, did you put the bungs in?' he shouts.

I scamper madly around the boat for a minute until I realise that the bungs are in. Rob is now doubled over.

I slip the oars into the rowlocks and sit on the seat. It's much higher off the water than the Rowbug, which is good — much less chance of getting my arse wet. And certainly a whole lot more stable. That is also good. I lean forward, raise my hands to put the blades into the water, and pull. My hands come back to me very slowly as the boat reluctantly begins to move. Boy, it feels heavy — and this with the boat completely empty. Once it's moving it keeps moving. It's like being on a big barge. It takes me a full minute to turn the boat around — it's so big I don't know who's rowing who.

I get the boat back to the ramp and Rob jumps in. I put my head into the cabin to get a seat out and immediately feel a convulsion in my stomach. Could I be seasick in the first two minutes on a flat-calm lake? But back on deck and rowing I soon have other things to worry about. In the gentle, enigmatic, Zen-like manner of the Buddhist masters, Rob begins instructing his new grasshopper on the subtle mysteries of the art of rowing.

'Jingoes, Kev, your technique is crap! You won't beat an egg doing that. Rowing is like makin' *lurve* — slow it down and lengthen out!'

Today we are working on the 'catch', the all-important moment when the rower's blade first enters the water. This is a mysterious ballet of motion and timing that is crucially important to efficiently transfer the rower's strength into boat speed. Unfortunately it combines a number of factors — your speed up the slide, the small arc made by your wrists as they lift, the angle of your torso, and numerous other intangibles such as local barometric pressure and sunspot activity. But like learning how to ride a bicycle, there is only so much you can be taught.

After some brief pointers Rob sits behind and grades each stroke as either pass or fail: 'Nup . . . nup . . . nup . . .' Then every hundred strokes or so, 'That's a good one.' Then 'Nup . . . nup . . . nup . . .' until the planets swing into alignment again. I thought I had been getting pretty competent with my rowing, so this critique is very frustrating.

Finally, after visiting every corner of the lake, we return to the boat ramp, chat to the curious onlookers who gather around every time the boat is taken out, and head home. This becomes the pattern for many similar trips. Sometimes, on sunny days, Rob's wife Rachel joins us with Finn. They bring lunch and we putter around the lake as if we are on the Serpentine. Sometimes, if we are very unlucky, Rob will burst into song. He does a fine version of 'Pokarekare Ana' that could bring any amorous walrus to the surface.

Little by little I begin to become competent in some of the hundreds of things that I will need to know. I learn how to use the foot steering, how to keep a course into the wind, how the compass wobbles as you row, how to lay out the sea anchor, where to stand and not to stand on the boat, the best way to pee into a bucket, how to do simple repairs on the watermaker, how to use the stove and cook a meal, how to step over the swinging oar of the person rowing so that I can change position without them missing a beat, what foods taste best and which hatch is most convenient to store them in. And always, always, there's more practice on the catch.

✕

I am in the doorway of one of the boat-building sheds at the Unitec campus in West Auckland. It is impressively large and lofty, as big as a college gym, with huge ventilation tubes winding up from large machines into the ceiling. There are skeletons of boats lying around, their ribs exposed, giving the building an air of a dinosaur graveyard. There is a sharp, clean smell of fresh sawdust. A small stack of pre-cut plywood sheets leans against the wall in the corner — that is our kitset, newly arrived from the UK.

Rob has asked Unitec if they would consider having one of their boat-building classes build our boat, and they have kindly agreed. I follow the course instructor, Paul Donahoe, into a room where he unrolls the plans on a large table. There is an older guy with a large beard in the room too. I introduce myself and ask him who he is.

'I'm just an older guy with a beard,' he replies. It turns out he is Chris Lovegrove, the programme director. We all peer at the plans.

'How does it look?' I ask nervously. 'Too difficult?'

'Hmm, maybe too easy,' says Paul. 'There's not much to it.'

Over the next hour, Paul and I discuss how the boat is to be built. I am particularly keen that the boat is built so that it is exactly 'true' — dead straight from bow to stern. I'm also there to meet the students and to help them feel they are part of a bigger project — show them that a real person is going to be using this boat and is relying on their craftsmanship.

The students are all baggy jeans, baseball caps and attitude as they slouch in their chairs. Some of them look as if they would rather be skateboarding than here.

I end the presentation dramatically. 'We don't need you to make a rowboat — we need you to make a *rocket ship!*' I thunder. 'Any questions?'

There is an uncomfortable shuffle. One guy finally puts his hand up.

'Are you allowed to take drugs on board?'

Paul Donahoe walks me to the door. 'They're good kids,' he says. 'I'm sure they'll do a good job.'

I nod. 'How far through their training are they?'

'Ahh . . . not too far.'

'Have they built anything yet?'

'Oh yes.'

'What's that?'

'Their toolboxes.'

I am obsessed about my bum. My increasingly long sessions on the Rowbug are only made bearable by putting down a combination of carefully folded towels. Every workout reminds me that I have still to come up with a good seat solution. I start thinking about people who spend a lot of time sitting down, and what they use. People like paraplegics. I start calling physios and specialists to see what seat solutions are in the market. One of them recommends that I go and see Andy O'Sullivan from a company called DME at their offices in Birkenhead.

Andy is a man who Understands. He nods as he listens to my story, then he asks me, 'Do you know a couple of guys called Matt and Steve?'

'Sure, why?'

'They were here a couple of days ago, looking for a seating solution for the same race.'

'That's a coincidence!' I splutter.

'Not really,' says Andy. 'People try lots of different things but every-one comes here in the end. Let me show you what we've got.'

We go out to the storeroom that backs onto Andy's office and he shows me a Roho, a strange-looking rubber mat about the size of a wheelchair seat. On the surface of the rubber are rows of egg-shaped rubber pods. It looks a little bit like supersized bubble wrap. But unlike bubble wrap the pods are all connected, with air channels set into the rubber, so that pushing down on one rubber bubble causes the others to inflate and compensate. I try it out. It feels incredibly comfy.

On the way home I go to a hardware store to buy a seat-sized piece of wood. I replace the seat on the ergo with the wood, and plop the Roho on top. I'm in heaven — it's like sitting on a La-Z-Boy. A slightly wobbly, rubber La-Z-Boy. It isn't perfect, but it's a fantastic start.

'Well, do you want to win, or do you want to take the fastest course?'

This question is posed by Andy Philpott, a professor at Auckland Univerity's engineering school. I am meeting with Andy and Geoff Leyland, who has recently returned from finishing his PhD in optimisation in Switzerland. They have agreed to give me a hand to find the best way across the Atlantic.

'There's a difference?'

'There can be. If you're coming second you might choose to take a riskier route where there might be a chance of better conditions. It will be slower on average, but you might get lucky.'

Basically, the main call is whether to take the longer, more southerly route that makes the most of the prevailing weather systems — the old sea captains used to say 'go south until the butter melts and then turn right' — or to take a route that is closer to the shortest course, or to take one somewhere in between.

But there are other things to consider. What if we work out a route based on the average weather conditions then face non-typical conditions? How should we deviate if we get headwinds? What if we are coming second to Matt and Steve — wouldn't they just cover us, making sure they stayed close enough that they are being affected by the same weather. Isn't that what they did to the Aussies in 2001?

'They might not cover you if you were the third boat,' says Andy. That might be the answer — to let another boat become a threat, and then take a different route! But they will ignore us only if they think we aren't their main opposition. Not for the first time it occurs to me that it's very important that we are perceived as the underdogs.

There is much talk of isochrones, orthorgonals, polars, sea states, admiralty charts and racing strategy. The whole business of optimisation is much more complicated than I ever thought.

'The issue is that from day to day there are lots of different optimisations — it's going to be impossible to come up with a single route before the race. Are you going to have an automated tiller system on the boat? If you want we could just crunch the numbers on the university's super-computer and steer you from here,' suggests Andy.

'Thanks, but maybe next race!'

They say they will think about coming up with a solution, and in the meantime I could source some weather charts of the Atlantic for the months of the year we will be out there.

De: Biggar Kevin
Para: 'Palomares H & Q'
Asunto: RE: A question about your pigeons
Buenos Dias!
I will be in the Canary Islands in October of this year to take part in the trans-Atlantic rowing race. Have you heard of this race? It has taken place in 1997 and 2001 with the boats leaving from Canary Islands and going to Barbados.

We have a little problem — I hope that you can help us! We would like to take video while we are on the boat but we have no way of sending the video back to land. We would like to place the video on a Sony 'memory stick' which is a very small light piece of plastic (please see photo) and then attach the memory stick to a carrier pigeon. I understand that pigeons can fly for 1–200kms over sea? So we could have the pigeon on the boat for a few days and then release it to fly back to the Canaries.

Is this possible? If so let's talk some more.

Regards
Kevin

Using an online translator, I manage to translate the reply into English.

To: Biggar Kevin
Subject: RE: To question about your pigeons
Dear to sir:

I to answer your questions, but I to prefer to do in Spanish because it is more easy for me, excuses me. There are many problems for which you solicit, and that would be the following ones:

1. In October the doves still are in their period of dumb, that is changing their plumage, which makes difficult its flights.

2. The normal thing is that the release of the doves is made from a earth place, although soon must fly on the sea. To conduct this operation from a boat on the high seas, by experiences already had, is very complicated and the results are negative, since the great depths that there are in that route do not allow a correct direction of the doves when not being able to perceive the terrestrial magnetism normally that he is basic apparently to orient itself.

3. The number of doves to also loosen can be handicap, because since minimum would be necessary to loosen 2 together doves.

It seems to us very interesting this ready proposal and we will to help him, but he would be very difficult to guarantee that a dove in those dates and circumstances can arrive at the destiny with 'memory stick'.

We know the trans-Atlantic rowing race, and are to your disposition to continue studying this subject, and we would like to know, if it is possible, since points exactly of the route from to leave Tenerife, or to that distances think to send the video. A greeting and we hoped to know something but,

Esteban Hernandez

The race organisers require participants to do a number of courses, like survival at sea, a marine medic course, and navigation with a sextant. This last obligation is imposed by the Spanish maritime authorities. I suppose they had a bad experience with Christopher Columbus, who was so disoriented that when he pitched up in the Caribbean he thought he had arrived in India, but nowadays using a sextant is about as relevant as learning how to splice a main brace, load a cannon and walk on a peg leg.

Taking a sighting with a sextant is difficult; you have to stand on the deck of your heaving boat, and at a certain time *exactly*, take a reading of the angle between the celestial body you are looking at and the horizon. This certainly doesn't sound easy, although I wouldn't know personally because the actual use of a sextant is not a required part of the course. Nor did we have to take one on the boat — we just needed to know how to do the calculations. The course could even be done by correspondence.

If the Earth was a perfect sphere, travelling in a perfect circle around an infinitely small sun . . . then the maths would still be mind-bogglingly difficult. From the angle the sextant gives you, and the time of day, you use a series of arcane tables to do certain calculations to which you apply an increasingly obscure series of corrections, including your height above the sea, the motion of the planets, where you think you are and many other things, including variations in the Earth's orbit. For example, from my course notes:

> The 'v' is an extra correction for additional longitude
> movement of the body, and 'd' is an extra correction for
> additional declination movement. The sun has no 'v' correction
> and the stars have no 'v' or 'd' correction. The sun needs the
> 'd', and the planets and moon need both 'v' and 'd'.

All of this will only tell you where you probably were when you took the sight, and that was several hours ago, when you still had the will to live.

Fortunately, the other courses are applied, practical and useful. The medical courses that I attend are run by Brent, a stocky former SAS medic, who has plenty of stories from the battlefield to hold our attention and emphasise his points.

The course is very hands-on, literally. One of our tasks is to carry out a 'primary survey' on a person, where the aim is to determine the location and extent of the injuries that an injured person may have. After we have practised doing this on other people in the course we do it again with blindfolds. Then with blindfolds and oven mitts on — to simulate working with cold hands, or in case we have to resuscitate a hot muffin that has fallen out of the oven.

We learn how to give injections and how to put in stitches, using real flesh, at least real pig flesh. So if a flying pig happened to explode over the boat in the mid-Atlantic, I could do a pretty rough job of stitching to put it back together — although it might look like Franken-swine.

It is when boils are mentioned that my ears prick up. In the books I have been reading about ocean-rowing, boils sound almost inevitable and make rowers' lives absolutely miserable.

When I bring up the subject of boil avoidance with Brent he suggests I contact a friend of his, Shamus, whose company designs joint braces and prosthetics, and is apparently a genius at inventing medical devices. He might be able to help make the trip as boil-free as possible.

Shamus's offices are in the back streets of Newmarket. Hanging on the walls are enough plastic body parts to assemble a rugby team of Robocops.

Shamus is in his late thirties, with a mop of black hair and a big grin. He is another man who Understands. He Understands so well he is finishing my sentences for me. When I show him the Roho, and start to describe the race and my concern about my backside, he is sketching before I finish talking.

'So you are going to want to keep your skin dry, that's the most important thing. If the skin is dry it is much better able to resist the sheer forces. And it has to be as light as possible too — the more weight you are moving back and forth on the slide the more strain you're putting on the skin. And you are going to want your bum to be cool. Can you sit down and show me what the rowing action looks like?'

So I sit on the floor of his office, mimicking the different positions of the stroke.

He walks around me, still sketching, and muttering to himself: 'So, looks like some lower back support would be useful as well . . . Need to keep pressure away from the ischial tuberosities. Trim out channels here to support the sacrum . . . and then build up the foam here to protect the pivoting coccyx.'

He stops and shows me his sketch.

'Here, I think it should look like this. The Roho will go in the middle, but on the sides we will carve out some foam to provide lateral support, and here at the back we will bulge the foam out to provide some lumbar support. You might not be able to lean back as far as in a normal rowing seat, but protecting your back is going to be important.

'Give me a call at the end of the week; by then I should have mocked up a prototype in plastic, but you will probably want to make the final version out of carbon fibre.'

A week later I am back in the office. Shamus comes out from behind his desk and pumps my hand.

'Come and have a look.' He brings out an object that resembles a snug miniature armchair that someone has cut the legs off.

'It looks like a throne!' I say, turning it over. 'Where are the drink holders?'

'Try it out.'

We put it on a chair and I sit in it. It is very comfortable. The tendency to wobble around is completely eliminated. Seat solved!

Shamus now becomes the resident inventor for the team, and our expert on anything to do with the boat–body interface. He has an incredible knowledge of anatomy, physiology and physics, and a feel for materials — and if he doesn't have something in his storeroom he knows where in Auckland to get it.

The boat assembly is finally completed. All the parts have been glued and screwed together, and the plywood shell sanded into shape. The Unitec team have done a very thorough and professional job. Now it's time to get the boat painted and fitted out with equipment.

Silverdale is a little to the north of Auckland. Far after the suburbs have stopped, the motorway swings in gentle curves through seductive green farmland, until near the end a road takes you behind a hill to an incongruous collection of warehouses, mostly to do with the marine industry.

Here Gordon Robinson, of GR8 Design, carries on the great Kiwi tradition of blokes in sheds. His building is much like the others in the industrial park — a large corrugated-iron structure, with high windows that let in shafts of searching sunlight that illuminate the carcasses of various small boats and kayaks; crowded workbenches;

buckets overflowing with small parts, piles of scrap metal — and, in the shadows, a deflated one-person hovercraft. There is the inevitable old radio with a coat hanger for an aerial, tuned to a station playing classic rock.

I back the boat into the workshop. Gordon stares at it as if I have brought him the equivalent weight in doggy doo. He shakes his head, whistling silently. 'This is what happens when you get a bunch of schoolies onto it,' he says. Then eventually he adds, 'I suppose they could have done a worse job — at least it's straight.'

'How long will it take to get it ready?' I ask nervously.

'How long do you have?'

'About six months.'

'Yep, it'll take about that.'

'How much will it cost?'

'About twice as much as you think.'

Gordon worked on both boats for the 2001 campaign, so he is the natural choice to finish the fit-out of our boat. For the 2001 race Rob had commissioned him to design and build a foot-steering system, and he had come up with a clever arrangement of pulleys and a balanced rudder that enabled the steering to be adjusted with a twist of the heel. This was a vast improvement, and he has already been contacted by overseas crews wanting to use the system for the next race.

I am keen to learn from his experience in putting the boats together — to avoid any mistakes that had been made in 2001, install the great ideas they ran out of time to do, and learn from what happened on the boat during the race.

After much thought, Gordon comes up with a number of ideas. Firstly, we will do away with most of the plastic containers that hold the ballast water. Each boat is required to have 150 litres of fresh water on board, which in an emergency also serves to stabilise the boat and ensure that it rights in a capsize. In previous years dozens of plastic containers sat just under the main deck, linked together by a leak-prone combination of plastic pipes and junctions. Gordon's idea is to coat the actual inside hull of the boat with a waterproof sealer, creating a large wooden bilge tank. As well as increasing the stability of the boat by moving the centre of gravity lower, this would also do away with much of the plastic plumbing. It is altogether a simpler and more robust solution.

But I am nervous about having water constantly against the wood of the boat, knowing that swelling can add kilos to its weight. But as Gordon argues, that is exactly what happens on the other side of the hull. It is just a question of using the right sealant.

We will also try and trim the boat to run slightly nose-down, to decrease the wetted surface area, and therefore drag. This means making a number of subtle changes, including moving the watermaker from the middle of the boat further up to the bow and, when we put the rails on, making them slightly higher at the bow than at the stern, to ensure that we aren't pulling ourselves up for the next stroke.

There will be many other minor changes as well. The casing for the main solar panel will be made so that it can tilt sideways as well as up and down, to enable better tracking of the sun. To protect against the heat we will coat the entire inside of the cabin with a full inch of rigid insulation. We will augment the main solar panel by gluing individual solar cells onto the surface of the boat. This will also allow us to use a much smaller battery on the boat, which will be an enormous saving in weight.

So begin the many months spent finishing off the boat. Progress is painfully slow, as most parts and fittings and mountings are custom-made. Then, a few weeks into the fit-out, Gordon moves to larger sheds two doors up the road and all work stops for several days.

Gordon will have his head down in the bottom of the boat and you'll hear a muffled voice shout, 'I need a five-eighths wrench!' A disembodied hand appears out of the hatch and flails about by the tools on the deck then, when it doesn't find the right item, Gordon gets out of the boat, puts on his shoes, and goes over to one of the workbenches, cursing the mess and reminding everyone of his clear instructions about where tools are to go. After several more minutes of searching he leans his head back and addresses the cobwebbed rafters, his arms outstretched: 'How can I soar with eagles when I have to walk with turkeys!' The searching continues until the phone rings. Then a chat ensues, interrupted only when a sales rep for vacuum seals comes in. Some time later, after everyone else has gone, you hear a shout from some dark corner. 'I've found the wrench!' Gordon appears, triumphantly holding the wrench above his head, before his features cloud. 'What did I want it for?'

I give myself whatever low-skilled jobs I can, mostly sourcing supplies, although as my confidence grows I start to do little jobs on the boat. Gordon never fails to come over and examine my work carefully, nodding his head in appreciation. 'Kevin, you may be slow . . . but you're bloody rough!'

Day after day I coax the Starlet up from Howick, across the Harbour Bridge, and up through the dew-covered fields north of Auckland to Silverdale and the workshop.

I might be cutting and gluing the insulation for the back cabin, putting on the deck tread, mounting a compass — or carefully measuring the place for a hole, drilling it, finding it was in the wrong place, filling the hole, remeasuring and drilling another.

The boat-building is certainly slow and frustrating, but at least I can see progress being made. Unlike finding sponsorship or a second crew member.

The best times in the boatshed are in the late afternoon, with the sunbeams stabbing like chisels through the skylights at the wafting clouds of sweet sawdust, the gentle grooves of Goldenhorse's 'Maybe Tomorrow' playing on the radio, and Gordon's muffled shouting echoing in the background.

CHAPTER NINE

Man wanted for hazardous journey

Man wanted for hazardous journey. Small wages,
fierce heat, long weeks of unrelenting effort,
constant danger, safe return doubtful.
Honour and recognition in case of success.
— The Shackleton-esque newspaper ad we should have used

Late 2002

I'm back at Performance Lab to get my next exercise programme from Jon Ackland.

'So what are you giving me this time to make me faster than Steve Westlake?'

Jon steeples his fingers.

'We can do it, but it won't be easy. There might only be a few dozen people in the country who are better rowers than him. Have you found someone to row with yet?'

'No.'

'OK then, get one of those people, then you only have to be better than Matt Goodman. Don't compromise on this — you want the BIGGEST, HAIRIEST, TOUGHEST BASTARD YOU CAN GET!'

Our lack of success isn't through lack of looking. Since day one Rob has been working his way through his contacts in the rowing world.

Several times he has rung to say that he thinks he is on to someone, only to have the lead melt away. I am continually surprised. The idea of rowing the Atlantic is so appealing to me — isn't it appealing to everyone?

By the end of the year we are getting desperate.

The phone rings. It's Rob.

'I think I've got someone for you.'

'What's he like?'

'He's really good, he was a member of the New Zealand bobsled team.'

'So he can go fast in the cold. Can he handle slow and hot?'

'Look, he's really keen. He's already been training by going for runs with a 40-kg pack. He's . . .'

'Rob.'

'Yes?'

'It's a rowing race.'

A pause.

'Right. I'll keep looking then?'

'Good idea.'

The thing is that we really need the other person to be a rower. We are running out of time to get a novice up to fitness. By the end of 2002 we are starting to get desperate. I call up Rob.

'Rob, what if we could get Rob Waddell on board?'

Rob's answer comes in three even descending tones.

'You would win.'

'Well, let's ask him!'

'I have already, he said no.'

'Let's ask him again. We'll go and see him.'

Rob Waddell is about as good as rowing gets. He's the current Olympic single-sculls champion, and holds the world record on the ergo. In fact, he could average for six minutes a force that I could barely pull on one stroke. With him on the boat, my job would be like the stoker on an old-fashioned train. I would just need to stand at the stern and shovel food at him, while he frothed the water in a frenzy. Maybe I could even do a bit of waterskiing.

Rob Hamill makes the calls, and a few days later we are standing outside a block of flats in central Auckland. Even if I didn't know the number it would be easy to spot which one Rob Waddell lived in. Next to one door there is a neat stack of the most enormous shoes I have ever seen, like Ronald McDonald's shoes at the McDonald's playground.

We are early, so we wait. After a few minutes a car pulls up and out comes Rob Waddell. I see him as he comes up the stairs, and he keeps getting bigger and bigger. He resembles a giant. It isn't just the height of him, it's the depth — I don't think I have ever seen more muscle in one place. Would he even fit in the boat? If he wanted to lie out flat we would have to build a little extension out the back.

We give it our best pitch, but no luck. Rob is very supportive, and has advice about rowing seats and bum problems, but rowing the ocean doesn't excite him. In any case, he has obligations with Team New Zealand for the America's Cup that is about to start. After an hour we are back out on the street.

The phone rings. It's Rob.

'I've found another guy.'

'Any issues?'

'Oh, he has a bit of a temper, but he's usually bluff and bluster. If the worst comes to the worst we'll just get a padlock for the cabin door. She'll be right. Come on down to Raglan on the weekend and you can have a bit of a row with him.'

The Starlet races through the unfolding green countryside on a still spring morning. There is mist rising off the paddocks, revealing tottering little lambs. We are heading south of Auckland, out to the west coast and the beautiful Raglan Harbour.

Rob pulls into the marina parking lot with the boat, followed by another station wagon, out of which pours a swarm of small blond children and a bloke who introduces himself as Ian. Rob's plan is to take the boat out into the harbour and down to where the river meets the sea, and perhaps even into the open ocean. Fresh from my

Boatmasters course, this seems a little risky. Even if we had checked the weather, knew the tides, had lifejackets, a working VHF, a life raft, flares and had consulted the coastguard, there is still the small matter of the warning signs posted around the marina advising of the dangers of going through the heads in a small boat. I point this out to Rob.

'Oh yeah, nah, nah, she'll be right. It'll be great fun.'

Ian was with Rob in the Olympic team and is well used to his gung-ho, damn the torpedoes attitude. He jokes as we get the boat ready. 'Where's the handle for these oars, Rob? Oh f--k it, no worries,' he mimics. 'What's this loose bolt doing here? Oh, no worries, come on, f--k it, let's go!' He has me in stitches.

Things start out well enough as we ease out down the river. At first the rowing is very smooth and Rob stands up Napoleon-like in the footwell, issuing instructions. We are making excellent progress towards the rivermouth, in fact suspiciously good progress. The GPS tells us we are doing 7 knots hardly touching the oars. There is clearly the mother of all currents underneath us.

Soon we can make out the rolling, heaving churn where the rivermouth meets the ocean. Before we arrive we are passed by a motorboat with two guys in it. They disappear over the top of one large wave and are lost from view for a few seconds. Suddenly they reappear, spat back up into the air before falling back into the waves.

'No worries! We can make it!' shouts Rob.

'You've got to be kidding,' I yell.

'Biggar, you're a poof!'

'We could go out,' says Ian, 'but we'll never make it back in again.' I'm starting to like this guy.

With his crew mutinying Rob turns us around and we have some fun surfing a couple of rollers that are pushing in up the river. Then we start to row in earnest against the current. It is hard, honest work, but I am enjoying putting my back into it. I glance out at the bank. There's a small boy eating an ice-cream and watching curiously as we flail away. A minute later I look again. The boy hasn't moved and neither have we. It's like walking up a down escalator that is getting faster and faster. The bank is tantalisingly close but we are rowing at full racing speed just to stay in the same position. Even to turn slightly towards the side would mean we would be sucked out into the huge, thumping waves on the bar.

The beads of sweat on my brow begin to join together and run down into my eyes. But I can't stop for one stroke in case we lose precious ground — the current is doing its best to suck us to Australia. The little boy has finished his ice-cream and been joined by his family. More people are arriving and staring out curiously. Some are laying out blankets. They are clearly hoping for a spectacular end.

Ian's jokes have been getting fewer, and he is also starting to struggle with the pace. We can't keep it up for much longer; soon our strength will falter and we will be sucked out into the maelstrom. What we need to do now is close the hatches quickly — try to make the boat watertight. Then turn the boat around, run at the bar head first, hold our breaths and hope for the best.

Suddenly I hear Rob say, 'Here comes the cavalry!'

I look around and see a red semi-inflatable skimming down the channel towards us. It's the Raglan coastguard. They throw us a line and tow us back to the boat ramp. There are goofy smiles all around. My sense of relief is even large enough to overcome my embarrassment. We donate generously.

At least I have got to see Ian at work, and he seems to have the goods — a strong rower, with a good sense of humour. Unfortunately, shortly afterwards family commitments rule him out — and we are back where we started.

Voicemail message:

Rob, I just thought you should know we have been a victim of some industrial espionage. I was at Les Mills on the erg and I didn't see Steve Westlake come up. I had been working out for about half an hour when he came up and said hi, and the cheeky bugger walked all the way around so he could see what was on my monitor, and unfortunately I had been pulling quite a good pace. It's a shame actually; if I knew he was coming I could have been flopping about all over the place doing 2:10 or something. Anyway, he asked if we had found anybody yet and I said no, we were still holding out to have him on the team . . .

'Have you managed to write to them yet?'

'Yeah, finally. I've been negotiating with Westlake. We have agreed to disagree, so we are going to mediation.'

'That's been dragging on a bit?'

'Yeah, I've been getting some emails from Steph Brown that have been a bit . . . unhelpful.'

December 2002

The phone rings. It's Rob.

'I think I've found you a rower! A guy called Scott Kensington.'

'Any issues?'

'He doesn't know how to row.'

'Mmmm-kay?'

'But he's bloody good though. Yeah, he's pretty special . . . he's represented New Zealand in about five different sports.'

'Really? Which ones?'

'Uhh, soccer, cross-country running, swimming, cycling, triathlons. He's just taken part in the Mizone endurance race down the length of New Zealand.'

'How did he do?'

'Pretty good I think.'

'But he can't row?'

'No, but he must be bloody good at picking things up. He only started kayaking during the Mizone and apparently ended up beating Gurney in one of the legs.'

'Sounds good . . . when can we meet him?'

'I think we should take him out for a row in the Atlantic boat. I have an idea.'

It's just before Christmas and the Louis Vuitton series, the races to determine who will be the challenger for the America's Cup, are in full swing. One of the favoured contenders is Oracle, and Larry Ellison is in town with his extraordinary jet-engine-powered superyacht *Katana* — complete with basketball court, helicopter and jacuzzi — to watch his investment in action.

Rob's idea is to drape a banner over our cabin — something along the lines of 'Sponsor wanted! Your name here' — then row out to the spectator fleet. Our unusual appearance should be sufficient to temporarily distract Larry's eye away from the bikini-clad models lounging in his hot-tub. He will quickly comprehend the worthiness of our cause and write a cheque for the amount required. This he will put in a bottle, or tie to a supermodel, and throw to us. If this brilliantly simple plan somehow fails to work then at least we will be able to see how Scott does in the boat, and maybe even see a bit of the America's Cup action up close.

My training programme also requires an overnight row, so after we've dropped Scott off, Rob and I will carry on rowing through the night. Rowing for two hours is now not an unusual part of my training. A week earlier I had rowed for four hours straight on the ergo at 2:10 pace and felt good. But this will be a huge step up in terms of duration, and the first real taste of what the Atlantic row is going to entail. It will be a big milestone, and I am excited. What is sleeping at sea going to be like? What is it going to be like to have to get up every two hours? What will it be like rowing in the dark?

I meet Rob down at the marina at Okahu Bay, and we start throwing equipment and food into the boat.

'So how did the mediation with Westlake and co go?' I ask.

'Yeah, we finally got it sorted out. It took a few hours but we got there in the end. It's good that it's over.'

'What's the outcome?'

'Oh, we just split up the money and split up the gear.'

'So did you have to give back the money that's in dispute?'

'No.'

'And they have agreed that you should get paid more?'

'Yes, they have.'

'And they get a final payout?'

'Yep.'

'So it's all sorted out then?'

'Yep, should be.'

The conversation tails off as Scott arrives. He's tall and lanky and doesn't say very much as we get ready. Rob and Scott take the first shift, out to the America's Cup course behind Rangitoto. For someone who hasn't spent a lot of time rowing Scott's technique is exceptional. Or, as Rob cheerfully tells me, 'He's making you look like shit, Kev!'

It's a fine day and there's a blustery southwesterly wind ruffling the gulf and speeding us out to the race course. I am enjoying the unfamiliar feeling of being in the boat without having to contribute to the motion. Despite the assistance of the tailwind, it takes over an hour to get out to the course. Scott takes it all very matter-of-factly.

Just north of Rangitoto we join the spectator fleet close to the downwind buoy. The dozen enormous private yachts jostle for position with hundreds of smaller craft of all shapes and sizes. There is much horn-blowing, shouting and salty language as hundreds of square metres of glossy fibreglass surge and roll within a few feet of each other. We get a few honks ourselves as we bob in the swells set off by the fleet.

It's not hard to spot the gleaming white *Katana* sitting back at a regal distance from the mob of boats.

'Let's row over to him,' says Rob. 'Kev, you take over.'

So with Rob in the footwell steering we begin our stealth assault. Unfortunately, shortly before we arrive the racing yachts round the downwind buoy and begin to beat away upwind. Immediately all the spectator boats, including *Katana*, surge away in a cloud of diesel to the other end of the course.

'After them!' shouts Rob.

So we follow, but before we are halfway down the course we almost run into *Katana* coming back the other way. She speeds past, a white cliff of glistening burnished steel. Somewhere high above, near where the sun comes through the clouds, is that a glimpse of a supermodel in a bikini and a heavily sunglassed man at the rail? But then the yacht is gone, with just the churning sea left behind.

'He's over there, let's go!'

So the afternoon progresses, with *Katana* running up and down the course being chased by a tiny rowboat with three men on board, one of them waving his arms manically. It's like a mouse trying to catch a cheetah.

More interestingly, Scott is doing exceptionally well. He has been rowing more or less continuously for over four hours without it seeming to faze him. It's a very impressive rowing debut.

Then the race is over, the tenders begin towing the race yachts back to the marina, and the bulk of the spectator fleet chug back around North Head. By now the best part of the afternoon is over and it is time for us to head up the coast to the Whangaparaoa Peninsula, a finger of land that juts out about 10 km into the inner Hauraki Gulf. But we are about the same distance away in the exposed part of the harbour and the wind is determined to blow us out to South America. It's awkward rowing in a crosswind — the boat kicks and bucks, and my hands are never level so that all the rowing strokes are a compromise.

I wouldn't mind so much if I knew we were getting closer, but the GPS mounted on the bulkhead is not working and it is not obvious to me that we are making any progress. Not having a GPS has a diabolical effect on mental health. I wonder how many back-ups we should have for our crossing. Maybe half a dozen.

'Is this what the Atlantic was like in '97?' I ask Rob.

'Nup, waves are bigger in the Atlantic.'

It's an hour before I can believe the peninsula is getting larger, and nearly sunset before we reach the tip of the point and slowly start to make our way around into what should have been the lee side. It takes much longer than it should for the wind to die away, and for a while I wonder if it hasn't perversely changed direction, but then slowly the rocking begins to ease. The stroking becomes more rhythmic and the boat begins to run smoothly, as if gliding on ice. The sun peeks out from beneath the clouds, and my sore, raw hands start to uncramp.

Scott has impressed the hell out of me — this is by far the most rowing I have ever done in a day, yet he didn't seem at all fazed. As we row down the peninsula, Rob and I try to do a sell job on him, trying to get him enthused about the Atlantic. Scott's concern is mainly around his responsibilities to the swim school he runs in Rotorua, and the amount of time the race would take from this. He has said he will think about it, and we have agreed to talk in the New Year.

We pull into a little bay where Scott's girlfriend is waiting to pick him up, and with a few perfunctory goodbyes he jumps out. I get out the little gas stove and cook up a freeze-dry, enjoying the serenity and chatting with Rob about Scott, trying to delay the row back for a few precious minutes. We adopt the typical shift routine for the return leg, two hours on, two hours off, with Rob going first.

I crawl into the back cab and shut the hatch. It's a strange feeling being inside the cabin with someone else rowing. I am completely reliant on the competence of the other person. If I close my eyes will the next sound I hear be the crunch of fragile plywood on barnacle-encrusted rock? Will I wake up with an avalanche of cold water pouring through the hatch? Or will the bow of some boat, unseen in the dark, be coming through the cabin?

There is a certain solidity to Rob's rowing, a definite feeling of the blades locking into the water and the boat being tugged along. I scrunch up a fleece jacket to use as a pillow. My squashed cheek jerks in time with every stroke.

'Wake up, ya scurb!' It's brutal waking up to find yourself in a cold boat bobbing on a disgruntled sea. I push open the hatch door — it's dark, cold and windy. Shit. I have to go out into that?

'Where are we?'

'Just off the end of the peninsula.'

'How has it been?'

'Not good. We might not make it back to Auckland if this wind keeps up. See how you go.'

It's decidedly uncharacteristic of Rob to be concerned, and if he isn't making progress then I don't like my chances. So I very gingerly step over Rob's oars.

'Put your hand on my head!' he shouts as I almost lurch overboard. I sit down abruptly on the bow seat, and put in a few strokes before Rob gets up and disappears straight into the cabin.

I am rowing with short, fast strokes to try and make progress as the boat bucks into the wind. I feel rising unease as I try to work out in the dark if I am making any progress at all. I try to line up lights on the land to see if they are passing in front of each other. Sometimes it looks as if they are and sometimes it's just hard to tell. It's one awkward, swearing stroke at a time. I try to breathe through my nose and not worry.

Very slowly the bays of the peninsula slip away into the darkness. Slower still the wind dies down, the chop subsides, and the beaches of Auckland's North Shore start to reveal themselves. Time crawls by. How does time at sea go? Just like time on land. One second at a time. What is it like rowing for two hours at sea? Like rowing for a minute on land, but 120 times.

It's time to call Rob out. 'Wake up yourself, ya bastard!'

He appears and when he sits down I take two steps over his swinging oars and get into bed. 'Good on ya!'

By the time we get to North Head, at the entrance to the inner harbour, dawn has begun to streak the sky. I take a shortened break and rejoin Rob at the oars. Instead of rowing back to the boat ramp Rob wants to make one last chance to meet Larry, by sneaking up on him before breakfast. He isn't up. Nor is anyone else.

It's a long row back up the harbour to the trailer at Okahu Bay. 'How was that, Rob?'

'It brought all the horror back. I'd forgotten how tough it was.'

The worst part is always the packing up. Removing all the stinking and soggy gear. Scooping out all the half-eaten food. I am bitterly tired, and have to try hard not to fall asleep on the drive home.

My brain feels spacy and distracted afterwards, and irritable. My arms are aching and my back is stiff, and my brain is whispering to me something that I really don't want to hear.

You know the worst thing about that row . . .

Don't think it.

. . . that was just for 20 hours. Imagine doing that for six weeks.

I can't imagine it. It's not possible. Anyway, I've got plenty of time to improve. I have to focus on the positives.

Six weeks.

Yes, it had been tough and daunting. But just maybe I have found a rowing partner.

There is one other bit of good news to finish the year. Somehow I have managed to find a girlfriend, one who doesn't mind being driven around in a Starlet, or seem too embarrassed when I have to leap out and hit its engine with a hammer. Although Irena does wisely insist that our relationship will only be for the summer.

It's the Monday just before Christmas. I give Rob the first call of the day.

'Any news on sponsorship?'

'Absolutely nothing.'

'It's not looking good, is it?'

'No.'

'How does this compare with '97 or 2001?'

'In some ways this is harder.'

'So the book is going to go ". . . by the end of 2002 it looked like not much had changed"?'

'Yep.'

'I got a letter this morning from the race organisers. There's lots of writing in red saying that if we don't pay a deposit we are going to get kicked out of the race. What shall I do about it?'

'Tell them we'll pay them out of our winnings.'

'I thought there weren't any cash prizes.'

'There aren't.'

'Any word from Scott?'

'Yeah, I spoke to him last night — he said he's still thinking about it. How's the boat-building going?'

'Slow. Have Matt and Steve ordered their kitset yet?'

'Yep, and apparently they've taken the foot-steering plate off the boat. Probably to get it made in carbon fibre. Does that put a little shot of acid into your stomach?'

'Yep.'

At least it's Christmas, which happily coincides with a break in my training. Two whole delicious weeks in which I can try to completely forget about rowing and let my body and brain heal.

Instead I go to Morocco and come back loopy.

CHAPTER TEN
Dividing by zero

Some friends have kindly offered to subsidise a trip to Morocco with them; in return they ask only that I officially name the boat's poo bucket in their honour. I could sure use their company and their inspiration, and it would be great to get that perspective on life that only travel can provide. So I go.

I stop off in London just long enough to pick up a vicious and persistent cold, then for a few blissful days I wander the souks, drink hot sweet mint tea, sleep on coarse wool blankets out in the desert, trek in the Atlas mountains and run down giant sand-dunes in the Sahara, laugh and talk with my friends. The campaign is another world away.

Near the end of the trip we stop the car at a small, dilapidated seaside town. There is a fresh breeze blowing out to sea, flapping the flags of the run-down hotels and the pennants of the tent cafes near the beach. This is the sirocco, which blows the fine Saharan sand miles out to sea, even to the Canary Islands over 100 kilometres away. Here at last is the Atlantic.

The waves look reassuringly peaceful. It doesn't look that much different from the Hauraki Gulf, but without the islands. I find myself wondering what is behind the curve of the horizon.

My heart starts to sink with the whine of the descending jet engines. By the time I am in the car driving home from the airport I am breathing hard and feel sick. I am sick, my cold still lingering, robbing me of energy. I feel as if I am waking up after a huge party with an enormous hangover — without having had the party. There is so much left to do, and the start of the race is less than ten months away — there is a boat to be built and tested, a rower to find, tens of thousands of dollars of money to raise, and hundreds and hundreds of hours of training to fit in.

I call Rob.

'Any news?'

'No, it's been really quiet.'

'Any word from Scott?'

'I haven't heard from him for a while. I think he's going a bit lukewarm.'

'Don't say that.'

I look over at the alarm clock and it's 3am. A gale is whipping the trees outside my window. What if I was out in the Atlantic right now? What sort of beating would I be taking? My unconscious must have been thinking the same thing because my heart is pounding and the sheets are wet with sweat. My mind is racing.

I should quit. But then I'll look like a complete idiot to all those people who thought this was a waste of time, and were proved right. What will I do now? Still no money, and soon the big bills will be coming in. My friends are having second babies and owning houses — I am 33, broke, and soon to be very broke, and now there are strange gaps in my CV. *I should be married, the seat still isn't right, how are we going to get the books on tape into the computer, we aren't going to have time to get the music for the trip . . . There isn't time, there's no time, we should pull out . . . no, I am committed now, I have told everybody, I am going to look like such an idiot . . .*

I try to sleep but nothing seems to shut up the doubting voices in my brain. Instead I am at the gym when it opens at 5:30am and I row on the ergo for a couple of hours. But even with two hours' worth of exercise endorphins inside me there is no change. My brain has turned against me, every thought an accusatory stab. All the chores that make up everyday life seem pointless. There is a knack to living that I have lost.

I force myself to do my little daily tasks, and slowly I get some wins and start to feel a tiny bit better. It occurs to me that the amount of work I have to do is finite — as long as I am making some progress, no matter how small, I will get to the end. A finite distance divided by a finite speed gives a finite time. I just have to make sure I'm not dividing by zero.

I wake up that night and look at my alarm clock. It's 3:30am and the wind is whipping the trees outside. I put some Blu-tack in my ears to keep out the noise and try to think happy thoughts but my mind is running away again.

I have forgotten to have children now I am too old even if I met the right person tomorrow it would be two years before we were married and another year after that before I had a child which I couldn't support anyway and I would be 56 at their twenty-first birthday party and all my friends have kids they will have finished school just about before I start.

The next night it happens again, and when I throw back the sheets I am steaming. I can't tell if I am anxious or whether I am just hot and trying to attribute it to anxiousness. Maybe I'm just jet-lagged. Or maybe I'm losing my marbles.

Everything seems hyper-real. I have lost all perspective. If I don't get a boat to the start line at the Canaries then I am a failure. Not a 'Oh well, let's try again later' failure, but a permanent Failure. I will never amount to anything.

Every thought is prioritised as critical. There are so many things to do and every one of them is the most important one to do. I force myself to lie in bed until 6am because I have to rest. When it is time to get up I have no energy, I have only dread about the day ahead. I feel like I have sandpapered my fingertips — everything I touch hurts. I look at the people around me. How do people afford those cars? How do they take risks? I look at their faces. There seems so much sadness and futility in the world.

I talk to a friend about my appalling situation, the overwhelming, inevitable failure that I have strapped myself into: the feeling of being in a barrel about to go over Niagara Falls. She recognises the symptoms and tells me that it is not the situation that is the problem, it's the way I'm feeling about it. She gives me a strip of Aropax.

That night I am worried about going to sleep because tomorrow it will all repeat, and I will have to roll the boulder up the cliff again. I wake up at 3:30am and again I have The Fear. Outside the rain hitting the windows sounds like handfuls of thrown gravel. But this time I can beat the thoughts down.

I don't know whether this success is me or the pill. Then I think that it is highly unlikely that one pill would have worked.

Today the plan is to go down and catch up with Rob, then to go to Rotorua to see Scott. Which means I get to drive for two hours down to Hamilton. I'm looking forward to the drive — when you are driving you have purpose and motion and everything is all right.

If only I hadn't read *A Voyage for Madmen* before Christmas, the story of the first solo around-the-world yacht race. One of the entrants, Donald Crowhurst, mortgaged himself heavily to enter and became so overwhelmed by the preparations that he would go for long, pointless drives to get small pieces of equipment when he should have been getting the boat ready. He eventually started late, and soon discovered that his poorly built boat was breaking up underneath him. He ended up doing circles in the Atlantic and sending in fake position reports until finally he went completely nuts and stepped off the back of his boat.

By the time I arrive at the Hamills' my face still looks like George, their Labrador. But as I sit on the porch with a cup of tea, feeling the brilliant Waikato sunshine, I slowly, slowly start to feel the gloom lifting. Rob's enthusiasm helps: 'Of course it's going to happen!' he says. Somehow I believe him, even though I know his confidence is completely groundless. But there are only ten months to go until the start, and surely I can hang on for ten months. With two of us working on it surely we're going to get somewhere. We just need to convince Scott, raise the money, finish the boat, freight it to the start, and train, train, train.

'Hey, you know I'm doing this Inzone school tour thing,' says Rob.

'What's that?'

'It's a roadshow. A whole lot of people from different backgrounds go around schools and talk to the kids — it's aimed at inspiring them to set goals and achieve their dreams.'

'Well how long is that going to take?'

'About six months.'

'Six months! Full-time?'

'No, I'll still be available, but I'll have to manage my time better.'

We drive down to Rotorua and meet Scott at a pub for lunch. He looks reassuringly solid, even photogenic. We eat lunch and then go back to his house to give him the full razzmatazz pitch, showing him the movies of the Atlantic, talking about the excitement of the start, the drama and satisfaction of the finish, all while a summer thunderstorm passes overhead. Scott listens then says, 'So what's all this shit I hear's going down between you and Westlake, Rob?'

So Rob tells him. Scott wants to know if we could all work together. I say I don't think there will be any problems with that, as he is clearly a guy you can have a frank conversation with. He still has concerns about the swim school he's trying to build up, but says that he will think about it. One thing he doesn't have any concerns about is the rowing. He is very confident that he can take on the physical challenge.

By now it is late afternoon and time to go. We shake hands and I leave feeling positive. It has stopped raining, the sun is out and the streets are steaming.

I sleep on the way back to Hamilton, lulled into calm by the exuberance of the Waikato summer. Rob convinces me to stay at his place. It's a good idea — my bed at home isn't working anymore.

Scott calls up. He wants to do the race. He has been lent a rowing skiff, he says, and he has done three hours today. I put down the phone and feel better than I have for weeks.

Slowly as the weeks go past the heaviness lifts. There are good days and bad days, but the bad days stop being as bad and my ability to sleep through the night comes back.

Maybe it is the pills helping, but not because they have solved my problems. I wake up each day and have all the same problems. The outlook is nearly as bleak, but I don't have the same response. The only conclusion is that it isn't my situation that is causing me to feel the way I do. It is my interpretation of it. I have stopped being able to distinguish between what I am doing and who I am. I just have to remember that I am not my participation in the 2003 trans-Atlantic rowing race, it's just what I am doing at the moment.

It seems impossible, almost inconceivable, but there will be a time when the race is over. There will be a time when all this is history. If that time doesn't come soon enough then, if push comes to shove, I can jump on a plane and in 24 hours I could be sitting on the beach in Rio, in the sunshine, surrounded by people who have never heard of the race and wouldn't care even if they had. I stop taking the pills.

CHAPTER ELEVEN
The good ship *Holiday Shoppe*

God bless this boat and all who sail in her
God bless all the things that take place on the edge of life
   that make us more interesting people
God bless the Trans-Atlantic Challenge and all those who
   pit their strength and endurance against one another
Bless their watermakers and lubricant manufacturers,
   keep their bodies and their minds safe
And above all bring them back to those that love them,
   fulfilled, satisfied and ready for another adventure.
— Blessing said at the launch of *Holiday Shoppe Challenge*

The leaves are falling, the wind is cooler, the summer is over and so is my unusual relationship with Irena. She has moved to Sydney, but is over for our last weekend together.

She wants to have coffee with a Polish friend of hers, and I go along. Her friend is a doctor from Tauranga and turns out to be very cute, smart and entertaining. She has me laughing about the perils of being a bridesmaid — although I think I would have been laughing if she had been reading out a grocery list. Unusually for someone of her gender, she seems to be interested in hearing about the race. A few days later Irena forwards me the Hot Polish Girl's email address and says goodbye.

March 2003

Today is a special day out at Gordon's boatyard. TV3 is going to do its first piece about us in the sports news. Hopefully this will raise the profile of the campaign and lead to more interest from potential sponsors. Scott is coming up from Rotorua and we are going to take one of the 2001 boats for a row for the cameras.

More importantly, our new patron, Sir Edmund Hillary, is going to be coming up with Lady June. Rob got to know Sir Ed after the '97 race, Sir Ed lent his support to Rob's 2001 campaign, and now he has kindly agreed to be our patron this time.

The last time I had seen Sir Ed was on a spring day fifteen years earlier, when his helicopter lifted off from the dusty field next to the Thyangboche monastery in Nepal. It was just after I had finished secondary school, and I had spent six weeks working with the Himalayan Trust helping to build a school. My lasting memories are Sir Ed's voice — in the morning coming through from the tent next door: 'June! Where are my undies?' and at night making us laugh with his mournful rendition of 'There is a bridle hanging on the wall' and telling stories at the campsite.

The TV crew arrives and they take some shots of us around the boat before interviewing Rob and Sir Ed. Then we drive down to the ramp at Stillwater, and row back and forth for the cameras.

That night the clip shows on the TV news. The phone stays resolutely silent.

There are two working Atlantic boats. *Telecom 1* was built for the 2001 race, and is owned jointly by the members of that campaign. *Telecom 25*, which was originally built for the 1997 race and later repainted, is owned by Rob and Phil Stubbs' estate. It's now permanently on the road with the Inzone tour, meaning there's just one for the 2003 teams to train in and to serve as a template for the new boats we are outfitting. So it is arranged that the two teams will share the boat, and exchange it on neutral ground. Rob is dubious that this arrangement will last, but I am more optimistic. Steve and Matt won't think of us as opposition. They won't care how much training we do in the old boat — it can only be a fraction of the time they've spent in it.

Scott and I are scheduled to have the boat at the end of March, so we start planning our first ocean row. There's a breeze predicted from the northeast, so we decide to spend a night rowing away from the coast, directly into the wind, and then return with the wind at our back.

On the day, Dad drops us off at the base of the Whangaparaoa Peninsula at lunchtime. Unlike Mum, Dad's been pretty supportive, although when I first mentioned the race his reaction was 'Don't be so bloody stupid!' Dad doesn't live in Howick, he lives on a little lifestyle block near Coatesville, northwest of Auckland.

There's just time to throw clothes, maps, lifejackets, stoves, food, batteries, water, rudders and radios on the boat and jump on before a squall hits. Scott takes the first shift, and for a while we make progress. By the time I take over we are out of the shelter of the bay. The rowing is brutal. The boat is pitching into short, sharp seas that slam into the bow and prevent us building up any momentum. But it's the wind that is even worse. If I let the bow stray away from anything other than dead into the eye of the wind I have to spend the next minute pulling wildly on one oar and even backing down on the other, or rowing in a big circle to try to get the boat around into the wind again.

The boat is pitching, rolling and yawing so madly that it's hard to stay in my seat. As the seas grow dark and the horizon disappears I start to feel myself descending through the telltale signs of nausea — the hollowness in the stomach, the dry mouth, the dodgy burps, then the over-production of saliva. I lean over the side and barf, trying to be as quiet as possible so Scott doesn't notice. Luckily he seems not to hear me.

On the fourth time, he does. But by then I am getting quite good at the routine. I can feel the nausea coming on, and as it starts to build uncomfortably over the next several minutes I start to look forward to the conclusion, as I feel a lot better afterwards.

After an hour I swap over with Scott. Shortly afterwards I hear a distinctive falling-liquid sound, and pop my head out of the hatch to see Scott leaning over and feeding the fishes.

'How are you doing?' I ask.

'Wouldn't want to be anywhere else!' he says.

Good answer. Bloody liar.

I try to get some sleep. But my brain is determined to remind me that I am on a thin plywood skin perched over hundreds of feet of water. Psychologically, it is strangely tiring being on the boat. It moves exactly as if four of your largest mates each have a corner of your bed and are trying to get you off it. When your whole world is moving it seems to take up a lot of your mind just dealing with that motion. Little things — like switching off the cabin light — seem to take a lot of effort.

Scott has a grim shift. When I emerge he refers to our sports drink as 'vomit propellant'. I swap back onto the oars and almost straight away I start being sick again. Then I have an idea. I am listening to the radio on the headphones, and I switch to the golden oldies nostalgia station. Now I can do what I have been wanting to do for a long time — listen and throw up. It's quite therapeutic.

The rowing is not therapeutic. To make any progress at all I have to shorten the stroke to just the most powerful part. Even then the boat refuses to budge, and as soon as the blade is out of the water it starts sliding back. It's as if we are rowing uphill. It's not pretty stuff.

Late at night, when Scott is rowing, I am woken by a shout. While he was leaning over the side the boat had slid backwards, and an oar had twisted in its gate until it broke. We jury-rig a replacement but it's only a matter of time before it breaks. It's time to call it a night. As Scott points out, there is only so much longer we can go on when we aren't holding down any food or water. So we turn around and enjoy a wild ride back into the bay, with the seas and wind now pushing us along. Our progress has been so pitiful it takes just an hour to get back to where we started about seven hours ago. It's eerily peaceful behind the little headland when we arrive. I let out the anchor, make myself a very tasty freeze-dry and enjoy it in the stillness.

In the morning Dad arrives to pick us up. There is a small group of early-morning walkers on the beach who see us rowing in. They start to clap as we pull up on the beach. I feel like a phony — we have only been sleeping at anchor in the bay and they're treating us as if we have just rowed in from Madagascar.

I confess to Rob that I'm disappointed I am not exactly Captain Cook in the stomach department. Rob just laughs. 'I was like that, and Westlake was a big fish-feeder too. Don't worry about it, you'll come right — and if not there are some great sea-sickness tablets.'

I have tried to get another appointment with Rachel Brown to fine-tune our nutrition programme. She says she is now providing advice for Matt and Steve, and will have to check with them. The answer comes back no — they don't want her providing me with any more information.

×

April 2003

My training load is surging, and I am sticking to it grimly. Now I am rowing up to six hours at a time on the ergo. But it isn't an ergo race across the ocean. Scott and I should be out in the boat, not in the gym.

We are due to have the boat the next weekend, so I call Steve to arrange a pick-up. He says that he has taken advice and he isn't going to be returning it. I beg. He says he will speak to his advisers and think about it. He keeps his thinking to himself.

I call Rob's house. Rachel answers, says, 'I told you so,' then gets Rob who provides an update.

'The final settlement's been held up because they aren't giving back some of the gear.'

'What kind of gear?'

'Video camera, Suunto watches, a GPS, survival suits, that kind of thing. It comes to several thousand.'

'Why aren't they giving it back?'

'They say they don't have it, or it's been lost, or they've given it away, or it's been stolen — lots of reasons.'

'So now they're going to keep the boat as a bargaining chip?'

'They haven't said anything to me but that's what it looks like.'

I am mystified. If they wanted bargaining leverage they had plenty already. The boat isn't going to make much difference. This is unsporting. Now I'm training to row a boat across an ocean without a boat. Maybe they think I'm such poor competition that it doesn't matter if I have the boat or not. Maybe I'm just collateral damage in this feud.

A friend mentions a certain very successful middle-aged businessman and suggests I ask his advice. He's a man with a colourful past and has a certain softly spoken, unsmiling authority. As a result he is known as 'The Don'. He has heard about our campaign and has asked to meet me.

I meet him for lunch at a restaurant in the city. It's a weekday and the restaurant is mostly empty. The maître d' leads me through the neatly set tables to the window, where a middle-aged man with silvering but immaculate hair sits reading a menu. He shakes my hand very firmly while looking me in the eye. We sit down and exchange small talk about mutual acquaintances until the waiter comes and takes our orders.

Then I tell him about the preparations for the race — about our progress, about how the training boat has been kept from us, about shutting off our access to Rachel Brown. He picks the bread from the inside of his roll and speaks without looking at me.

'I know about these people. They are very confident. They don't rate your chances very highly. So it is your job to make sure it stays that way. It is clear that the winning of this race is done in the preparations. If they don't see you as competition then they won't prepare quite so avidly.'

'I agree.'

'Just before you go to the Canaries give me a call. I will have something to say to you.'

Hot Polish Girl and I have been trading emails. She works in Tauranga but is coming up to Auckland for Easter, so I suggest we go to the Easter Show. We eat candyfloss and shoot dodgy air rifles. We go on one of the twirly rides, where you get spun in a cage upside down. Hot Polish Girl laughs at my (manly) screams. We end the night at a cafe, where we soberly agree that as she is Irena's friend we can't go out. But we keep talking on the phone every other night or so, as friends do.

May 2003

It's now just two months before we have to pack our boat into a container to be sent to the Canaries. Five months before the start of the race, and we still don't have a sponsor. For most of the campaign Rob and I have been sharing the expenses, but now I have maxed out my credit card and Rob is having to pay Gordon's fit-out bills. And now our official campaign launch is pencilled in for the end of the month.

The dull throbbing pain has turned into a sharp throbbing pain. Rob and I are still spending hours and hours each week knocking on doors and giving presentations, and calling in favours to get intros to companies. Rob is fearless, treating corporate offices as if we are visiting a friend's bach over the summer. With total belief in the product on offer he'll pad up to the reception desk in his jandals, ask to see the big guy, and when informed that he is in a board meeting he'll reply, 'No worries, it won't take long. Is it this door?' He opens the door to a room full of dark-suited, slightly startled middle-aged men sitting around a large, glossy table and announces, 'Gidday Kelvin, how are you? Can we have a chat? Are you busy?'

A friend invites me to the launch of a new export magazine to schmooze with the big-noters who are going to be there, including the Prime Minister, Helen Clark. As people are mingling around afterwards I find myself talking to the PM, and I ask her if she would mind being at our official launch.

'Sure,' she says helpfully. 'I'll launch anything. I opened my hairdresser's new salon a few weeks ago.'

The phone rings. It's Rob.

'Gidday, any news?' I ask.

'Yup. Westlake and Goodman have been sponsored by CRC.'

'Don't they make greases and stuff?'

'Yep, they are two blokes sponsored by a lubricant company.'

'Oh well, at least we don't have any competition for sponsorship now. Any news on the gear they haven't returned?'

'No, but Steph decided to send me some emails again. The other day I got three all within an hour.'

'Really? Saying what?'

'Oh, just more of the same.'

The phone rings. It's Rob.

'I think I have someone interested.'

'Oh yeah?'

'Yeah, it's Holiday Shoppe. I spoke to their marketing manager on the phone. They're based in Auckland. I can't get away from Inzone at the moment so I've told her to expect a call from you.'

A day later I go to Holiday Shoppe's office in downtown Auckland to give a pitch to their marketing manager, a young Scottish woman called Anna. She doesn't seem very excited, but she asks a lot of questions. I don't expect to hear back.

But then she calls back and asks for another meeting. This time I meet her and her boss. We start to talk numbers. What they have in mind is not as much as we have in mind, but they can help us out with some of the flights we need. They say they will consider it.

A few days later I am on the way to Silverdale when I get a phone call from Rob. He sounds chuffed.

'We've got the money!'

At last. At long last. The steel bands that I hadn't known were there disappear from around my chest. I take my first deep breath in months. We are on our way.

May 16, 2003

It's the day of our launch party and we have hired out Float bar down on Auckland's waterfront. Inside there's an area fitted out like a mini-theatre, with a little stage, lighting and sound systems, and amphitheatre seating. The boat is outside, ready to be lowered into the water after it has been christened.

The PM's security people have cased the place out the day before. They warned us that her schedule was very tight and she might not be able to make it. But she arrives right on cue, followed by Sir Ed and Lady June. There's a little discussion as Sir Ed has to be persuaded to take his place on stage with the dignitaries rather than in the audience. Soon it is standing room only as the bar becomes crowded with our sponsors, friends and family. There are plenty of media too.

It's very strange to be in a room full of people, when putting together the campaign has been such a solitary experience. This crazy idea is starting to touch a lot of people's lives.

Kaye Parker from Cure Kids, and Becky, one of the Cure Kids ambassadors, speak first, then Rob invites Sir Ed to say a few words. The whole crowd goes quiet as he steps up to the microphone and starts to speak:

> I get constant calls from the media all over the world at the moment, because of the 50th anniversary of the ascent of Mt Everest, and almost without exception one of their questions is, 'Are there any challenges for young people left to do?'
>
> So I have to think up all the great mountains that still have not been climbed, the great sailings over the southern ocean still to be done, and the great journeys in the Arctic and Antarctic area. And I remember many years ago when I was selecting for an expedition to go to the Himalayas, and I got a note from a chap called Mike Gill. Mike was a very well-known mountaineer who had done fantastic things in climbing, but I had never met him, so I thought I would ask him over and see what he was like. So Mike came and he sat very quietly and didn't have much to say, and I found I had great difficulty in persuading him to relate any stories about his great adventures.
>
> Finally I discovered that, during the course of the last two years, he had actually won a New Zealand canoeing championship, and I was quite interested in canoeing in those days, so I said to Mike, 'Well Mike, so what do you have to do to take part in the New Zealand canoeing champs?' and Mike thought for a while, and then he said, 'The main thing is that you have to have a canoe.'
>
> One thing that we can rely on very strongly in our group that is about to paddle across the Atlantic is that we undoubtedly have a canoe, and I think that's the first step forward.
>
> I am also confident that our team crossing the Atlantic will reproduce the form that New Zealand teams have already done twice before.

So to Rob, Scott and Kevin, we wish you the best of luck. We know you will give it everything you have, and that all of New Zealand will be proud of you. Thank you.

After Sir Ed, the Prime Minister speaks, wishing us all the best and making a point of thanking the sponsors for supporting us. She jokes about how last time she launched a trans-Atlantic boat she managed to spray champagne over herself.

Then we go outside for the blessing and the christening. The boat is too soft to break a bottle against directly, so we place a champagne bottle on the bow and the Prime Minister swings away with a hammer. It takes three increasingly wild blows before the glass finally shatters and the fizzing liquid spills over the bow to the cheers of the crowd.

Then *Holiday Shoppe Challenge* is lowered over the side of the pier into the water. Scott and I get in, and more photos are taken. But the maiden voyage is short-lived — soon after, the boat is lifted from the water and goes straight back to Gordon's for more work.

The day has been a great success. As a friend says to me, 'If I had known it was going to be this inspirational I would have brought my wife and kids along!'

CHAPTER TWELVE
Sea legs

I'm back at Performance Lab. This time I have a challenge for Jon.

'Jon, I'm asking all of the suppliers to think of something that's going to give us an edge. Some little innovation, some new product or process or idea that we can use. Come on, what have you got?'

'All right, I'll give you something. You should be spending as much time as possible on the boat. You should be doing all of your training on the boat, doing all the things that you are going to do with the equipment that you are actually going to use, in the conditions that you are going to use them. In fact, in worse conditions. You need to be eating, sleeping and shitting on that boat. It's better if it's out on the Hauraki Gulf, but even rowing around in circles on Lake Pupuke would be better than nothing. You have got to be completely comfortable on the boat in all conditions.'

'I'm not sure that that's very practical. You know what the trans-Atlantic boats are like — they're a bathtub. You can't row into any kind of headwind. It's a real hassle to get them in and out of the water, you really need two people and often there's only me, and . . .'

'Of course it's difficult! You WANT it to be difficult! Because it's difficult for all the other crews too — SO THEY WON'T DO IT! Kevin, you HAVE TO BE THE BEST at dealing with your boat under ANY conditions. Then when the race starts you PRAY for bad conditions — the worse the better — then you will cope and they will struggle and THAT'S HOW YOU WILL WIN!'

I hear that Steve and Matt are going to be at the CRC stand at the Auckland Boat Show with their new boat. I try to observe discreetly from a distance, but it is just easier to get up close and gawk. The boat looks sleek. But it is so unfinished that there is really nothing to conclude. Matt and Steve say hi. They give me a can of CRC.

June 2003

There is one goal in our training that I am very keen to achieve, and that is a row out to Great Barrier Island. It's a respectable 40 nautical miles offshore, in the open waters of the outer gulf, so it will require exactly the right weather conditions if we are going to get there and back. If the wind is too strong one way or the other we risk either not making it or getting blown to South America.

Scott has been having a bad run with his health lately. First his appendix had to be taken out, then he needed an operation on his bum, then he sprained his ankle, and now there are some niggling problems with his back.

This coming weekend the boat being used for the Inzone tour will be back in Hamilton, so we have the chance to use it for an open-water row. Better still, the conditions look as if they are going to be perfect for a Great Barrier attempt. A large anticyclone is parked over the country and by Thursday the harbour looks like a turquoise ice-skating pond. I call up Scott, but he says his dentist has discovered that one of his teeth is very close to a root canal and he really needs to have it looked at this weekend. I put down the phone and slap my hand on my forehead.

Rob calls up to say that his mum isn't well and he needs to go to Whakatane to visit her. He suggests that Scott and I come down for the weekend and do a couple of day rows in the ocean there. It is still ocean enough to be useful, and it's close enough to Rotorua for Scott to get back to his dentist on Saturday. It's also close enough for me to visit Magda on the way down and continue our wonderfully ambiguous relationship.

The sun is setting as I go over the Bombay Hills, and by the time I reach the foothills of the Kaimais the colour has leached from the sky and the scene is in stark greyscale, like an Ansel Adams photo. The wide road sweeps into the hills and the Starlet putters into the sky.

Driving the Starlet is getting more difficult. The strap holding the oars on the roof hums like a kazoo in my ear. The windscreen dazzles from the glare of the oncoming car lights but I can't clean the glass because one of Dad's horses chewed the wipers, and they now make a nasty banshee shriek as the steel carves twin semi-circles in the glass. As the car rolls around the corners with the CV joint wailing I remember the disclaimer I had to sign to let the mechanic install new suspension on only one side of the car. He also told me not to power out of corners. Not that the Starlet powers out of anything. But I can't tell how fast I'm going because the speedo isn't working.

At the top of the ranges I can see the puddle of light that is Tauranga in the distance, and half an hour later I arrive at Hot Polish Girl's house. She looks very beautiful. We go to a restaurant called Astrolabe and she is very funny and the food is delicious and the pinot is very good and she laughs and puts a hand on my knee.

I arrive in Whakatane in time for breakfast and still have to get Rob out of bed. He seems very slow to get started and mumbles something about a party the night before. The sky is grey and overcast. I ring the coastguard, who tells me that the wind will stay from the north and will rise from 20 to 30 knots. Scott and I get the boat together with the rain lashing us, then with Rob in the stern looking rather pale we cast off from the riverbank and float down to the bar.

The seas are running very high and waves are breaking on the bar, which cheers Rob up. Soon we are being pitched up and down, and Rob is hooting and calling for more effort. A large wave breaks over the bow and dumps right on top of me, filling the footwell. Rob shuts the hatch just in time but emerges a moment later. 'Crikey, that was close!'

He disappears again as the next wave hits the bow. 'Jeez, this is great fun, eh fellas?' comes the muffled query from within the cabin.

Safely out over the bar we squint through the rain into the wind to get our bearings. The sea is lumpy and heaving as if squirrels are fighting under a duvet. Whale Island is a grey silhouette on a grey backdrop disappearing in and out of the clouds. Dark squalls rake the surface of the water. One hits us and in a few seconds the wind increases 10 knots and the rain becomes even more intense.

We are rowing directly into the wind. My oar skips the water or digs too deep; my back is taking a huge beating. As we struggle to keep the careering boat into the wind Scott and I spend minutes just pulling on one side to try and bring it under control. Yet, strangely, I don't seem to mind. I'm just focusing on each stroke and enjoying the challenge. It's tough, but I seem to be stronger and fitter than I thought I was. The GPS isn't working, but judging by the eddies our oars leave we are probably going at about 1 to 2 knots.

'Baby's awake,' says Scott. The rear hatch flicks open as Rob comes out to relieve himself over the rudder. He turns around to watch our work: 'Jingoes, Kev, you'll kill a seagull if you keep rowing like that!' He disappears again.

The closer we get to the island the tougher it gets. I am hoping there will be some lee, but even a hundred metres off the beach there are still strong gusts of wind coming at us. It is almost as if the blasts are coming directly from the rocks on the island. Then at last we get into the bay, with its steep-sided hills, and the wind switches off and the seas become calm. Ah, the serenity! The sheer blessedness of a sudden safe harbour! Muscles uncramp, raw fingers uncurl from the handles, ragged breathing becomes smooth and even. 'Honest work,' says Scott.

The boat noses into the sand of the beach. I jump out awkwardly and straddle the oar. The shaft breaks with a gentle snap. I am surprisingly unhurt — apparently the weight of my testicles has broken the oar. 'That's going in the book!' says Rob.

The sun even comes out for a little bit, but we can see a big squall coming so rather than shivering on the beach we push the boat out and start back. The return is much more pleasant without exactly being easy. Most of the swells are about as big as the boat, but occasionally there are some large waves that loom over us. We strain hard to get a surf on them, but they are too confused to offer assistance for more than a few metres. At least we don't need to stop for drinks, as it is raining so hard I can just open my mouth and put my tongue out. Whakatane frequently disappears in the clouds, and at such times we are surrounded only by murk.

When we get within sight of the bar we pull up just short of the breaking waves. We call up Rob and he comes out to assess the situation. I don't have time to do much looking as I am transfixed by the monster swells that are coming up behind us. Each passing wave sucks us a few metres closer to the Death Zone and Scott and I are kept busy rowing backwards, trying to keep the stern square-on.

'OK, we've got three options,' Rob says. 'We can try going through the main channel . . .'

'How big are the waves?'

'Ahh, looking bloody enormous . . . Then there's the beach, where the waves look only slightly less bloody enormous. So it looks like the dinghy channel is our best bet.'

'What's that?'

'It's next to the main channel — have a look.'

I quickly glance over my shoulder. As we rise up on a swell I see a narrow route to the side of the main channel, flanked by double-decker-sized rocks that would offer some protection against the swell if we could shoot the gap without being smashed to matchsticks on their barnacle-covered flanks.

'You can't be serious!'

The chute Rob is aiming for is about as wide as the boat is long. But Rob is very confident.

'Biggar, you're a poof! It's just a matter of timing. OK, here we go. OK, row row! NO NO NO WAIT!'

A cliff of water rushes underneath us before slamming into the rocks.

'Hell! That one would have munted us!' says Rob.

'ROB!'

The tide is coming in so there is no staying still. The waves are lurching us one way then the other, and mostly towards the rocks, so

Scott and I have our hands full backing out. Then a series of big swells heave us right into the area where the waves are breaking and there is much cursing and frantic oar-clashing as we turn the boat around and row back to a safe point where we can all take stock. Now a big black squall is almost on us, threatening bigger waves and more wind.

As desperate as the dinghy channel looks, the size of the waves pounding over the bar and driving into the beach means it is still our best shot. We carefully put the stern into the seas so that we are ready to spring forward as soon as Rob spots a break in the wave traffic. We wait. I feel sick. Scott turns around with a big grin on his face.

'See you on the beach, buddy!'

Rob shouts, 'ROW! ROW! ROW!' I pull as hard as I can — in the next five seconds we will either be safe or sushi. We surge forward and now have to do a nasty chicane to wind through the rocks.

'LEFT! LEFT! RIGHT! RIGHT! ROW! ROW!' Glistening, jagged rocks slide past on either side, scraping our oars. Then we are through, into the relative calm of the channel and safe from the waves.

'So, Rob . . . is this what the Atlantic was like in '97?'

'Nup, waves were bigger.'

Thursday night a few weeks later I am checking the forecasts for the weekend weather on the internet. Very strong northeasterly winds swinging to northerly are predicted, so a Great Barrier attempt is out of the question. Instead Scott and I decide to make a long plunge from the Gulf Harbour marina on the Whangaparaoa Peninsula down to Thames, weaving through the islands in the gulf where we can to get a little shelter. It's a trip of about 50 nautical miles, and it will be practice for doing long downwind runs at sea — and also good practice for getting seriously shat on by the weather. It will also be the first real sea-trial for our new boat, which is finally nearing completion. Just for fun we will do it overnight. By Friday night the wind is howling. The automatic weather station at the end of the Whangaparaoa Peninsula says it is blowing between 50 and 60 knots and still squarely from the northeast.

It's one thing to be drawing lines on a map inside a living room, with a nice hot cup of tea, and quite another to be preparing the boat down in the marina with the lanyards of the masts flapping hysterically and a gale shrieking through the rigging in the darkness. Rob is in Auckland and he phones to tell us not to go — the storm is too bad. Well, if it's bad enough for Rob that's good enough for us, so we sleep in the boat in the harbour hoping things will improve overnight.

They don't. Next morning the crackly marine forecasts on the VHF radio are still predicting that conditions are going to ease later in the day. So we go for a drive to the top of the ridge where we can see the other side of the peninsula. We watch the whitecaps and see the surf pounding onto the beaches. It is discouragingly wild.

By lunchtime we are so bored that being upside down at sea is preferable to hanging around, so we cast off from the marina. Immediately the wind shoves us rudely out into the gulf. As we pull away from land the wind gets stronger and stronger. I take a quick scan around — as far as I can see we are the only boat in a harbour that is flecked with foamy whitecaps. This is starting to sound like a coastguard incident report: 'Despite the extreme weather conditions, the lateness of the day, and the untested nature of their craft, the two crew set off . . .'

Then the sun goes down and we are thrust into the blackness of a stormy night, with the lights of the North Shore providing the only illumination. I am steering, constantly looking over my right shoulder for the dimly glowing whitecaps as they teeter towards us, so that if one looks like it is going to break on us I can try and angle in towards it so that it won't catch us completely broadside.

Out of the night comes a loud BOOM and the stern jumps a foot towards the beach, nearly toppling me out of my seat. A large, unseen wave has broken on the back cabin, slapping it like a drum. It's like my nightmare of rowing in a storm, only in real life it isn't that bad. It's even kind of fun in a rollercoaster-ride kind of way. The fact that the boat is handling it so well is a great comfort.

In theory we have now been rowing for so long it's time for someone to take a turn in the cabin, but there is no way I am going to lock myself in a wooden box when there is so much action taking place. It would be like trying to snooze while going over the Niagara Falls in a barrel.

We cut as close to Rangitoto as we dare, knowing that there are

131

plenty of rocks lurking just under the water. There are a few hundred metres of blissful shelter from the wind, then we set out for our next waypoint, the tip of Musick Point. But after an hour of rowing together into the wind we agree that we aren't going to be able to make it around the point. Disappointed, we row in the lee of the peninsula down to Bucklands Beach and tie up to a spare mooring. It's about 1am by this stage and we have been rowing almost constantly since early afternoon. It's been a great workout, and our confidence in our ability to handle the conditions has grown enormously.

Every time we come back from a sea-trial there is another list of things to fix and ideas for improvements. The poo bucket is slipping, the headphone cord gets caught under the wheels, the automatic bilge pump isn't working, the water coming from the ballast tanks tastes funny, the solar panels are tilting the wrong way . . .

'No they aren't,' says Gordon.

'Yes they are.'

'No they aren't. When you are on a tack from Rangitoto to North Head, the sun is over there, right? So the panel tilts that way.'

'That's exactly right. Except we're going to be in the northern hemisphere.'

'Yeah, so what?'

'So the sun's in the south.'

Our solar panel is mounted as a frame within a frame. It can tilt not only front and back to follow the sun, but also twist a few degrees to follow the sun off to one side of the boat — except it is the wrong side. Rather than pull the whole thing to bits, Gordon's cunning plan to remedy the error is just to unbolt the solar panel's outer framing and rotate it around 180 degrees. It means that we will have an unnecessary metre or so of cable run, but it saves a lot of time messing about.

I look at the GPS plots of some of our training rows. Even when it is dead flat and calm there is always a slight zig-zag motion in the path. I realise it's because we have to steer by a very wobbly compass, and so we tend to wait until it gets sufficiently out of kilter before we make a correction, then we weave back on course. Over a few nautical miles several hundred metres might be added to our course.

Also, the rudder acts like a brake — every time it deflects the water flow it slows the boat slightly, and the bigger the course correction the greater this effect. If there is a way we can take these course kinks out of the route then we will increase our speed to the finish for no extra effort. I mention this to Gordon.

'Oh yeah, the autohelm. We looked at it in 2001 but didn't have time to develop it.'

A month later I am looking at it in our boat. It is a long rectangular box with a protruding metal arm that moves in and out. You attach the top of the arm to the tiller of your boat, head in the direction that you want to go, activate it and keep rowing. A little electronic compass inside the autohelm then detects if the boat is veering away from the intended course and adjusts the arm accordingly. It's like magic — like it is alive. Gordon has engineered a clever system using brackets and levers to incorporate it into the foot-steering system. When we try it at sea it works beautifully. The GPS trails become dead straight. Almost better than that is the fact that now my brain is freed up from the constant task of steering I can concentrate on rowing faster.

The boat is a constant time-eater. Sometimes it feels like it's one step forward and two steps back. The insulation I have put on is coming off. The new watermaker is overloading its circuit breaker, so that needs to be replaced. The ballast water still tastes funny.

'What do you mean "funny"?' says Gordon.

'I don't know, kind of turpentine-y.'

Gordon tastes it.

'Well how long has the water been sitting in the ballast tanks?'

'I don't know. A while.'

'It's just residue from the sealant — flush it out.'

If the boat can now drink, pee and navigate, it still can't see. Each boat has to have a device for detecting the container ships that will inevitably be steaming around us. In theory all boats at sea are required to have a 24-hour watch; in practice standards slip. In the vast ocean it seems strange that ships can actually hit each other. But freighters don't just meander between ports — they need to take the shortest possible routes to save time and fuel. They pay specialist companies to optimise the routes for them depending on weather conditions. So do freighters coming the opposite way. Sometimes the computers come up with exactly the same routes.

During the sea-survival training one of the other attendees, the captain of a large container ship, told me how one night off the west coast of Africa he was woken up when he was flung out of his bed hard enough to hit the wall. The first mate had fallen asleep and they had hit another boat *bow on*. Apparently the other boat hadn't been keeping watch either.

We'll be particularly vulnerable as we are small, very low down, and made of wood, which makes us a very poor radar target. The solution is to have a device called an 'Active Echo'. This detects another boat's radar and amplifies the return signal to make our little boat look like a supertanker. Only they are quite expensive.

'When are you going to get me an Active Echo?' Gordon asks. 'We need to install it.'

'I'm working on it.'

July 2003

TV3 wants some aerial shots of the boats at sea, which they will play while running news updates during the race. They want us and *CRC* to go out and row in the gulf while a helicopter carrying a camera crew takes dramatic sweeps over us. It will also be the first time that we have really seen *CRC*'s new boat outfitted. After spending so many hours going over the different design options for our own boat I have a keen professional interest in seeing the solutions they have come up with.

With the wind a fresh 25 knots from the southwest it promises to be a lively row. The sky is sunny, with squalls passing over the city. I pick up Rob and we get down to the launch point at Okahu Bay early. While we have a coffee Rob briefs me on what is going to take place.

'They're going to try to psych you out. They'll try and be as slick as possible.'

'. . . and our job is to appear bungling and inept.'

'Exactly.'

Then we hear a car arrive and through the back of the cafe we catch glimpses of a sleek grey boat being backed onto the boat ramp. So we go out and say hello. Rob and Steve even give each other an uncertain handshake. Fortunately the TV3 presenter and cameraman arrive before the love evaporates.

While the CRC team are being interviewed we can gawk freely at their boat. There is a strange stubby aerial poking up out the back of the cabin which doesn't look like a satellite phone antenna. Their light stalk looks very professionally done — hey, they have an Active Echo! There is also some kind of ventilation system for the back cabin. But what's with the crazy tall pedestal seats? Oh I see, the rails that the seats slide up and down on are flush with the deck. That means they have to have very tall seats to get the oars to the correct angle. It makes for very clean lines and fewer stubbed toes, but more weight that has to be moved with the skin of your arse a million times or so.

Now it's time to put the boats in the water. Matt and Steve slowly back down the ramp and gently slide their boat off the back of the trailer into the water. Rob does his trademark Rocket Launch.

At great expense we have had our heavy metal footplates made in lighter carbon fibre, but there is no need for CRC to know that, so we have brought along the old metal ones. But we have brought the wrong nuts for them, and as I search in all the hatches for spares I wish that it was just a little bit harder for us to look as if we don't know what we are doing. Matt and Steve are all deft, stony-faced efficiency, and they are soon sitting in their rowing positions looking at us. Then they leave.

We eventually push off from the dock and are barely at the breakwater when one of the steering lines breaks, and we waste more time getting it sorted. By now *CRC* has disappeared into the boating clutter on the horizon. This is frustrating — it's hard to look bad when no one can see you.

We are nearly at North Head when I look over my shoulder and see the silhouette of *CRC* parked in the water.

'Scott, they're checking us out! Row like shit for a bit.'

So for the next few minutes as we approach we put on a display of schoolboy rowing, complete with clashing oars and caught crabs. I think that maybe, by the time we pull up next to *CRC*, we have laid it on a bit thick. But then Steve calls out, 'So I've heard you've been doing a lot of your training on Lake Karapiro?'

'Oh yeah, we've been out there a couple of times.'

With the wind behind us it doesn't take very long to get out to Rangitoto. We see the helicopter coming and start rowing in short little tacks, trying to look windswept, earnest and as if we're battling the elements.

The helicopter swirls around us and we try not to look at it — which is difficult when it hovers so low it blows off the BP logo that's taped to the solar panel.

To make things more difficult for ourselves we do most of our training at night. One time we loop around the back of Waiheke, another time out to Kawau, another time up the coast to Omaha.

The wrinkles in our routine start to get ironed out, we learn where to put our feet, where to hold on to. Which nuts like to work their way loose and the safest way to take a poo. I get better at reading the size and direction of boats from their lights. And our confidence in the boat grows as we see how it handles in different conditions.

The best part about the sea training is the sunrises. By the time the sun comes up it feels like it has always been dark. Then the soft morning light comes and it is miraculous. The sea becomes a glossy blue, the seabirds dive into the water around us, and the sunlight warms our bones. The boat glides smoothly toward the boat ramp at Stillwater and I feel incredibly tired, but good tired, as if my muscles have been washed, wrung out and dried.

But the sea-trials are just the weekends. During the week, strength training is done on the ergo and the Rowbug. I put bungy cords around the Rowbug's hull to drag in the water and increase resistance, and I'm making longer and longer trips up the Tamaki River to Browns Island. One morning I get up at 4am and spend six hours rowing out to Rangitoto, Motuihe, over to the north side of Waiheke and back again.

One morning as I am putting the boat up on the racks at the rowing club, some young guys start talking to me about the Atlantic, and while we are talking I start to describe the Atlantic boat.

'You mean like the one that's stored in the boathouse?' one of the guys asks.

'What's in the boathouse?'

'You know, that boat that rowed across the Atlantic.'

I check inside. There it is, in the dark bowels of the downstairs area, hidden behind racks and racks of rowing eights, and just a few yards away from where I pick up my oars. There it is. Right under my nose this whole time. But now our own boat is working we don't need it anymore. At least, not most of it.

'There you go.'

I hand Gordon an Active Echo.

He sniffs. 'It looks a bit used. Where did you get it?'

'I found it lying around.'

CHAPTER THIRTEEN

How far is a million metres?

The problem with rowing across the Atlantic, from a spectator's point of view, is that 99% of the race happens out in the Atlantic. It occurs to me that it would be great if we could somehow bring the race, or at least the spirit of the race, closer to New Zealand.

So I suggest to Anna at Holiday Shoppe that Scott and I make an attempt on the million-metre indoor rowing record. The existing record for a two-person team is 87 hours, 34 minutes, 36 seconds. It was set by Chris Hanselman and Mark Sharp in Hong Kong in 1993, which means it has been unbeaten for nearly ten years. But when you do the maths it works out at a very comfortable pace indeed. In fact, I have worked out that we should be able to take ten hours off the record by rowing 2:15 splits — 2:15 is the pace I go when I am warming down. It's the pace I do when I am using one hand to hold a cellphone. Rabbits in waistcoats could do 2:15. Hippos in pyjamas. It should be a doddle.

Anna likes the idea too, and she morphs it into a 'Rowed Show'

— a travelling rowing extravaganza. One of her team, Natalie, has found a large flatbed truck that is used for street productions. One side folds down to reveal a stage, and it can be enclosed at night for security. The idea is to start on the truck outside the Holiday Shoppe branch at Lynnmall, in West Auckland, and then move to Botany Town Centre in South Auckland.

⤬

The large truck swings into the Lynnmall carpark on Thursday morning and pulls up in an area that has been cordoned off outside the Holiday Shoppe office. The marketing team get to work plugging in the big stereo system and putting up the backdrop. Matti, another of Anna's team, is dressed as a pirate, complete with a parrot stitched to his shoulder, and is on the mike, working up the crowd. There's a large plasma screen set up on the stage to count down the number of metres left, as well as displaying an animated 'virtual rower' we'll be able to pace ourselves against.

We'll be using a Concept2 rowing machine, and a second one has been installed as a back-up. It will also be used for a 'Keep up with Kevin and Scott' competition, with anyone who can stay abreast of us for two minutes going into a prize draw. There are colouring competitions and a barbecue as well. While all this is being set up Scott and I do interviews with TV3, TV1 and SKY Sport, and by lunchtime we're ready to go.

Scott loses the toss and starts off on the first two-hour shift, while I go for a wander around the mall. When I get back I see that Scott is working hard, averaging close to 2:00 splits.

'Mate, you only need to go 2:15 — take it easy!'

'No worries,' he says.

Then it's time for my shift. I feel a little self-conscious being up on stage, but it is a treat to have something to look at for a change while I'm rowing — the curious shoppers, the kids at the pirate's colouring-in competition and the people jingling buckets for Cure Kids. But for some reason the work is harder than normal. Maybe the truck bed isn't flat. Maybe it's because I'm going slower than usual. I speed up a bit and start averaging 2:06 splits, just a little slower than Scott. But it still seems difficult. This is a pace that shouldn't trouble me at all, yet today it feels quite tough. Maybe the ergo is stiff. At the end of my shift we swap to the other rower.

I towel off and wander around the mall. What the hell have we got ourselves into? Can we get this done on time? We're aiming for about 72 hours, which means we'd end on Sunday afternoon, but maybe it will take till Monday? The alarm bells are going off in my head. Hang on, those *are* alarm bells! A shrill, piercing noise is coming from speakers inside the mall. Is this for real? Shopkeepers start pulling down their security gates. I guess it is for real. Other people are ambling more or less purposefully toward the doors.

Suddenly the Rowed Show is the main attraction. With little else to do while they are waiting for the mall to reopen, a crowd of several hundred people are now watching Scott. More and more are stepping up to race against him on the spare ergo.

At the next changeover Scott says, 'Mate, you're going to have to go slower!'

'Why?'

'Because it's not going to be me who's the first to slow down.'

And so the day turns into night. During each shift I monitor the developing aches and pains and afterwards I go into the mall, blinking in the lights, to try to find cures. I feel a bit guilty going into the shops — by rights I should be making do with just the things that might float past us while we are at sea. It's unlikely that a hot Starbucks flat white is going to float by, but this is an emergency. It feels as if we are going to be lucky to get through.

By 10pm the crowd has melted away, the mall has closed, and it is just us and the usual hooded characters skulking in the shadows in the corner of the carpark.

'See you tomorrow!' With a clang Anna and Natalie shut the back door of the truck, then they're gone. There aren't any lights in the back of the truck, only the glowing flicker of the screens. I tape the head-lamp light onto the monitor of the rower so I can keep track of my pace. We have a couple of movies to watch through the night. The first is a James Bond, but it's hard to hear it over the roar of the rowing machine's fan blade. I have to guess what's going on. My bet is that the guy wearing black, with scars on his face, is the bad guy.

But right now I have other things on my mind. Most urgent is that there is something up with my bum. The rocking motion on the rubber seat has been causing some grabbing, ripping and tearing that has been getting worse through the afternoon. When Scott comes in to take over at midnight I totter down the steps of the truck as if I have been sitting on a sharp, spiky carrot.

Between shifts we are sleeping in the Holiday Shoppe office. I have a few energy bars, then I lie down on the floor to sleep. Only I can't lie down because of the throbbing in my derrière. It's time to try the suppositories in the first-aid kit. I've never used them before, and I read the instructions with disbelief. By the time the business is finished I am sweating and shaking. I wobble out to the footpath, where I stand hyperventilating. I try to compose myself in the cold night air, and ask myself what the f--k I have got myself into. But then the drugs start to work. I even got some sleep.

When I open up the back of the truck just before dawn Scott is looking drawn and pasty. He has turned the monitor away so that he can't see how he is doing.

'I'm not feeling so good.'

'Yeah?'

'I've been throwing up. I can't keep any food down.'

'Yeah? Shit.'

We agree that he should go to bed, and as soon as it gets light we'll get him to a doctor. So it is particularly heart-warming a few minutes later to see the two pink, scrubbed faces of Anna and Natalie opening up the door of the truck and letting in the sunlight.

Scott comes back on briefly at 8am, so I can go to the loo, have some breakfast and find him a doctor. I manage to get hold of Dale Speedy, a sports medicine specialist, and as it happens an expert on hydration. He kindly agrees to see Scott in his clinic as soon as he can get there.

It's lunchtime before Scott gets back. I am very happy to see him, and he looks much better for the break. Blood tests have been inconclusive but the doctor has diagnosed hyponatraemia, or overhydration, which seems odd as Scott has lost kilos of weight overnight. The doctor was not keen about Scott continuing, but Scott insisted. They have agreed that if his headache gets any worse, or if he vomits again, then he will have to stop before something terrible happens, like his kidney exploding or something. It's just good to see him back.

But now it is time to move the truck to the Botany Town Centre. I have been rowing for four hours straight and I'm keen to have a break. So with Scott on the rowing machine, they shut up the truck and we drive the half-hour or so to Botany Town Centre with me dozing on the floor. It's quite a bumpy trip and Scott is being tossed around. He does a great job of getting there without barfing.

Our new home is right in the middle of the mall, outside the supermarket. There are curious shoppers walking all around, and little kids dancing to the music and doing the colouring-in competitions, while their mums and dads eat from the sausage sizzle.

There is still a significant possibility that Scott isn't going to make it. Rowing on the moving truck was a bit too much too soon. He has a couple of hours' rest and then rows for an hour. Then for an hour and a quarter. I am still rowing two hours but the last half-hour is dragging on forever, so Scott and I agree that we will both row shifts of an hour and a half.

We are again taking our breaks in the local Holiday Shoppe office. The staff are still working, but they don't seem to mind as after every shift a dishevelled, incoherent rower staggers in to fall unconscious, face down between the boxes of brochures in their little storeroom.

Friday evening is the worst. With it comes the realisation that we aren't even halfway through the task. We have barely managed the first night, and now there are two more to go. Again the mall is deserted. At the end of each shift I grab my towel, stumble to the public loos and just sit on the throne and marvel at the warmth, cleanness and stillness. It is all white and shiny, like a temple. I take a long look at myself in the mirror then wobble to the back of the Holiday Shoppe office, where it is so deliciously warm and dark, then I give in to the overwhelming desire to sleep and lie out on the Thermarest.

Soon the alarm goes and I look at it incredulously. But then I have to get up, as we haven't factored in any time for disbelief. I have another mouthful or two of food, then it's back out into the cold.

We have been warned that on Saturday night some Girl Guides who are doing a 'No Sleep-A-Thon' may come and visit. But by the time it gets to 2am I have decided that they are unlikely to come. It's getting warm inside the truck, so I have stripped to the waist while I watch another DVD. If you have ever seen the Vin Diesel movie *XXX* you will know that despite the title it's actually a pretty standard action movie, with one brief bedroom scene. The Guide leader's timing, then, is unfortunate.

After knocking on the door of the truck a few times without getting a response she pulls it open to find a wild-eyed, half-naked man covered in sweat watching what is clearly a porno movie. The Guides don't stay long.

In the small hours of Sunday morning it gets cold in the truck, very cold, and I am feeling oddly shivery. My head is feeling strangely hot and cold, and my back is stiffening up. My thinking is making less sense than ever. I wonder if I am going a bit loopy. I just want to lie down. It would be so easy to stop. Despite my head being hot I try putting on my sweatshirt. Slowly I start to feel better. Was I suffering from incipient hypothermia?

Worse, Scott comes out from one shift complaining that his back has gone into spasm. Luckily his girlfriend Sarah is there to give him a massage. It says a lot about Scott's determination that he pulls through and keeps going.

First thing in the morning a friend visits with a video of an All Blacks match that was on TV the night before. I can see the players moving around the field but I can't make too much sense of what's going on. But it is very good to have someone to talk to, and something to distract me.

At breakfast time Rob rings me sounding uncharacteristically subdued. He says he won't be able to be there at the finish. His mother died in the early hours of the morning. He and his family are going to Whakatane. I offer him my condolences and we ring off. It will be strange not to have him there at the end of such a significant milestone for the campaign — it won't be the same without his enthusiasm and support.

By mid-morning we know we are going to finish late that afternoon — barring any more major physical malfunctions. It's a little later than we had originally thought, but still several hours within the old record.

I am sleeping down the back of the Holiday Shoppe office when a friend comes and wakes me up. 'Hey, Scott's going ballistic — if you want to be at the finish you'd better come soon.'

So I pull on my shoes and walk out into the afternoon sun. Only this time I'm not feeling dread — I'm feeling pure joy. A large crowd has gathered around the truck and Matti is on the mike whipping them into a frenzy. Scott is burning it up, pulling under 2:00 splits, and there are cheers as he goes through each milestone. There is even applause for me as I get up on stage and swap in. This is rowing how rowing should be. Every time I go through another 1000 metres the crowd gives another yell. With 2 km to go Scott comes back on stage and rows on the other ergo.

The crowd is shouting out the distance until the big odometer finally hits zero and Anna and Natalie spray us with magnums of champagne. We jump up and punch the air, then we shake hands and hug everyone while the crowd cheers. We have set a new world record of 76 hours 48 minutes. Despite all the setbacks we have managed to smash the old record by 10 hours.

Emma Keeling from TV3 manages to pull Scott and I away from the throng. The first question she asks is, 'So, what do you feel like?'

I'm lost for words and so is Scott — we look at each other and start laughing. Finally Scott manages to sum it up. 'It's like hitting yourself with a hammer — it feels great when you stop!'

We do some more interviews for radio and TV, and the crowd slowly melts away. Then, moving carefully, I walk over to the Starlet, lower myself gingerly in and drive home.

The two things that surprise me most about doing the million-metre row are the number of people who ask me 'How far is that?' and secondly, how far it really was. All that bum-ripping pain. All that muscle-grinding effort. All the endless hours. And that 1000 km was only 20% of the total race distance. And not really even 20%, because the real race doesn't take place at high speed inside a clean, dry shopping mall, with flush loos and washed clothes.

But there are some positive takeaways. We have broken a world record, even if it was a slightly flabby one. We have certainly learned that something thicker than Lycra is going to have to go between the rubber of the Roho and our bums on that seat. But most of all, we have to find out what is up with Scott.

A week or two later I am on the ergo at Les Mills when Steve Westlake comes into the gym, sits down on the machine next to me and starts rowing. I force myself to slow down.

'So how did you find the million-metre row?' he asks.

'Pretty tough, actually.'

'Yeah. I thought you might.'

We make a little more small talk, then he leaves to do some weights. I keep on rowing. I'm still rowing when he leaves the gym.

CHAPTER FOURTEEN

Captain Kirk meets Mr Spock

The top five things you don't want to hear from
the lab technician when having to use a rectal probe:
'We've been keeping yours in the fridge.'
'Sorry, we've run out of the thin ones.'
'I'm not getting a reading — can I put it in further?'
'That's strange, it worked fine when we used it on the sumo wrestlers.'
'They come out of the box that colour.'

The young guy in the lab coat is holding up a long, slender instrument. It looks a lot like a sparkler. In his other hand is a tube of lubricant.

'Sorry mate, it's the rules. No one goes inside unless they are wearing one of these.'

Rob has contacted the Centre for Sports and Exercise Science at the Waikato Institute of Technology, and they have kindly offered us the use of their heat chamber so we can start acclimatising to the heat we can expect out in the Atlantic.

The Starlet shudders to a halt in the parking lot of the institute's sprawling grounds. When I find the room, it's smaller than I expect — only about as big as a double bedroom. The technician is hosing down the floor.

In the heat it is quite possible for someone who's working out to cook themselves and fall over, so the policy is to continually monitor your temperature to ensure it stays within safe limits. Not your skin temperature, your *core* temperature. So I take the probe to the bathroom and waddle out a few minutes later, all wired up. It's funny how something as small as a pipe cleaner can feel as big as a baseball bat.

I have researched the weather off the coast of South America using data from a weather buoy that suggests we can expect about 32 degrees, and 80% humidity. So the technician dials up the heat and I sit on the rowing machine and start rowing. With a hiss a stream of hot fog starts to pour out of a little grate on the wall. Soon sweat is running off me, down onto the floor and into the drain. My heart is pounding as my hypothalamus tries to flush blood through my skin in a futile attempt to cool down. It is becoming much harder to keep up a normal pace.

The lab technician's voice comes over the intercom.

'Hey, we've lost the core temperature reading — can you check the probe?'

I wriggle on the seat. 'It's definitely in there.'

'Yeah, it has to go in a bit deeper, eh.'

'How much deeper?'

'You should feel it tickling your tonsils.'

Since the million-metre row Scott has continued to suffer from migraines. But three weeks later the training schedule requires us to do a 24-hour row, so we decide to do it in the heat chamber where we can be thoroughly monitored. We will eat and sleep in the chamber, and the lab will measure our electrolytes, testosterone, cortisol, glucose, food and water intake, and our psychological state every two hours.

TV3 send a crew down and we do a piece with Emma Keeling before we start, then they leave and we begin for real. The monotony quickly sets in. Rowing at sea can be boring, but rowing in a small, hot, white room is desperation. Time slows down, and effort goes up. I suck in hot air and blow sweat off my nose.

I get through the first shift, but it is afterwards, lying on the Thermarest in the stinking remorseless heat and feeling the clinical white walls pressing in, that I start to feel my will begin to crack and my mood begin to plummet. Maybe it is too soon after the pain of the million-metre row, but all I can think about is the next 24 hours stretching out in front of me — staring at white walls, busting my gut, shredding my muscles, spitting into tubes, eating fat, all with a probe up my arse. All to die pointlessly in a ridiculously futile race over an ocean. The room starts to feel very small. There is nowhere to escape to, and the heat feels like a claustrophobic blanket.

What doesn't kill you makes you tough. What doesn't kill you makes you tough.

It's Scott's first time in the chamber and he is keen not to overstress himself, so he is rowing a little slower than usual. But by the middle of the night he is starting to look waxy, his work output has dropped away, his breathing is laboured and he is shiny with sweat.

'Scott, are you feeling OK?'

'I've been better.'

Then a few moments later: 'I think I'm going to have to take a break.'

That was Scott for the rest of the night. He goes outside, and when he doesn't improve we decide he should head home. I keep rowing until the next day.

It feels sensational to get out of the heat chamber and have a shower. I feel burnt clean. Every deep, unlaboured breath of cold, clean air is a gift. Every step without a baseball bat up my bum is a gift.

A couple of days later I talk to the professionals who were monitoring us. Is there something wrong with our diet? Were there any clues in our blood tests? But despite all the data that has been collected, what is affecting Scott is still a mystery. We schedule another 24-hour row in the chamber for a few weeks' time.

The phone rings. It's Rob.

'Hey, I've found a reserve for you.'

'Does he know how to row?'

'Oh yeah, he's bloody good.'

'Any issues?'

'Oh no, he's a good bugger. Hard as nails.'

'How do you know him?'

'He's the captain of the Waikato crew for the Gallagher Great Race. I've been talking about it with him for a while, and the idea has finally gained traction.'

'So he's still at university? How old is he?'

'I don't know — 22, I suppose.'

'That's pretty young! Has he rowed much?'

'Oh yeah. All his life.'

'How good is he, on a scale of 1 to . . . you?'

'Oh, he's bloody good. Yeah, no worries. You know how Ackland said to find someone better than Westlake? Well, this guy's one of them. He was with the New Zealand elite rowing team at the world champs in 2001.'

'So what did you tell him about the race?'

'I told him we were looking for a reserve and asked if he was interested. He's been thinking about it for a while, and now he's agreed.'

'OK. That's great. What's his name?'

'Jamie Fitzgerald.'

September 2003

In early September I go down to Hamilton to watch the Gallagher Great Race. For the last two years Rob and two friends have organised a rowing race up the Waikato River in which Waikato University takes on a top university from overseas. This year it's Oxford.

I don't rate Waikato's chances very highly. I know that the Oxford crew train incredibly hard all year round for their race against Cambridge. Plus they are stacked full of German Olympians and world-championship winners. But it should be a fun day, and I will get to see this Jamie in action.

Rob has got me a pass to watch the race from the corporate lounge area of the clubhouse. He has also invited Jim Shekdar, the crazy Englishman who rowed the Atlantic in 1997 and went on to row solo across the Pacific a few years later. I have just finished reading his book, *The Old Man and the Sea*. Jim is here as part of his preparations for an attempt to row the Southern Ocean later in the year. It sounds completely nuts, but then who is to tell a guy who has rowed the Pacific what he can and can't do?

Jim is larger and perhaps more portly than I would expect from an international endurance athlete, but full of good cheer and stories. Like the time in the Atlantic rowing race when he couldn't agree with his crewmate about what direction they should take. One thought south and the other thought west. They couldn't resolve the debate so in one shift one rowed south and the next shift the other rowed west! I ask him if he has any advice for me.

'I'm sorry to tell you this, but us Pacific Ocean rowers call the Atlantic a training pond. I wouldn't be too worried if I were you.'

We turn our attention to the race as the TV monitors begin the countdown to the start. When the gun goes off the boats are too close together and immediately start clashing oars. There is such confusion and clatter that I feel sure they are going to start the race again. But the boats pull apart, with Oxford taking an early lead.

Waikato edges up alongside Oxford but Oxford put on a spurt and stretch away. Then, incredibly, the Waikato team charge again and this time Oxford can't shake them. They go into the final straight neck and neck. The crowd along the banks are beside themselves. Slowly Waikato begin to move in front. The close-ups from the TV shots show the intensity of the pain on the faces of the Waikato crew. They cross the finish line just in front, with the crowd on the bank going crazy.

But I am only looking at one person — the captain, who at the moment is leaning over the side with his shoulders heaving, his face a mask of agony from the effort. So this is the Jamie Fitzgerald that Rob has been talking about.

Scott makes it through the second heat-trial, but he is not looking very good and his back is still troubling him. We still don't know what is wrong.

We plan another overnight row but this time it's going to be outside on the water. We launch from the Takapuna boat ramp on a Saturday morning and row together up the North Shore beaches. I tell Scott that we really need to find out what's wrong with him as I am concerned that he's not going to make it across the Atlantic.

Scott is offended and thinks I am doubting his ability. I try and tell him it's not that I'm doubting his ability, it's that we need to find out what's going wrong so that it doesn't happen when we are in the Atlantic. Scott says that his body has never let him down. We go back and forth on the subject for half an hour until there is an uncomfortable silence.

Scott says he needs a beer. Suddenly I do too.

Neither of us is in the mood for rowing anymore. A very sombre party returns to the boat ramp.

The following Tuesday night Scott calls a meeting at Rob's house and I drive down to Hamilton. Scott is affronted that I would doubt his ability; he has every confidence in himself and thinks that I should too. I say that we need to do some more research and pin down some of the health concerns that seem to be affecting his performance. I ask for a week to get more information and make a decision. But Scott is not happy with this.

'What will you know in a week that you don't know now?'

'We can speak to some experts, try and get some opinions about what's wrong and whether or not we need to be worried about it.'

'These people don't know me. I know what my body can do. It has never proven me wrong.'

But he reluctantly agrees.

I spend the next few days calling up anyone who might be able to help. I speak to chiropractors, osteopaths and sports doctors about what might cause someone's back to play up like Scott's. I speak to heat acclimatisation experts to get their opinion about the validity of the tests. No one can shed any light at all. But all of them are concerned.

I try to imagine that the campaign has a board of directors. Would I rather explain to them that I had ditched the guy who knew all the boat systems and had done all the training to bring on a complete novice just before the race? Or that I had gone with Scott even though we knew he wasn't well?

The strange parallels to the events just before the 2001 race aren't lost on me either. Am I doing to Scott what Westlake did to Rob?

No, it isn't the same. I want to find out what's wrong with Scott. Westlake agreed to row if Rob passed certain tests, then he changed his mind and said he wouldn't row with Rob regardless.

I decide to call The Don. I explain what's going on, then I ask him,

'So what do you think I should do?'

'You know what to do.' Click.

In fact I don't. But I will wait until the week is up at least.

Another physiologist associated with the Centre for Sports and Exercise Science has another theory and wants Scott to do some more tests.

I am at the high-altitude clinic in Mt Eden when my cellphone rings. It's Scott. He was on his way to do the tests when he had an epiphany. The call ends.

The woman across the table is looking at me strangely.

'Bad news?' she asks.

'My rowing partner has just pulled out.'

I call Rob right away.

'Rob, Scott just pulled the plug.'

'Shit.'

'I know.'

'How do you feel about it?'

'I don't know. Relieved that I don't have to make a decision, I guess . . . I suppose we need to get Jamie into the heat chamber?'

Rob gets onto it, without telling Jamie about Scott.

Later that afternoon I call the lab tech. 'How did Jamie go?'

'The guy's a monster. It didn't worry him one bit.'

Rob gets Jamie to drop by his house after the test.

'Scott's pulled out. We need another rower and so . . . you're it.'

Jamie looks stunned and stares at the corner of the room.

'Far out . . . far out! I'd better tell my mum!'

Scott's withdrawal from the team is reported on the TV3 news that night. In an interview he says that it's due to 'cultural and philosophical differences'. On another channel he says, 'Kevin was speaking Russian, while I was speaking French.'

The next day I drive down to Hamilton to meet Jamie and go over what has to be done in the two weeks we have left before we fly out. After all the agony of trying to find the right person to row with, now it comes down to a spin of the wheel. He's our last chance.

I pull up at Rob's house and Jamie answers the door. He's taller in real life than he appeared on the boat. He has a mop of brown hair, and he walks with a kind of loping gait. It's a slightly surreal experience — it isn't often you meet a person and your first words go something like, 'Great to meet you finally — let's row an ocean.'

There's quite a lot to get through — we have to find a safety-at-sea course for Jamie to do, and a medical course, and we need to finalise the preparations for our leaving party. I also want us to see a sports psychologist before we go, to help us work out how we are going to get along.

Throughout the meeting Jamie is enthusiastic and pragmatic, and best of all he laughs at my jokes. I start to think that maybe this is going to work out after all.

⚔

There was only one possible theme for our leaving party — 'Pirates of the Caribbean'. As well as a send-off for us it is also a charity auction to raise funds for Cure Kids. Sir Ed agrees to do one of his famous sketches of a mountaineer going up a mountain. Rob and I turn up at his house in Remuera, where we are met at the door by Lady June and invited in for morning tea.

Over scones we chat about how the campaign is going, particularly about the departure of Scott and the arrival of Jamie. Then it's time to start the drawing. Sir Ed gets a large piece of white paper and a pen. He looks around the room. 'I need a mountainous profile. C'mon then, Rob, put your head back and let's have a look.' He finishes the drawing with a few deft strokes and holds it at arm's length. 'Oh, that's quite a good one,' he says, pleased with himself.

The Novotel in Ellerslie have donated the venue and the catering, and Anna and the Holiday Shoppe team do a fantastic job of decorating the room with a tropical theme. Irena is over from Sydney and she and Hot Polish Girl come dressed as lusty wenches. They look fabulous. Jamie comes in wearing ripped jeans, a waistcoat and nothing else.

Irena asks me, 'So, who's the new rower?'

'That guy over there.'

'Oh, you mean Mr Muscles?'

The auction goes well, we raise over $9000 for Cure Kids, and the party goes on until they have to kick us out.

The day after the leaving party is not the ideal time for another overnight row, but Jamie needs to go out at least once in one of the Atlantic boats before we get to the Canaries.

We head north to Stillwater and slide the boat into the water, then we stroke out with the tide, heading out between a line of boats toward the Hauraki Gulf. At the end of the Whangaparaoa Peninsula we turn towards Tiri Tiri Island.

This seems like a good opportunity for Jamie and me to get to know each other a little, but after the festivities of the previous night neither of us is feeling very talkative. In the end our conversation is limited to the necessities of getting around the boat. But Rob wasn't fibbing — Jamie really does know how to row. The oars are like matchsticks in his massive paws, and the boat surges with a purpose into the light chop.

As the sun sets, a fierce electrical storm that has been strafing the mainland rolls down the peninsula. We find some shelter in a bay, drop the anchor, and manage to fall asleep with the sound of thunder exploding around the boat.

I see Jon Ackland for the last time.

'How are you feeling?' he asks.

'Well, pretty energetic I guess. A bit apprehensive.'

'Good,' he says. 'Let me tell you a story. I was training someone for the Ironman in Hawaii a year or two ago. She was a good athlete, a very good athlete. She had a pretty good chance of winning. And the night before the race I went to see her to see how she was doing. We had a chat, and as I went to leave she burst into tears. And then I knew she was ready.'

'How did you know that?'

'Because she had finally realised what she was going to have to do to herself to win.'

The phone rings. It's Gordon.

'I was having a chat with Steve the other day and he was saying that he had seen you rowing and that you aren't going to be a threat. He reckons you'll probably pull out of the race in the first week.'

I am having my final lunch with The Don. He picks up the oversized wine glass and gives it a little flick with his wrist to send the contents spinning around. He watches it carefully.

'This race is going to push you to your limits. You will question yourself about why you are doing it. You need to have the strongest possible motivation to gouge every last scrap of effort out of you. So why are you doing the race?'

'Mostly to prove to myself that I can.'

'That won't be enough.'

He finishes his glass in one swallow. For once he looks me straight in the eye with an unblinking stare, and he speaks in a low, menacing growl.

'You need to think of all the injustices that have ever been done to you! All the insults that you have ever received! All those little people who doubted you and stood in your way and tried to make you mediocre. You have to show something to those people.' He puts a clenched fist on the tablecloth.

'Don't take part in this race to create something beautiful — win it to destroy something awful.'

Hot Polish Girl is up from Tauranga and offers to make me lunch while I pack and do some last-minute things. She is looking particularly cute, in a sleeveless white t-shirt. She makes a pizza that is one half Spanish and one half Caribbean. I don't get it — she has to explain it to me. I'm too busy thinking how lovely she is. She gives me a St Christopher to keep me safe, and a kiss.

I go to the ergo up on the mezzanine floor at Les Mills one last time. More than eighteen months ago a flabby fatty first sat here and bitched and moaned his way through an hour of sloppy rowing. I sit down on the rowing machine, put the resistance to maximum, get hold of the little handle and start rowing.

I think about the changes that have taken place in me over that time, physically and mentally. Now I don't weigh any less but my muscle mass has increased considerably. My forearms have grown ropey, my thighs are bulging, and my back feels like a steel bar. I've had my technique pulled apart by Rob and put back together. I've been in the boat out in the gulf in conditions so horrendous that we were the only craft on the water. I've spent hours, mostly at night, rowing into oar-bending headwinds. I've seen litres of my sweat trickle down the drain in a tiny, hot white room. I've been bucketed with rain, seen lightning stab the seas, been grilled under the sun, and nearly frozen myself senseless rowing in the back of a truck. Now I am a world record holder for long-distance indoor rowing.

I row for an hour at 1:48 splits. Eighteen months ago I could barely have pulled one stroke at this speed. I've never been so fit in all my life. I'm fizzing with energy. Now I'm ready.

I almost didn't want anyone to come to the airport. If there are a lot of emotional people there I know I will feel like we are actually going off to a watery grave. I just want to get onto the plane and out at the other end.

But in the end there's a crowd of family and friends milling around to say goodbye. I meet Jamie's girlfriend Kate, another former New Zealand rower. I give Mum a hug, and realise for the first time how hard it's going to be for her while I am away.

Jamie's mum is wailing. I promise I will look after him. She wails louder. Then at last we are through the departure gates and sitting on the plane.

CHAPTER FIFTEEN

'Are you the good Kiwis or the bad Kiwis?'

From 30,000 feet you can see a lot of the Earth, and a lot of the Earth that I am seeing is ocean. For hour after hour I have my nose pressed against the window as it rolls underneath us.

I don't know much about the Canary Islands other than that the world's worst aeroplane crash took place there and that a lot of Brits go there for holidays. As our plane comes out of the clouds we can see the island of Tenerife for the first time. It doesn't look like a tropical island paradise, it looks like the desert-like Central Plateau back in New Zealand. Lots of scraggly brush, tussock grass, and much bare, sharp volcanic rock, sweeping dramatically up to the clouds. In the air-conditioned coolness of the cabin we could be landing at an abandoned Siberian airbase rather than a tropical island.

We get our bags and wait outside for our ride. Rob hasn't told us much about Chris — just that he is some expat Kiwi bloke who lives in the Canaries and was a great help in the last two campaigns, and that he is happy to host us until our boat arrives.

Eventually a small car screeches up. A wrinkled face on a wiry frame appears out the window. 'You look like Kiwis.' He gapes at Jamie. 'Look at the size of him!'

We squeeze in alongside Chris's two lively daughters, Grace, aged eight, and Tayla, six, who happily gabble to us, and Bonita the puppy, in a mixture of Spanish and English. We drive around the island, eventually winding our way down a narrow road past a block of palm-like trees that are wrapped in a huge quantity of clear plastic windbreak.

'It's a banana plantation,' explains Chris. We turn into a break in the plastic and drive some more. Suddenly the path opens out into a clearing and there is a house, completely hidden from the outside.

'Does the council know about this place?' I ask Chris as we pull in. 'What council?'

We sit on the porch and have a drink. Not Chris, he is recently on the wagon. It turns out he is one of the original bungy-jumping pioneers. He has plenty of tales of wild jumping in the early days.

'So we go to jump off this bridge and we hook up the bungy and AJ says, "OK, I'll go", and I say, "No hang on, we have to test the length is right." So I find this old railway sleeper that's about the right weight and we tie it to the bungy and we chuck it over and it sails down and sticks about two feet into the mud!'

Apparently Chris developed a lot of the materials and techniques that turned bungy-jumping into a sport. In fact, he still holds the world record for the highest bungy from a fixed structure. He ran various bungy operations around the world and was in the original team that started the X Games before finishing up in the Canaries. He started an amusement park here called 'Sky Park' that has a bungy tower and other aerial-type rides. Then things took a horrible turn for the worse. His young wife, Donna, died suddenly and inexplicably. His business partner sold out to the Spanish mafia, who have since been trying to muscle Chris out of the business. He has recently been locked out of the park, and is waiting while his case winds its way through the convoluted Spanish justice process. With the stress his health is failing, particularly his liver. Now there have been death threats. He keeps a baseball bat by the door.

Waking up the next morning I experience an unfamiliar feeling. There's nothing I have to do! Since our boat hasn't arrived yet, we can enjoy ourselves for the next few days.

Chris thinks he can get us a jump at the bungy park. Jamie is not hugely keen. 'Come on, Bushman! It'll toughen you up!' shouts Chris. Then he goes and looks out the window. 'Hang on, the winds might be too strong!' Jamie perks up. Chris makes some phone calls. 'No they aren't, let's go!'

He drops us off near the back entrance of the park. Soon a muscled, tight t-shirted, long-haired Spanish guy saunters out and introduces himself as Alfredo. I'm thinking that if he pays the same attention to tying the knot around my ankles as he does to his hair I'll be fine.

The tower is enormous. It goes up fifteen storeys and sways a little in the breeze. The elevator quickly ascends to the edge of my comfort zone, and then keeps on going up and up. I try to focus on the view out over the ocean, which is outstanding. Jamie goes first, then Alfredo ties up my ankles. I shuffle my toes to the edge. Who's the boss here — me or Fear? Am I ready for this race or not? I bend my knees and jump out.

The funny thing about bungying is that the relief of having finally committed to a decision is so great you actually feel good on the way down.

Chris and his friends take us to Los Gigantes, the harbour that hosted the start of the first rowing race. The landscape is dramatic — huge cliffs fall out of the clouds and plunge into the sea. On a small headland there's a little marine company. We visit the bar where the rowers went to party. The owner still has photos from that time on the wall. I look at the happy, flushed faces of the rowers, and hear an echo of laughter and music from six years ago. They would have had hardly any idea what they were getting into, or how many of them were going to make it across. Fourteen of them didn't. No one plans to fail. No one thinks it's going to be them, but Fate always picks a few. What's in store for us?

Each evening I walk up the outside stairs of Chris's house to the roof-top terrace. I look out over the large slice of ocean to the island of La Gomera silhouetted in the distance. This is where our race starts.

Over there the other crews are arriving and getting set up.

'You're better over here,' says Chris. 'There's nothing over there. Nothing!'

But I'm thinking about our plan to row over to the start. I have heard about the 'acceleration zones' where the wind is funnelled to a furious pace between the islands, enough to blast boats out to sea. There looks like a lot of sea to get blown into. Starting the race a week early would be embarrassing.

In the evenings, when the blazing heat of the day is tapering off, Jamie and I go for runs to kill some time and burn off some energy. From the banana plantation we either jog down the hill to a large hotel and sneak into one of the pools, or we jog up the steep, winding lanes that go up the mountainside.

It seems a good idea to try and get to know this guy that I'll be stuck on a boat with for the next few months. I'm worried that we might not have much to talk about as our backgrounds and ages are so different. But Jamie is a good talker, and a natural storyteller. We chat as we run, and I try to keep up with the lingo.

'So I'm going to have to redo the semester when I get back; it's going to be pies.'

'What's it like hanging out in Hamilton? Are the locals friendly or is it . . . ahh . . . pies?'

'Very friendly after a few Waikato Draughts. I'm in the pub the other day when these twins walk in and . . .'

'Hang on! Is this a good story?'

'Well it's not pies . . . why?'

'Can we save it for on the boat when the weather gets really really lousy and we are locked in the cabin for two days or something? It will give me something to look forward to.'

'Yeah. Sure. Primo.'

A few days later Rob, Rachel and baby Finn arrive. Shortly after that a large flatbed truck with a 12-metre container on top somehow makes its way down the narrow lane through the banana plantation to the house. The container has to be taken away empty right away so we rush to unload everything, transferring it from the chest-high container to the asphalt in front of the house. Chris has organised a group of his young friends, mostly the bungy operators from the park, to help.

The boat inches out and teeters on the edge of the five-foot drop. I promise myself that I will dive under it and use my stomach as a fender rather than let it drop. But many hands grab the frame, t-shirts bulge, sweat and hair product trickle down brown foreheads. Slowly the boat is lowered safely to the ground.

Rob has persuaded us to make a last-minute change to the paint on the bottom of the boat, using a new super-slippery paint he has found. This involves two days of hot, unpleasant work lying on our backs to sand back to the undercoat. But when we are finished the hull is gleaming and astonishingly slippery.

'Primo!' says Jamie.

Ten days before the start of the race we need to go over to La Gomera to attend the first official briefing. This will be our first chance to see the other crews and boats. Rob wants us to go barefooted to show what wild savages we are. I put my sandals in the car. He throws them out onto the drive.

Down at the ferry the security guards won't let us on without footwear. So we go to the gift shop and buy tiny pink jandals, which satisfies the guards but does make us slightly less intimidating.

We sit in one of the upper decks for the trip and look out at the enormous, glittering blue ocean. It looks calm and definitely manageable. I start to feel hopeful. 'Is this what the Atlantic is like, Rob?'

'This is the bloody Atlantic!'

Just off the coast of La Gomera the water changes rapidly, beaten into steep, choppy whitecaps by a sudden vicious wind. There would be no way of rowing against it, or even through it. We would be blown south away from the island and out to oblivion in half an hour. Is this the dreaded acceleration zone they talk about?

The ferry pulls in at San Sebastián, a small, pretty town flanked by steep brown hills. We shuffle our pink jandals down to the civic centre. Inside, milling about waiting for the briefing to start, are the other crews, smiling and shaking hands. Some of them look pretty fit.

Rob points out two of the biggest, Alan Watson and Miles Barnett of *Bright Spark*, who have both rowed for Cambridge and are likely to be very highly placed. Westlake and Goodman are there in their grey racing outfits, carrying water bottles. We exchange cool nods as we take our seats. I whisper to Rob, 'So how's the Dispute going?'

'Yeah . . . lots of heat and not much light.'

'What's left to be decided?'

'Mostly it's just this issue with the equipment thing, but with Westlake seizing the boat we're now trying to negotiate a deal that sorts out the equipment and the boat at the same time. They don't seem to want to compromise, and they're saying the same about me. If it's not sorted soon we may need to get arbitration after the race.'

A petite, pretty blonde woman calls us to order and introduces herself as Teresa. I recognise her voice from the phone — this is Teresa Page, who is the head of operations for the race. She tells us that starting from tomorrow each boat will be scrutinised to ensure compliance with the rules regarding safety equipment and general seaworthiness. In addition, all boats are going to be weighed, which means that everything in them will need to be taken out.

'Wow, what a pain in the neck!' I whisper to Rob. 'Did they weigh the boats in 2001?'

'No, they said they might, but they never did. I guess it was too much hassle for them.'

After the briefing Rob stops to chat to a reporter who recognises him from the 2001 race. The reporter asks what his role is in this campaign. When Rob explains, he suggests, 'So you are like a Yoda to their Luke Skywalker?'

I like the analogy, and as we walk out I quiz Rob, 'So what does that make Goodman and Westlake?'

'The Dark Side.'

Rob introduces us to a young, square-jawed, blond-haired Brit called Simon Chalk, who he knows from the '97 race. Simon's company, Woodvale Events, is the new owner of the Atlantic race, having just bought it from Chay Blyth. But I recognise Simon's name as one of the guys who had been capsized off the coast of Australia attempting to row across the Indian Ocean. Over lunch at this year's adopted bar, the Blue Marlin, Simon tells us about his successful re-attempt earlier in the year. His rowing partner was not keen to do the trip again, so Simon ended up going solo. It took him a mammoth 107 days in seas that were apparently far rougher than the Atlantic. He saw waves 15 metres high and capsized not once but four times during the crossing.

At one point in the conversation the sky dims and the air cools as a cloud passes over. Simon stops talking and looks up as the Dark Side saunter past in their long grey outfits and dark sunglasses. He watches them walk away then takes a sip of his drink. 'Seeing those two makes me want to jump in a rowboat,' he says.

Then he adds, 'Talking about boats, did you know theirs hasn't arrived? Apparently the container ship is held up and won't be here for a few days.'

'So what have they been doing?' asks Rob.

'I've seen them go for a few runs. I think they have been helping out some of the other teams with their boats as well.'

That's not all they have been doing. After Simon leaves, Rob gets to chatting to a group of English people at the bar. It turns out they are there to support one of the other teams. They ask Rob which team he is supporting.

'The Kiwis,' he says.

'Oh, we've heard about them. But are you with the good Kiwis or the bad Kiwis?'

On the way back to the ferry we pass the rows of trans-Atlantic boats that are up on the hard. Many are being worked on. It is very interesting to see what solutions other crews have found to the problems we have faced — where they put their seats, the types of hatches, handrails, ventilation, what they had done about insulating the cabin.

We walk around saying hi to the crews and introducing ourselves. 'It's a festival of handshakes,' Jamie says. 'Every country has their own thing.'

We meet one of the two mixed crews, Marcus Thompson, a comedy writer, and Sally Kettle, of *Calderdale — The Yorkshire Challenger*. Marcus is an epileptic and they are doing the race to raise funds for an epilepsy charity. They have already raised a colossal £200,000 and have set themselves the target of £1 million! They seem to get a giggle out of calling us The Happy Shoppers.

Rob calls us over to meet Chris Hall and Richard Pullan from *Team Altitude*. Rob met Richard when he spent a season rowing for Auckland, and he rates him pretty highly. They seem solid blokes and well prepared.

The Royal Air Force crew, Matt Stowers and Mark Jacklin, are already in the water. They have squeezed their race preparations in between working at their normal jobs until almost right before the race. Their boat *Per Ardua* seems a little low in the water and they are still squeezing food into every hatch. When I ask them about it, Matt says, 'We've had to spend so much time on exercises out on the field being starved that we aren't going to let that happen this time!'

They also have an absolutely enormous teapot, big enough for the whole barracks — it could just about double as a lifeboat. I envy the camaraderie and good-natured banter between the crews, and it is refreshing being around people who wouldn't even dream of asking you why you are doing the race. I'll be glad when we move over here.

On the ferry back to Tenerife Rob talks about the atmosphere he experienced before the start of the first Atlantic rowing race. Leading into that race the statistics for ocean rows were not good. There hadn't been that many attempts, and of those about half had failed. Five boats and their crews have been lost at sea.

'Those stats were hanging over all of us,' Rob says. 'There was a real intensity in the air. It felt like we were going off to war.'

'Did anyone die in your race?' asks Jamie.

'No, but six boats didn't make it, and a couple of people were injured and taken off their boats. I can't put my finger on what makes me think this, but the crews there today seemed a bit too casual. It's a worry — the risks are real.'

Chris has planned a big leaving party for us and all the people who have been helping out. He produces two enormous iron saucers, over a metre across, one of which is filled with firewood, the other with ice for the beer.

Before the guests arrive Grace and Tayla start acting uncharacteristically coy and bashful. They want Jamie and me to come into the living room for a presentation. They know that greenstone gives you strength, and they think we should have some. So they have taken the clasps off their greenstone bracelets and made them into necklaces for us, so that we can be extra strong for the race. It's very sweet.

Soon the guests arrive and so does the rain. The kids run in and out of the house, delighted because they so seldom see rain. 'It's raining on *both* sides of the house!' they say with surprise. Salsa music plays and flames lick up into the night.

We have a busy day tomorrow — the truck is coming early to pick up the boat and put us into the water — so I make my excuses at a reasonable hour and go to bed. Jamie stays up later to absorb some more of the local atmosphere.

Early the next day a flatbed truck winds its way down the lane through the plantation and hoists the boat up onto its back. I watch with a knot in my stomach. I can't wait for all this boat dangling and undangling to be over. Chris yells increasingly offensive instructions in English to the Spanish driver. Alfredo, who is translating, turns to me with a smile. 'It is such a good thing that the driver does not speak English.'

The closest port is Puerto Colon, but the truck can't drop the boat into the water there. Instead we drive miles up the coast to another port just south of Los Gigantes, where the truck parks on the breakwater and the boat is swung gently out and onto the water. It floats! Jamie and I get in.

We push off from the pier and I take a few gentle strokes. I am light-headed and breathing deeply with joy. Here I am in the friggin' Canaries with my boat in the water! This is what I have imagined for so long. Sunny skies, silky seas, and a cleansing spot of exercise to look forward to.

There is a distinctive sound of gurgling and splashing liquid. I look down and see Jamie leaning out over the side. Rob calls out from the pier, 'Are you guys all right?'

'Yep, sweet. Jamie's just checking the waterline.'

Soon Jamie is back into the swing of things and we pull out of the harbour and head down the coast to the marina at Puerto Colon, where the rest of the food and equipment can be put on more easily. The wind is behind us and we make good time.

I flick the circuit breakers on and the boat clicks and whirs into life. The watermaker begins growling happily, the autohelm starts twitching and, after a brief pause, the Navman GPS finds itself. This is reassuring, since it's going to be giving us vital information.

The GPS is mounted on the bulkhead of the cabin, so that when you are rowing you can see it all the time. Depending on what screen you are on, it tells you some combination of the time, your speed, your position and your distance from any coordinate you have programmed into it — so it can tell you how far you have rowed in the last 24 hours, or how far you are from the finish line.

I close my eyes. I'm having another Moment. I've made it to the start line at the Canaries. Everything is Perfect.

I hear another funny noise.

'Jamie, what are you doing?'

'I'm taking a pee!'

'Oh man! That's the snack bucket!'

After piling on the rest of the food and equipment we spend the night sleeping on the boat in Puerto Colon. The next morning we begin rowing north, back up the coast — if the wind between the islands is going to be blowing us out to the south I want to have plenty of north to lose.

The water is still and calm, and as blue as a bottle of Bombay Sapphire. We row under the blazing sun for some hours while 15 miles of startlingly rocky coastline slide past. Mid-afternoon we finally reach the dramatic cliffs of Los Gigantes. There's a little marina with a breakwater surrounding it, and we tie up to a buoy outside this. Then we swim to the beach and wait for the evening, when hopefully the wind will be at its quietest. At 7:30pm we point the stern at the cliffs and begin to row. Soon the cliffs are shrinking as they retreat, and we are making excellent time, really excellent time. The rowing is very pleasant, and it is calm enough to have the portable radio out on deck tuned to a local English rock station.

We are in the middle of the islands when the wind picks up

suddenly. The whitecaps coming out of the darkness are slapping us hard on the beam, causing the boat to roll and lurch. I watch the GPS very carefully to see if we are starting to lose ground. So far so good. Then the amber light on the GPS flickers and it goes blank. It seems to have had some sort of power failure. Shit. But we can make out the flashes of the lighthouse at the entrance to San Sebastián harbour on La Gomera, so we aim for that.

The waves continue to get bigger; for some reason they are standing up quite steeply, and really shoving the boat around. We are still OK, but if things continue to deteriorate at the same rate it is quickly going to get sporty.

'Is this bad?' shouts Jamie. I have completely forgotten that he has had almost no time in the boat, certainly in nothing like this.

'Nah, it's sweet. Nothing to worry about.'

Something is up. We have the wind in our faces, and following seas, yet we aren't making much ground at all. The lighthouse is staying stubbornly in place off the starboard side of the boat. There must be a very strong tide that is pushing north against the wind. That might explain these strangely agitated seas.

Finally we make it to the end of the long, long breakwater and gratefully turn into the calmer water of the harbour. Against the wind it is still a stiff row back up to the marina. We find a berth and tie up. It's 2am. We have been rowing for 10 hours today, and the last six and a half have been without a break.

So this is what the Atlantic is like?

CHAPTER SIXTEEN

Countdown to the race

Monday, October 13 — six days to go

I am woken by a crisp, hearty English accent. 'Good morning guys! How's it going?'

I nudge open the hatch and let in the bright sunshine and a view of the dock. The voice belongs to a guy wearing shorts and a polo shirt, carrying a clipboard, and looking obscenely chirpy for this time of the morning. He introduces himself as Andy, and he wants us to move to where the boat crane can lift us out of the water onto the hard, in preparation for scrutineering.

With that sorted Jamie and I grab our bags and wander through the streets to find our hotel. Luckily it isn't the sort of place that minds, or even notices, if its patrons turn up in two-day-old rowing gear. Our rooms are small and bare, side by side on the third floor. Mine has a window that looks out over a park, where it looks like they are setting up for a rock concert.

The race is scheduled to start on Sunday, just six days away. My head is full of all the things that need to be done by then. There is a hose tail around the bilge pump that needs to be clamped. The compass light needs to be fixed. The gearing on the oars needs to be changed. A circuit breaker needs to be switched over, a pair of molegrips has to be bought.

The main boatyard where the rest of the boats are parked is full, so our boat is placed on a cradle a little way away down the pier next to the Barbadian boat, *Rowing Home*. Rob arrives on the early ferry and we spend the rest of the morning getting the food and equipment out of the boat, ready for the scrutineering.

We introduce ourselves to the Barbadian crew — Phil Als, a black, taciturn, multi-sport athlete, and Randal Valdez, a white, gregarious fisherman and windsurfer. I love Randal's accent: 'You haf to wotch dat wader at da norf of da island, mon. It can chop up ruff.'

In the corner of the dock, a little way down from us, is a much older boat sitting up on tyres. It's being attacked by a middle-aged bearded man with a saw and hammer. I introduce myself, and as he bashes at different parts of his boat he tells me his story. His name is Graham Walters, and he took part in the '97 race in the same boat he is working on now. He came tenth, which is a stunning effort given that he doesn't trust watermakers and took all his own water.

The boat came back to live with the gnomes at the bottom of his garden. To help it fit in, he painted flowers on the side. There it stayed for four years. Then in 2001, just three months before the next race, he rescued the boat and joined the field again, this time finishing 22nd.

Now, two years later, he has the bug and has again decided late that he wants to row solo across the Atlantic. In fact, the plan is to row across the Atlantic, through the Panama Canal and then across the Pacific. Well, that puts what we are doing into perspective.

The sound of my cellphone ringing wakes me up. I look at the alarm clock — it's 3am.

'Hello?'

On the scratchy line I hear the gravelly voice of The Don.

'A business associate has contacted me from the Canaries. He has contacts at the docks. He has offered to arrange to have the container carrying CRC's boat dropped as it is being unloaded. This service will cost 5000 euros. What shall I tell him?'

What? How does he know these people? Is he joking? To have them taken out before the race? What would that prove?

'No thanks. We don't need it.'

There is a brief pause.

'Excellent. Good luck.'

Tuesday, October 14 — five days to go

We are up early to get the boat ready for scrutineering. Rob calls me to the side of the boat.

'Hey, have you seen this?'

'What?'

Rob points to the port deck rail. There is a big dent in it, cracking one of the solar cells underneath. Rob nods knowingly.

'Sabotage.'

Possibly, but who and why? In any event, because the cells are wired in series it means that the chain of solar cells going up to the bow is probably stuffed.

The Challenge people come by to do the scrutineering. As well as Andy there is a stout, freckled, cheerful, thirty-something woman who introduces herself as Lin. This is Lin Parker, who is also the captain of the support yacht, and so a good person to know. They are very thorough, and pore through all of the safety equipment, the food, radio, battery systems, toolkit and solar panels. Finally the crane is brought over to hoist the boat off the cradle via some industrial-sized hanging scales. When the calculations are done we come in at 416 kg. Six kg above the minimum.

Back at the boat in the afternoon I am still trying to get the compass light fixed, and chatting to the steady stream of people coming over and saying hi and talking about the boat. One set of visitors aren't so chatty. The Dark Side come over and say nothing, but they stay for a long time in the same place watching us enigmatically from behind their dark glasses, occasionally sipping from their water bottles. Eventually they saunter away. Is this part of their Psych Ops?

The afternoon sun beats down on the dark asphalt of the dock, turning it into a black fry-pan. Jamie is lacking his usual zip. He is walking around with a towel wrapped around his head. I point this out to him.

'Yeah, I'm looking very Gisborne,' he admits. 'I'm not feeling great. I think I've picked up a bug.' He and Rob keep working on the oars while I go into town to pick up the bilge pipe we need. When I come back there are Woodvale race stickers stuck onto the bow of the boat, completely covering the solar panels. Apparently Teresa had come over and insisted on applying them. Race rules. Bugger. So now we have really lost the bow solar chains.

The team from Barbados are supported by Mount Gay Rum, and they are throwing a party to try and make a dent in some of their generous sponsorship supplies. They are based in an apartment on the hill overlooking the town and the view is sensational. Jamie still isn't feeling well and soon heads back to the hotel. The Dark Side are there drinking glasses of Sprite. I chat to Mick Burke of *Two Blokes, No Smokes*, who complains that they are infecting his rowing mate with early sobriety. We agree there will be a time to stop drinking — it just isn't yet.

When I get back to the hotel it's difficult to sleep. I lie in bed watching CNN and sweating into the thin cotton sheets until oblivion finally comes.

Wednesday, October 15 — four days to go

The morning finds us back working at the docks. It's not long before we are distracted by the arrival of a truck on the pier. Out of the back of the truck, like a landing spacecraft, a large object wrapped in a type of silver reflective foil emerges dramatically. The Dark Side's boat.

It looks very similar to when we last saw it. Although now I notice a strange acrylic hatch that goes right through the hull of the boat. I ask Goodman what it's for. He says it's for glass-bottom-boat tours.

The Dark Side's foil appears to be in high demand. I see a few crews starting to install it inside their cabins as insulation.

That night some friends from the UK arrive, and we go out to the Blue Marlin. We start chatting to a couple of tanned, blond-haired surfer dude-looking guys, who turn out to be Jason McKinlay and Philip Carrington from the British boat *Pura Vida*. They are both outdoor education instructors, and they have spent a lot of time preparing for the race. They have even spent two months in the Canary Islands, on Lanzarote, doing sea-trials and acclimatising. The only catch is that they have had all their equipment stolen from the boat, and they are now scrounging around their sponsors trying to get replacement GPS, radios, satellite phone and so on. They look like big, fit guys, with a good boat, and they have been preparing hard. Why would we beat them?

Thursday, October 16 — three days to go

I'm awake at 4:30am and see Jamie's light on. I go and knock on his door. He's feeling much better, and says he thinks he must have had some 24-hour bug. That's good to hear.

Later that morning we are working down at the boat when one of the RAF guys comes by for a chat. After a few minutes he says he has to go as he wants to watch *CRC* being weighed.

'It'll be interesting to see what they come in at,' I agree.

'If I know them it will be BANG on,' he says, his face glowing with admiration. 'Exactly!'

The Barbadians are getting ready to put their boat in the water and there are a lot of good-natured jokes going back and forth between them. Rob is bogging a hole on the side of the boat, and when he finds he has some left he asks them if they need any filler.

'Does it work on ears?' Phil asks.

'Either my ears or his mouth!' says Randal.

We are put back in the water ourselves later in the afternoon, and row over to where the rest of the boats are tied up at the main esplanade. It's now looking very colourful, with the boats flying flags, piles of equipment being loaded into hatches, crews and supporters laughing and talking, and tourists walking by taking photos. Rob comes back to the boat looking excited.

'You won't believe this! The Dark Side have come in underweight!'

'No way! How much? A couple of kilos?'

'More like twenty!'

'You are absolutely kidding.'

'No. I was having a chat with Andy and saw his clipboard. They've been caught completely red-handed.'

'Are they going to be disqualified?'

'No ... I don't know ... I don't think so. They'll probably just make them carry more weight.'

This is a bombshell. Does this mean that the Dark Side took a punt, based on their experience at the start of the 2001 race, that the race organisers were unlikely to go to the trouble of checking the weight of the boats? Does that mean they had knowingly submitted a dodgy weight certificate before the race? Is this just the first of a bag full of dirty tricks? Or are they innocent and for some reason their boat lost several per cent of its weight while it was locked in a container coming over to the Canaries. Maybe termites?

Friday, October 17 — two days to go

I wake up at 6am feeling fresh. Fresh and stressed. Two days to go.

We have breakfast then take the boat out for a row at 9am, when the tide is the same as it will be on race day. Rob looks at my rowing in amazement.

'Shit, Kev, who'd have believed it! You're actually rowing bloody well!'

We slide out of the harbour and row offshore. We are looking for the current that had tried hard to push us north the night we rowed over. It should be going the other way about now.

A hundred metres off the breakwater there starts to be a big difference between the log (the speed of the boat through the water) and the GPS (the total speed of the boat). It's the tide roaring south, a moving conveyor belt that we could hook into to sling us away from the island. And it's unlikely that the other teams know about it. Can we use this at the start to our advantage?

That afternoon a large gleaming-white launch pulls up to the wharf with Chris at the helm. It will be the base for our supporters over the next few days. In the evening we all go down to a barbecue that the race organisers have arranged at the end of the pier. It's another warm night, with a beautiful tropical sunset, and it's very pleasant to have a cold glass in my hand as the sunset colours light up the sky and frame the clouds.

I have just finished talking to two friends who have come in from London and am walking through the crowd when I hear shouting and see a scuffle up ahead. One of the raised voices sounds like Rachel Hamill. When I get there it looks like Rob is holding Rachel back. Matt Goodman is standing over them both, with a very agitated Steph Brown and Steve Westlake alongside. Jamie has got there before me and is now trying to separate people. There is plenty of heat on all the faces and short words going back and forth, and for a moment it feels like the men might start exchanging blows. Steph and Westlake eventually start to withdraw down the marina. The two women continue a shouted conversation, as if neither is keen to let the other have the last word.

'Why are you trying to ruin our lives?' Rachel cries one last time before she turns away, wiping her eyes.

When things have calmed down and people have returned to their food, I ask Rob what had happened. He explains that earlier in the evening, Steph had come up to him and Rachel saying, 'Hey Rob, me ol' mate, how much have you stolen from the team this time?' When Rachel responded, Steph had grabbed her by the cheeks and started pushing her head from side to side. Finn, who was in Rachel's arms, began to cry. Rachel managed to free a hand and push Steph away. Marcus Thompson, who was nearby, described Steph's behaviour as very peculiar.

Rob and Rachel had then left the barbecue but returned later to look for me and Jamie to tell us what had happened. But before they could find us, Steph had approached them again, shouting that Rob had stolen money. There was a scuffle between the women and punches were thrown.

The rest of the rowers and their supporters had stood and watched, baffled and horrified, until the women were pulled apart.

I am still trembling from the adrenaline when I go down to meet my brother Grant and his girlfriend, who have just arrived on the ferry after flying in from London. Afterwards we all go back to Chris's boat to debrief and plan our next steps. Outside the tropical night suddenly seems particularly inky. Rachel is distraught. 'The first time she came at me I was scared,' she says; 'the second time I was defensive. It's just horrible and embarrassing.'

There is a discussion about whether to report Steph to the police, and speculation about whether she will do the same. Chris keeps saying ominously, 'I'll make a few calls. It will all be taken care of.' The air is thick with talk of what might be done to our boat as revenge. Jamie volunteers to sleep on our boat. As I help him take some stuff down, I see Goodman is getting ready to sleep in *CRC*.

I can't wait for the race to start. It's going to be safer out on the water.

Saturday, October 18 — one day to go

Last update before the race!

Posted by Kevin Biggar on 18/10/2003

Well it's Saturday afternoon now, possibly a little bit cooler than it has been the last few days but still sweltering.

We have just had our final race briefing, it looks as if the weather is going to be exceptionally calm the next few days, which is better than the headwinds that were predicted a few days ago! So now at 11am tomorrow we just have to slip out of the harbour with the tide and head south and west and try and make it around El Hierro, the last island in the Canaries. That's the last land we will see for six weeks!

A French crew turned up yesterday after driving down through France and Morocco and taking the ferry across to the Canaries! Arriving two days before the start is cutting it pretty fine! We are completely ready ourselves now, just a little housekeeping inside the cabin. Our boat stacks up well against the other competitors; it's amazing how from the same kitset there can be so many variations on the boats!

This weekend is a continuation of the festival that they are having on the island at the moment. This means that tonight there is a large rock concert outside our hotel room! I am tempted to row the boat out into the harbour and try and find a quiet spot!

I am looking forward to the start tomorrow. All of our supporters have arrived from Tenerife and the UK and will be following us on a chase boat for the first few hours, but I am even more looking forward to settling down into the rhythm of life at sea.

Kevin

CHAPTER SEVENTEEN

Into the infinite

Sunday, October 19 — Race Day!

I last until about six o'clock in the morning, sweating into the thin white cotton sheets, before I turn on CNN. A few minutes later the door opens and Jamie walks in with a towel wrapped around his waist. We look at each other, not saying anything. I finally speak.

'I suppose we should go row an ocean then.'

The corners of Jamie's mouth turn down and he nods grimly. 'Might as well. Not like we're going to get any action in *this* town.'

I get out of bed, pull on my bike shorts and long-sleeved race top, and pack the last few things that haven't already gone into suitcases for Rob to take to Barbados. There is just a few minutes for breakfast, in the dark and strangely still dining room, then Jamie and I emerge blinking into one of the more spectacular Canarian mornings. Even though it is still early the sun is throwing sharp, dark shadows across the cobblestone streets. The sky is cloudless and still. You can tell that the price we are going to pay for this loveliness is extreme heat later on. We walk in bare feet down to the marina, where the sea is perfectly calm. Extraordinarily calm, definitely water-skiable.

Jamie stops at a phone booth to call Kate and the rest of his family. When we arrive at the launch and peek into the main cabin we can see sleeping bodies strewn everywhere. The bungy-park crew and their girlfriends have arrived. With everyone wearing white, and lying there with their limbs entwined, it looks like a Gucci perfume shot. I ease my way around the launch to where our boat has been tied on the front. We had decided it was better for Jamie to sleep back at the hotel last night, and I had had a dark thought that someone might have drilled a hole in the boat in the small hours. But there it is, still floating. Good. Everything looks as it should. There isn't much to do but go through some more checks. What was it Peter Blake used to say? 'I don't care if you've checked it, check it again!'

Soon the support team are up and a second breakfast is being organised for us. Grace and Tayla want their photo taken with us on the boat. I look at my watch every 30 seconds, but big chunks of time are flying by. The 11am start time feels scarily close. My blood is fizzing. In some ways it feels just the same as before any long training row. Except people are looking at me. Except this trip is strictly one-way.

The dock is filled with a colourful crowd of crews and smiling supporters now, as last-minute equipment and food is crammed into the boats. Jamie and I join the other crews walking up and down the line wishing each other well. I meet the excited French crew and wish them good luck. My cellphone is ringing constantly as friends call from all around the world.

Dave Pearse from *Petrel* comes up with his hand outstretched and a look of mock seriousness, as if patiently explaining important instructions: 'Now, if you get to Barbados first . . . I take two sugars.'

Jamie meets the Dark Side on the dock. Steve wishes him well, saying, 'Be safe, and see you at the finish.'

By 10:15 I am back at the rowboat. Things are becoming real very quickly. Now it is time to get going. I look up at the faces lining the rail of the launch.

'Has anyone seen Jamie?'

Blank stares. Rob volunteers to go look for him. He is back in a few seconds with Jamie, who is panting and looking flushed.

'Where did you go?'

'Oh, I just went for a bit of a warm-up run.'

In response to our incredulous looks he adds, 'Force of habit, I guess.'

Just before we get in the boat, Rob takes us aside to give us one last piece of advice.

'This is going to be the greatest adventure of your lives,' he says. 'The fact that you are putting yourselves out there just to have a go is something to be proud of. But don't underestimate the effort required to win. You are going to have to extend yourselves further than you ever thought possible. And when it really hurts just remember that it's proof that you're alive, and that's gotta be good!

'From what I've seen I truly believe you guys have what it takes. All you have to do now is believe it's possible and do it!'

We get into the boat, untie from the launch and join the line of crews gently stroking their boats out of the marina. As each of the sixteen boats passes the support yacht they do their radio check. At last it's our turn: 'Woodvale, this is *Holiday Shoppe Challenge*, how are you reading us? Over.'

'Loud and clear *Holiday Shoppe*. Good luck.'

We row slowly up to the breakwater end of the start line. The *Rowing Home* crew come and park next to us, looking very natty with their long-sleeved, skintight white rowing tops and black camel packs. Looking through the bobbing boats, I can see someone wearing a giant afro wig. One of the RAF guys has a pair of waterwings on.

I take out the video camera.

So here we are at the start with twelve minutes to go. It's pretty exciting, quite unreal — the calmest day we have had on the trip. It's unbelievably calm. It's going to be a bit of a sprint, so we'll see how it goes. It's hard to imagine that we will be doing this for 42 days . . . I guess we'd better do it faster then!

At five minutes to go the hooter blows on the deck of the support yacht and they hoist a flag. Damn, is that what the start is going to sound like? Only five minutes. Damn. I feel as if I am in a small boat just about to go over a waterfall. Wait a minute . . . I am in a small boat. I try to concentrate on my breathing, and stare at my hands holding the oars. I glance up at the people lining the rails of the spectator craft that are starting to fill the bay. I feel like I am a gladiator on the floor of the Colosseum, looking up at the crowd . . . just before they let in the lions.

I hear some strangely familiar chanting and look down the line of rowboats to see a pair of red-shorted rowers standing up doing a wobbly haka, to the delight of the crowd.

'Is that *Two Blokes, No Smokes*?' I ask Jamie.

'No, I think it's the Dark Side.'

The voice on the VHF announces 30 seconds. With 10 seconds to go the watching crowd start to shout out the countdown. Jamie and I move to front stops, arms out in front, blades in the water. Muscles tense ready for the first big pull.

Five

Four

Three

Two

One

HOOONK!

Jamie surges backwards quickly in a short half-stroke then races back to the front. I rush to keep up. Then another rapid stroke and then another. I am taking in big gulps of air. There is no time to look out to the side, but behind us I can see that some of the other boats are in a frenzy like us, while others are just rowing gently in an uncoordinated, unhurried way.

Behind us the spectator fleet surges forward, and I can hear the crowd yelling encouragement. Soon we are past the end of the breakwater, and Jamie tweaks the foot steering so that we start to angle southeast out to sea. I take a quick glance over my left shoulder. It looks like the Dark Side is in the lead, with *Team Altitude* right behind them and the rest of the fleet following. Now we are going through some surprised spectator craft as we head toward Africa. It seems that we are the only boat taking this course. Good.

I keep a close eye on the GPS, looking for the surge that will tell us we are in the current. For several minutes we keep rowing, but nothing.

No current at all. Now we are well past where we were on our recce a couple of days ago. This is bad. We slow down from our frantic pace.

I glance over at the rest of the fleet. Hundreds of metres away, the Dark Side are a silver dot against the high brown cliffs, leading a pack that is starting to stretch out behind them. The only boat that still seems to be chasing hard is *Team Altitude*. 'Good for them, I hope they give them a run for their money,' I think. It's hard to tell how we are doing exactly because of the diverging angles, but it looks more and more as if we are falling behind the pack. Bugger. I look over at the Dark Side again and wonder what it would be like to be leading the trans-Atlantic rowing race.

Meanwhile our support boat, which has been over to film the other crews, now motors up and swings up on our port side. 'They're definitely flagging,' Rob shouts out. 'They're working really hard!'

Bloody hell, so are we.

Just then another rowboat passes a few metres in front of our bows, heading almost 45 degrees to our course.

'Where did they come from?'

'Dunno!'

'Who were they?'

'Dunno!'

And how did they get in front of us? This is just silly now. We should be near the front of the fleet, and for some other team to leave the pack and cut in front of us we must be officially getting our arses kicked. So either we are very slow, or in a bad current, or both. It's time to admit defeat, change tack and join the others.

It's so hot there is water coming out of my nose. My face is permanently varnished with sweat. I keep blinking and rubbing my forehead on my sleeve to stop the stinging salty fluid getting into my eyes. There isn't a lot of talk going on. Just hard physical work and quick gulps at the water bottle. I look over at the cool shadow of our support boat on the water and wonder if it would be considered assistance if they brought it just a little bit closer!

On our new heading we start to pick up with the other crews quite quickly. But by now the pack has made enough ground towards the south that the island is no longer in the way and the Atlantic Ocean opens up in front of us. All the secretly guarded routes are now being revealed as the boats begin to fan out. It seems that the only thing everyone agreed on is that you can't row through La Gomera.

Soon nearly all the crews melt away towards different parts of the horizon, leaving us following *Team Altitude* following the Dark Side. Then we overtake *Team Altitude* and it is only us left doggedly rowing after the Dark Side, who are a small but distinct silver blob several hundred metres ahead.

At 1pm we are about eight nautical miles away from the start. Our support boat comes over for the last time and motors along beside us. I look up at the row of tanned Euro lovelies draped over the railing, their faces lit up by the sparkling sea beneath them. Rob sees my gaze. 'Think of all the girls in bikinis who will be waiting for you at the end,' he calls out.

We have left the island behind now, and we are out on the strangely placid Atlantic. Now it really is time to say goodbye.

'Hey Rob!' I shout. 'You were right — the waves were bigger in '97!'

'Make us proud, boys!' Chris calls out from the helm. Then the big white boat surges forward and turns away from us in a graceful arc toward the island. Rob and Rachel stand at the back and wave and wave, until the boat becomes just a white dot in front of the island. I twist in my seat to look over the bow. The Dark Side are still visible, but barely.

Ahh, well. This is pretty good, probably better than we could have expected. After all the days of uncertainty and angst about how we ranked against the other crews it has turned out pretty well in the end. The Dark Side were always likely to be in the lead, and there is no dishonour in coming second. It will still get us a beer in a bar. It's a shame now that we have to spend months rowing an ocean to confirm what the first few hours have shown. Oh well, certainly the weather could be a lot worse — these are absolutely perfect ocean-rowing conditions. Now we can just enjoy ourselves.

Jamie snatches a look over his shoulder. And then again a few seconds later. This time he's scowling.

'Mate?'

'Yep.'

'Have a look over your shoulder.'

I do. That can't be right. I wipe the sweat out of my eyes. There is the white stern of the Dark Side just a hundred metres away.

After the next drink break, 20 minutes later, we have closed the gap to about 50 metres. Jamie is worried.

'Mate, let's just take it down a notch and think about this. Are you allowed to board another boat in this race?'

'What do you mean? What? Do you think they're going to attack us? No! Maybe they've broken something.'

So we gradually draw up along their port side, but about 50 metres away. Now we can see the reason for their slow speed — they only have one person rowing. Goodman is up messing about with a pot, probably cooking lunch.

We stare at them as we go past. They don't seem to be too concerned. It's only just after 2pm and they have already gone onto single shifts. We keep staring, watching them carefully, and keep on rowing past them. After an hour they are well in our rear, their oars barely visible as tiny toothpicks occasionally flashing off the side of the boat.

Now it's 3pm, and the plan calls for Jamie to take an hour's break. He flicks in his oars, gets up, switches the steering over to me, and starts making a recovery shake. It's never pleasant when one person stops rowing — the boat feels very heavy, you struggle to try and keep the speed up but inevitably it slumps back. With the Dark Side still distant but visible I spend the hour imagining that they are getting closer. And I am tired. This is my fifth hour of continuously rowing the fully laden boat in the midday tropical sun.

When Jamie finally comes back on deck the first thing he does is squint out over the back.

'Yep, they're still there,' I say.

'Don't worry, mate; I'll sort them out.'

So Jamie sits down, and I creakily stand up and step over his swinging oars. I swig a recovery drink before gratefully stepping out of the scorching sun and into the delicious coolness of the cabin. I doze for an hour, still too wired to sleep well. *We're rowing the Atlantic!*

When I get back up, the first thing I do is look over the stern to see where the Dark Side are. Jamie is doing a great job, they are definitely further away. And after we row together again for another half-hour they are a tiny speck, only occasionally able to be seen, no bigger to my eye than the houses on La Gomera, which itself is now a shadow in the distance.

At my next break I get out the sat phone and ring Chris's house. Rob answers and I tell him about the events of the afternoon. I can hear lots of excited voices in the background as Rob relays the information. After the call I do a little video diary:

So it's 7:50pm, Sunday, October 19. Jamie is doing a shift and I'm just waiting for the pasta to cook. I've had 20 minutes of my break so far. Had a wash. Put too much water in the pasta so just waiting for that to fix itself.

I have to say, it's just amazing watching the sun set. The seas have been incredibly benign, a very gentle swell, tiny tiny tiny little chop. Only about five knots of wind WNW. The big mountain on El Hierro is in the distance, with just a little cloud on it, and we are just rowing into the horizon.

I guess we are pretty happy because we smoked past the Dark Side. Went past them at around 2pm and now can barely see them.

When I come out again it is dark. And after Jamie disappears inside the cabin I am left rowing alone, with a fair caressing wind, a tranquil sea, the outline of El Hierro sharp against the stars. Surely this is as good as life gets?

I look over my shoulder to the horizon, where the blackness of the water meets the grey of the night sky in a perfect straight line. Somewhere over there is Barbados! Only an occasional ruffle breaks the silkiness of the water, there are no waves. So this is what the Atlantic is like! It's thrilling. It's perfect. And what is even better is that I can enjoy it.

I don't have to worry anymore. I have spent two years not just having to consider but having to *believe* that the worst things are going to happen to us, so that I could make sure we were prepared for them. Now I am out here I can stop being the Woody Allen of ocean rowing and start enjoying myself. Whatever else I should have done to get the boat ready it is too late to do anything about it now. The weight is lifting off me and I am able to take full and easy breaths and decompress. As always, the doing is far less scary than the anticipation. So now I have time to try and digest what has happened today, and what it means that we have gone past the Dark Side.

Firstly, that our worst fears aren't true, we aren't complete crap. Secondly, that Westlake and Goodman are beatable. At the end of the day they are just a couple of grunts out on the water, like we are — they are nothing supernatural.

Thirdly, they are still very confident that they can pull us in. They were so nonchalant in the way they let us go by them. Westlake even rowed with one hand while he was taking a drink. They did everything but wave. Racing purists would say that they did the right thing — they have a race plan and a race pace, and they aren't going to break it for us. After all, in 2001 they trailed the Australian team for two weeks before they pulled them in. But if the situation had been reversed I couldn't have been so casual about it. Psychologically it is a huge boost to be in front of them. Now we have a sniff of what it is like to be in the lead, and I like it.

Fourthly, two people rowing are faster than one. We always knew that, but the speed difference didn't seem worth the lost sleep. No crew that I had ever heard of had rowed anything other than two hours on, two hours off. But it's one thing to know that, and another to see the Dark Side disappearing into the distance because there are two of us rowing and only one of them. Suddenly the idea of lost sleep doesn't seem so bad. In fact, it seems a good idea to overlap as much as possible and sleep as little as possible, although what exactly *is* possible I don't have any idea.

So when Jamie suggests that we do two hours on with only an hour and a half off, there doesn't seem any reason not to. They might come along and spank us like babies later, but for the time being let's put a bit of a burn on and create some excitement. We are winning the trans-Atlantic rowing race! (well, probably) so let's enjoy it while it lasts!

I open my eyes, it's dark, I don't know where I am. Oh yeah, that's right, I am in the cabin of a small boat crossing the Atlantic. I move my toe up to the light switch and flick it on. With the hatches shut I can't hear anything except the gentle squeak of the rowlocks. Has the wind got up? Has anything broken? I crack open the hatch and look out. No, it's still calm — just Jamie rocking back and forth. I have slept in my clothes to make it faster to get up, so in just a few minutes I am back on deck and sitting in the bow seat. I pick up the oars and start rowing in time with Jamie's massive back. After a few minutes, when the action has once again become automatic, I am able to look out of the boat.

Man! Those stars are something else. I had always heard that the stars in the southern hemisphere are supposed to be more plentiful and brighter than in the northern, but I've never seen stars like this. This is extraordinary. There are stars out from horizon to horizon. The night sky isn't black, it's milky grey, and even in places white with stars. El Hierro is visible on the horizon because it is a black shape against the milky grey night sky.

And every few minutes there are meteors. In five minutes I see more shooting stars than I have seen in my entire life. Some blaze across the sky in half a second. Others are slow, leaving a sparkling trail, and others fall quickly as sharp points in different colours.

There's a star over the stern and close to the horizon that seems to be moving around more than you'd expect from just the motion of the boat. Could that be the mast light of the Dark Side? No, I don't think so.

It's even harder waking up for the next shift. Miss Adrenaline has packed her bags and Mr Fatigue has moved in. My brain is struggling to get used to the idea that there won't actually ever be any break for the next few weeks. Maybe some chat will pass the time.

'So, tell me about yourself,' I suggest.

'Where do you want me to start?'

I look over my shoulder where an infinite sparkling sea merges into an infinite sparkling sky.

'I think you'd better start at the beginning.'

October 20 — Day 2

I go to bed after my last shift just as the first hint of light is starting to show on the horizon. When I wake up an hour and a half later, morning light is coming through the slightly open hatch. I'm worried about Jamie — this is as long as he has ever rowed. How is he coping? He must be wondering what he has let himself in for. But when I open the hatch he is still there rowing strong, looking fresh.

'Gidday Gorgeous!'

'Hi Honey, how's the rowing?'

'Fabulous!'

'Any sign of the Dark Side?'

'Nup.'

The seas are still calm and there is very little wind to speak of. El Hierro is still off the starboard bow, still looming disappointingly large. It is important to get as far away as we can while the weather is still benign. Apparently there are strong tides around the island and some crews have reported being sucked back towards it. As if to remind us that we aren't that far from land a little butterfly alights on the cabin and stays for a few minutes before fluttering off.

I look at the GPS; we aren't going very fast, perhaps around 2 knots. And there are some odd streaks in the water; strange flat patches that are devoid of any ripples, almost as if oil had been dumped. Some high cloud whitens the sky. There is a strange air of expectation.

From nothing, the wind grows to a gentle caressing breeze from the southwest, cooling our backs. But then it stays and swells stronger and stronger, and with it the seas begin to grow lumpy. By mid-afternoon the rowing has become difficult and unpleasant. By late afternoon our progress has slowed to less than a knot with two people rowing, while one person could barely make any ground at all.

In the cabin I flick open the isochrone booklet to see what we can do. The isochrone map was the routing system Geoff and Andy had come up with. An isochrone is a line on a map that represents a series of places where you are the same time away from the finish. So for parts of the ocean that typically have more wind and currents this could be a greater distance than parts where there was less wind and currents. So the isochrones look like a series of concentric rings.

Our isochrones were set to be about a day apart. It was very simple but very clever. All we had to do was follow whatever course would get us to the next line fastest. I run the end of the pencil over the map to our approximate position. The next isochrone slopes diagonally — it is as far away to the south as it is to the west, and the wind is coming from the southwest. So we could go south or west.

But then I look at the isochrone after that. It plunges away to the south. If we head south we might be OK today, but tomorrow, if the wind stays up, we would be stuffed as we would never get to the next isochrone. South is No Man's Land. We have to go west.

And if we can't make any ground west, then we always have the option of the sea anchor. Perhaps with the giant chute locked in the water we would not go backwards — we might even make a little ground if the current for some reason happened to be against the wind.

But for now at least that is out of the question. There is no way that the Dark Side are going to put out their sea anchor this early on in the race. In fact, they will be relishing these conditions as it gives them a chance to use their strength and experience to pull ahead of the fleet. And if they aren't going to use their sea anchor, then neither can we.

The rowing is getting harder and harder. Waves are buffeting the bow of the boat erratically. I drop the oar blades into the water and strain to move my hands backward. The full force of my legs is transferred to my back through my shoulders, my bulging eyes, and down my arms, stretching the joints of my hands until it turns my fingers white with pressure. Slowly the boat moves a little forward. I rush back up the slide so as not to give the wind a chance to slow the precious momentum. Then I jerk up my hands to shove the blades back into the water.

With the seas this rough one hand is often at shoulder height while the other is at my waist. Then the wave that my oar is set into disappears, and as I lurch backward the blade flicks around uselessly in the air. This sets the bow turning, and as the side of the boat sees the wind it begins to turn even more. So now I am coming out of my seat with short vigorous strokes to get some steering speed. I come down hard. There is an angry hiss and a few moments later I start to feel my bum coming to rest on something hard. Damn, I have popped the Roho seat! And it's only Day 2! Precious seconds are lost as I pull out the spare from the locker beside me and sit down again.

And so the afternoon goes on, until finally the light bleeds from the sky. There is something unnerving about being in a small boat at sea with the sky darkening and the wind picking up, and the enormous boiling anvil clouds forming over a heaving sea. As bad as everything is during the day, now it's going to be worse. And now we won't see it coming. At least it isn't raining here yet, though it must only be a matter of time. We have lost all sight of the horizon and it is impossible in the darkness to tell where sea and sky meet.

It is such hard work that we decide to do hour-on hour-off shifts through the night. I try to lock the boat into the eye of the wind, but it is devilishly tricky. If the wind for any reason gets a sniff of the broadside of the boat it swings away, and I am left rowing madly with one oar to try and bring the bow back into the wind. Sometimes I just let it go and try and use the boat's turning momentum to finish the circle, effectively doing a pirouette on the spot.

When I have a chance to look up the sky is featureless and dark, but every so often there are flashes of lightning that illuminate the *inside* of the thunderclouds, revealing their tumour-like convolutions and bulges. The effect is like a flickering, misshapen Chinese lantern — or a Norse god arc-welding himself a new axe.

I am listening to the iPod, the music up loud enough to drown out the crashing seas and the sound of my own grunting and cursing. It is on random play. I glance over at El Hierro, which is staying firmly put off the back of the boat. Then for an instant I see a giant pair of yellow horns. My heart races.

As the clouds pass by I see what is happening. It is an enormous moon rising behind the jagged peaks of the island. Right on cue the iPod starts playing heavy organ music from an album called *Chiller* — the music from horror movies. I don't know how it got on there, nor do I appreciate the irony — it is freakishly sinister.

The rowing is getting worse, the continuous strain is immense. We are very lucky that neither of us has shredded some tendon or caused some bulging muscle to split its casing. There is only so long our bodies and our wills can hold out.

Maybe, just maybe, it would make sense for us to dash north and try to get some shelter in the cove at the south end of El Hierro. In fact, Rob and Phil stopped there while they fixed their watermaker during the first day of the '97 race. They tied up to an empty mooring. So even if we didn't get any shelter, maybe we could do the same. With the wind at our backs we might be able to get there in a couple of hours of very easy rowing.

But that would mean giving up our hard-earned ground to the south. And when I look closely at the chart during the next break, it doesn't look as if there would be a lot of shelter from a sou'wester in the bay. Unless we found a mooring we would run the risk of being driven onto the rocks. Still, if it is going to be like this for days it might be a better option than being blown back to Africa. It's very tempting.

Around 1am, at the end of my shift, I decide that we are taking too many chances with our health and should try the sea anchor. It's a hard decision. I know from training that when things start getting tough my brain is wonderfully creative about coming up with rationalisations for stopping, so I am deeply suspicious of any 'logic' that says I should stop. But there is just a chance, depending on what the current is doing, that we could lock into the water and just stay where we are, which would be a whole lot better than risking a muscle or back strain to achieve the same effect. At the next shift change I talk it over with Jamie and he agrees.

The sea anchor is all set to go in the bow locker. With Jamie at the oars keeping us into the wind, I crouch on the heaving deck in the darkness, pull out the large bag, drop it into the dark, sucking sea, and play out the line until it goes tight. We both go back and watch the GPS closely. Well, we certainly aren't being pulled into the wind, but then we aren't going backwards that fast either. We agree to take a break for an hour and assess the situation after that.

Neither of us can sleep. I feel uneasy about being locked in a dark box on a dark night on a heaving sea. Through the insulation I can hear the muffled noise of rushing, tumbling water. The boat's motion feels strange; the bow is constantly being jerked as the sea anchor line goes alternately slack and tight. I imagine the chute in the black water pulsing like a jellyfish. Having a large hairy, sweaty bloke rolling into me doesn't help either.

What else is out there on a night like this? We have put our mast light on, but it is hardly certain that on this kind of a night a container ship would see us as it approached. We are putting a lot of faith in the Active Echo.

Before the hour is up I go outside quickly and check our position on the GPS. Shit! We have lost nearly a mile to the east! I call out to Jamie, and while he rows into the waves I am back on the bow pulling hard on the sea anchor rope to get some slack and pull up the chute, which has to be wrestled out of the water and into its bag. With the deck rolling and jumping it is difficult, and I am cursing as I get thrown onto hard parts of the boat. I have almost finished when Jamie calls out.

'What are those lights over there behind us?'

It's a ship! A big one, and not far away. Is it coming towards us? No, it is going to cross a few hundred metres behind our stern. But not a peep out of the Active Echo. If we had stayed on the sea anchor how close would it have been? I decide that I don't like being on the sea anchor very much at all.

To punish ourselves for our weakness we agree to row together for an hour to try and make up some of the lost ground. Then it's back to single shifts. It is gruesomely unlovely. The chunder row and the row to Whale Island were good training. The night just turns into a game with the GPS, trying to make it give a positive speed and any angle between 180 and 270. I'm trying to get smarter with the boat so that when it starts to go backwards and veer around I flip the rudder the opposite way and buy myself a few more seconds of time to try and arrest the backward momentum.

><

October 21 — Day 3

A few hundred times I look at the horizon, willing it to be just a little bit lighter. A few dozen times I imagine it is. And then at last it is lighter. Then lighter still.

In the half-light the overcast sky breaks up, and now there are just a few puffy cumulus clouds scudding along to set off a brilliant blue sky. It's the sort of weather that although too windy for a picnic would be great for flying a kite, or a bit of windsurfing . . . but not for trying to move a tonne of reluctant meat and milk powder across the Atlantic. If it had been the Canaries to Morocco race we would be having a ball. Instead we keep rowing just as we have the previous night. Only now we can see — and that is at least some comfort.

Day 3, Tuesday morning, 10:15am. We are pushing into this f---ing westerly, probably even a bit sou'westerly, and we are supposed to be having nor'easterlies. And all I'm doing at the moment is keeping the boat from going backwards. Which is pretty much what we did all last night. We've got our backs to the wall. Not as much of a leisurely vacation as I would have hoped. Wish you were here, Rob!

During my next shift I notice that the boat is locked into the wind at almost due west. This is promising. If the wind would just come around towards the north a tweak more then we could head south and perhaps a little west and be on our way towards South America, instead of bobbing around in the water next to this friggin' island. During my next break I plot our position on the chart.

'How are we doing?' shouts Jamie.

'Pretty good. We've made some ground west.'

We have been pushed quite a bit north as well, but I don't want to sour the boat vibe.

Around noon I think that the wind has swung around to the north enough to make an attempt to go on a more southerly course. So I try, but it's no good. The best I can head continuously is a bit east of south. Three hours later I try again, twist my heel, and swing the bow down. It works. We can only head just a little west of south, and we are only going at about a knot, but it is enough. We can finally get going. Halfway through Day 3 and it feels like the race has finally started.

Throughout the afternoon the swells follow the wind around, getting larger and better organised until they are as high as the boat.

My arms feel strangely leaden. I have very little energy. I should be eating more but everything about eating hurts. Anything coming into my mouth scrapes the blister on my lip, then irritates the ulcer in my mouth, grates past some kind of irritation in my throat perhaps caused by reflux, before finally landing on a very tender stomach.

I'm trying to distract myself with an audiobook, but the audio is very quiet and it isn't making a lot of sense. With five minutes of my shift to go I start to feel peculiarly light-headed and unconcerned. The aches disappear from my joints. I feel like I'm floating. I'm moving like I'm a Thunderbird puppet.

I'm starting to switch off, and I need to switch on. Once again there

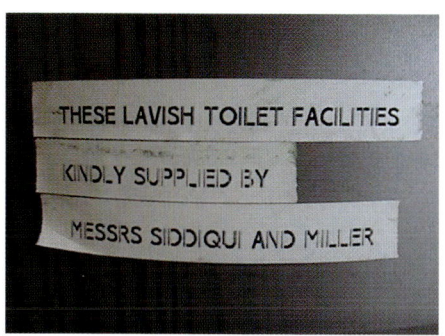

'These lavish toilet facilities kindly supplied by Messrs Siddiqui and Miller' — my friends sponsor our toilet bucket.

The original Naked Rower, Rob Hamill, at the launch of *Holiday Shoppe Challenge*.

Sanding the hull at the banana plantation in Tenerife — hot, nasty work.

Holiday Shoppe Challenge, tied up with the fishing fleet at the marina at La Gomera. See the 'mystery' hole on the solar panel frame?

Race day, on the start line. Five minutes before the starting gun, our blood is starting to fizz!

One and a half hours into the race, we swing around the bottom of La Gomera and out into the open Atlantic. *CRC* is next to the yacht in the distance and behind them is the island of El Hierro, about 50 miles away. Behind that is Barbados, about 2500 nautical miles away.

Sunset out on the Atlantic.
Funny how the darker it gets,
the bigger the waves seem to become.

A spot of water skiing anyone?

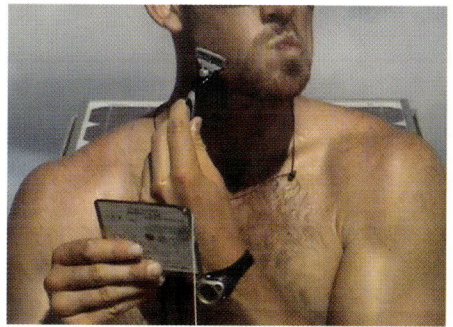
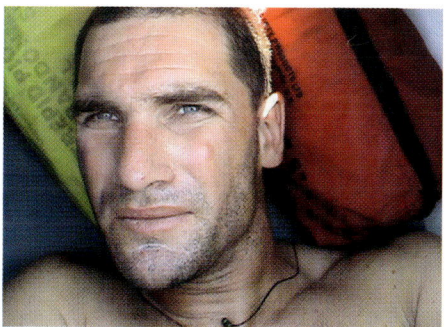

'I want to be an Atlantic Man,
shave myself with a Pringles can.'
Jamie is using the reflector from the
survival kit as a mirror.

Day 10 — the physical strain of round-
the-clock rowing is starting to tell.

The morning after the capsize we made a replacement for our lost
seat from hatch covers from the cabin and a deflated Thermarest.

The support yacht gives us three cheers as we cross
the official finish line off the northern tip of Barbados.

The welcoming committee. There are two men in this picture.

Landfall at Port St Charles, Barbados. We are the new world-record
holders and undisputed winners of the 2003 Trans-Atlantic race
— for a couple of days anyway.

Fat-boy rower before the race (left). Skinny-boy rower,
15 or so kilos lighter afterwards (right).

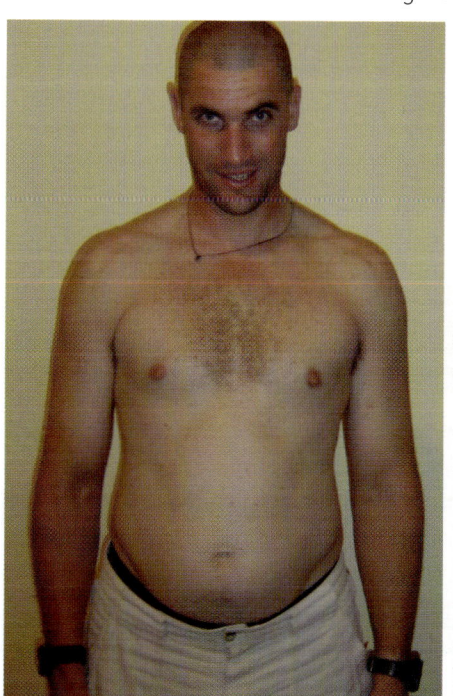
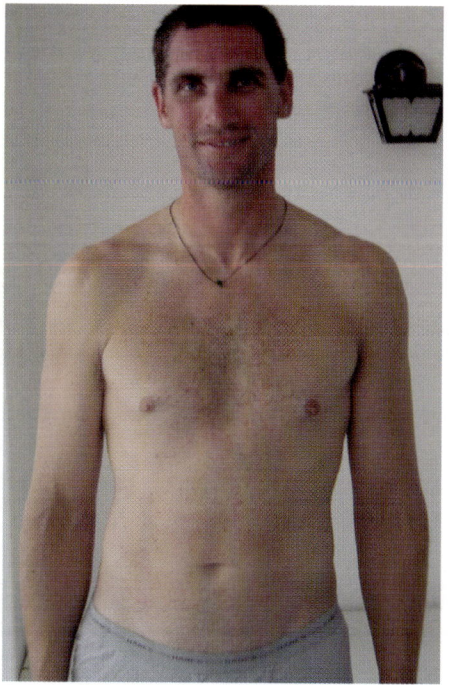

The protest is hatched. Shortly after they arrive in Barbados, Steve Westlake and Matt Goodman allege that during the race we had removed the restraining arms of our solar panel, allowing it to be swung upright and used as a sail. In Barbados, Lin Parker tests out this theory, on *CRC*.

If we had been taking the restraining arms on and off the solar panel during the race, then the screws shouldn't look corroded. Lin pauses while removing this screw from our frame — is it corroded or not?

A photo taken from the support yacht as it passed us a few days before the end of the race. This was the photo Westlake was referring to in *CRC*'s protest submission when he said, 'When we zoomed in on the hole in the solar panel it could not be seen, despite the fact that the photograph was of sufficient resolution to pick it out.'

Here is the same photo zoomed in, showing that the above statement might be true, but only if you don't look at the photo.

Flying back from Barbados on the much dreamt-about business class — now that's what I'm talking about!

We arrive back in Auckland to an incredible welcome from the Holiday Shoppe team.

is something strange happening. The seas are getting wilder and wilder until the waves are about 2 metres high, and topped with whitecaps. They're hitting us from starboard right round to the stern. There is something not quite right. Despite the size of the following seas we are only rowing at about 2 knots and we should be doing up to twice that. Maybe we are in an adverse current, perhaps some relic of the previous day's sou'westerly winds. The mountainous silhouette of El Hierro remains firmly fixed on the horizon.

I'm just exhausted, so exhausted I'm almost having an out-of-body experience at the end of each shift. It's amazing how safe and secure you feel in the back surrounded by the insulation. Then you have to wake up every two hours and deal with this shit.

October 22 — Day 4, the open ocean

In the morning I come out for my shift, sit down, and look up to see how far we have come from El Hierro. It isn't there. I turn my head around, slowly scanning the entire horizon. It is completely free of land. There is only the blue dome of the sky and the endless sea. We have passed through the Gates of the Atlantic. At last we are in the open ocean.

CHAPTER EIGHTEEN
Open-ocean madness

Top ten least appropriate movies for prospective ocean-rowers:
The Perfect Storm
The Abyss
Titanic
The Poseidon Adventure (original and remake)
The Deep
Dead Calm
Jaws (1, 2, 3, Jaws: The Revenge)
Deep Blue Sea
Shark Attack (Shark Attack 2: The Megalodon)
What Lies Beneath

On October 7, 2001 Debra and Andrew Veal started out as the only husband-and-wife crew in the second trans-Atlantic rowing race. After being hit with bad weather shortly after the start Andrew began to experience severe anxiety, which increased through the next few days as they rowed further from land. It got worse with lack of sleep and food. After they had been at sea for eight days Debra became concerned when her husband didn't appear for his shift or answer her calls. When she opened the hatch door she saw her 1.95-metre husband curled into the foetal position. As she put it in her book *Rowing It Alone*, he was 'groaning as if in pain and shaking violently from head to toe'. That night Andrew decided not to continue in the race, and five days later he was taken off the boat.

I knew before the race that there are a percentage of people who can't handle being in a small boat at sea, out of sight of land. What I didn't know was whether Jamie or I were among them.

So now I look around the horizon. There is nothing there, but my brain wants something to be there very much. I think I see land, and I swivel towards it. But there is nothing there. It happens again. Anything that can possibly be construed to be land becomes land to my confused brain — a wave in the distance, a low cloud. My brain knows there is land out there somewhere, and it wants me to find it. Still nothing. Oh well. Never mind, we've got the GPS.

During the day the weather improves and the sky is sunny and blue, with just a few scrappy cumulus clouds being pushed along by a frisky, helpful wind.

5:10pm. Here we are on Day 4. The nor'easterlies have finally settled in. When I say nor'easterlies I mean northerlies, but that will be fine. So all the battling that we have been doing for the last three and a half days is now over hopefully, and for the next few days we will have this kind of weather.

Each of the boats has a sealed beacon, an Inmarsat D+ unit, on board that sends a signal twice a day to the race organisers, who then put our positions on the race website. The plan is for Rob to text and call us on the satellite phone twice a day as the positions get updated. He'll also post news stories on our website. But as sunset comes at the end of Day 4 there is still no word from him.

The Atlantic-class rowboats are very hard to make out at sea. They are so low down and small compared to the swells that another boat could pass within half a mile and not be seen. But that doesn't stop me looking out over the stern of the boat every so often to check if I can see the Dark Side's mast light. Actually, there is a funny green-looking star. Then the star begins to move. Then there is a red star next to it. That's strange. I watch it for a few minutes before I realise it must be a yacht. Hey, it has to be the Woodvale yacht!

'Hey Jamie, get out the VHF! I think the support yacht is looking for us.'

'What?' comes the muffled voice from the cabin. 'Oh yeah, all right.'

Jamie stands in the footwell with the VHF pressed to his ear.

'Gidday! Hello, uh ... yacht, it's the Kiwis ... Over.'

'Hello *Holiday Shoppe* . . . How are you doing? . . . Over.'

'Yeah, good good. I don't suppose you have our position in the fleet? Over.'

'You're in the lead. You're about 20 miles in front of *CRC* . . . Over.'

'That's bloody good news! How are the other boats? Over.'

'Not bad . . . the crew from *Calderdale* has just been picked up. Marcus had got very sick and wasn't going to get any better. Over.'

'That's a bummer . . . that's a shame. No seasickness on your crew? Over.'

'Yeah, no, thankfully not. We have had a little change though. One of the crew, Jeremy, the one with the blond hair, he's jumped into number 7, the French boat, because the guy who did it last time around decided that he didn't want to go on, but his partner still wanted to carry on. So they got towed back to La Gomera and Jeremy has got on and they have set off again. Over.'

'That's insane!' I hiss.

'That takes the Challenge people to another level, doesn't it?' says Jamie. 'Over.'

'Just shows that we are getting more stupid every year! Hey, we probably won't see you guys for a number of days because you are so far ahead it takes a long time to get up. But we haven't forgotten about you!'

So it's official — we are in the lead! And by quite a lot! What is the Dark Side doing? They must have put out their sea anchor for hours on Day 2! And we thought *they* were the hard men. Maybe we are leaving them behind?

The rowing takes on a new urgency. It *does* matter that we row well. It matters that every stroke is a good one. Now we know how to win, we can make the right decisions. *We are in this race!*

I wake up a little early before my first daylight shift. During the night I have been cutting my arrival at the oars pretty fine, and occasionally even being a few unforgivable seconds late, pulling on my shorts or trying to untangle my earphones as I get into the seat. So now I decide to make it up to Jamie.

'I'm giving you a present,' I say as I flick open the hatch door. 'I'm three minutes early!'

'I'll give you a present!' says Jamie. He pulls his shirt away from his lap to reveal he's rowing naked.

'Ah, anything you want to tell me, mate?'

'Yeah, my arse has been playing up a bit and it's a lot more comfy like this.'

✕

October 23 — Day 5

When the sun comes up we are still fizzing from the news of the night before, and there is still an extra bit of oomph in each stroke as I imagine us pulling away from the Dark Side. I'm not imagining it — we soon receive a text message from Rob:

> 23/10 AS OF 8AM, LAST 24 HOURS HS 54, DS 43
> YOU 24NM IN FRONT!
> ROB

Now the weather has improved and we are getting what we have paid our money for. We have large sinuous seas that are rising and falling like the shoulder blades of a great cat. Mostly the waves come towards the stern, but there are the odd ones that come from the side, and even odder ones that come from anywhere.

Nearly all the waves I have seen in my life have been seen from the beach, and there all the waves come from the same direction. In fact they have to come from the same direction, because the land blocks all the other directions. Now it seems obvious, but I had never thought of it before.

Out in the open ocean each wave must have its own story. Maybe the big heavy swells from this direction are pumped out by a storm off the Grand Banks, and these little ones over here might be from a squall over the horizon, while these others are from a low-pressure system on the equator. The ocean skin is just a trembling membrane, fluttering with energy from all sources.

From mid-morning the sun is like a laser, boiling the surface of the water. Soon the towering cumulonimbuses start to form, as thousands of tonnes of water are hoovered up into the sky.

Each shift we are lathering the sunscreen on our faces, the backs of our hands and our knees. Jamie has a few more places to put it on as well.

During the day I watch as the clouds get fatter, like ripening fruit, and droop lower, turning the colour of ripe plums. By late afternoon they hang dramatically, great sacks of water teetering over the ocean, held up by the faltering grip of the sun. Just like the coyote in the Road Runner cartoons, who runs off a cliff and spends a few seconds poised in the air looking surprised — you know this can't last long.

It doesn't. I look out to one side and see that a huge purple thundercloud has begun to empty itself into the water. The downpour is ferocious. It's impossible to see through — it's like a waterfall pouring out of the sky. Even the sea swells are being smashed flat by the deluge.

Thunder crackles around us menacingly, and again and again lightning jabs the sea as the light fades from the sky. It occurs to me that with all this lightning it may not be a good idea to be waving a couple of long graphite poles about. Now there is a squall coming up fast behind us, and it is raining hard underneath. By the time Jamie comes out for his shift it is so close that I can hear the rain hissing as it hits the ocean. Here it comes.

As soon as Jamie is in position in the stern seat and has taken a stroke I pull my feet out of my shoes and, still in a crouch, take one step over his oars, plunge into the cockpit and pull the hatch shut. I hear a muffled, gargled 'Bastard!' as the rain explodes against the top of the cabin.

Lying on my front on the Thermarest I can wedge myself in using the dry bag stuffed taut with our medical gear on one side of my hips and the Pelican box, a hard waterproof container, on the other. With my hips firmly locked in place there is little sensation of movement. I get the nylon bag that holds the survival suit and lay my cheek down on its slick surface. It ain't the Ritz but it is dark and cool. It is also very quiet and strangely peaceful. I feel as if I'm on a different planet from the rest of the rowboat — as if I am rowing the ocean but somehow managing to sleep in my own bed every night. The rain is just a gentle muffled drumming.

I wake up when Jamie gives an eight-minute-to-go call. I crack open the hatch to check on conditions. It is utterly black. The boat is rolling and pitching. Rain is driving down and Jamie's dripping face is lit up eerily from the glow of the GPS. I close the hatch, and calm, order and warmth is restored. I wait for a few seconds, hoping that the channel will change, then I open the hatch again. Instantly I am back in a raging tempest. Nuts! I have to go out in this?

Soon I am sitting in the seat while Jamie is at high speed clicking on my steering lines, taking a gulp of recovery drink and heading for the hatch.

'How did it go?' I ask.

'Not bad, just a couple of Ovahks.'

'Ovahks? What do you mean?'

'You'll see.'

The wind has got up to around 20 knots and is blowing from due north. That means we are taking the waves at an angle, exposing part of one flank to the weather. Above, vast and dimly perceived clouds are blowing over, obscuring the stars. The sea is so dark that only the white caps of the waves can be made out, looming around and above the heaving and bucking stern.

Half an hour of awkward rowing later there is a loud boom and the boat lurches over to port, almost knocking me out of the seat.

'Oh f--k!'

OK — I get it now.

A wave coming out of nowhere has slapped the side of the cabin and dumped a pile of water on the boat. The bilge pump in the footwell starts grinding, spitting out water over the side.

In the dark I can't see these waves coming, so I try to guess what is happening by the occasional glint of the starlight on the water and the movement of the boat. With a little warning I might be able to get more stern on when the wave comes. My struggling brain starts to perceive fantastic shapes. I swear that the Auckland Harbour Bridge is over my right shoulder. But when I look that way it isn't there. I look away and there it is again.

I come out for my next shift in the darkest part of the night. I am making the awkward step-hop to get past Jamie's oars when the boat rolls unexpectedly. I sit down hard on the gunnel, arms waving, and I am still rolling over when Jamie's paw thrusts out of the dark and grabs my shirt. I teeter for an agonising moment and we stare goggle-eyed at each other before the boat rolls back up and I can wriggle on board.

'Ta for that.'

'No problem.'

October 24 — Day 6, dolphin day

Voicemail left on Rob's phone in New Zealand:

> Yeah hi Rob, it's Kevin here. Just watching the sun come up, completely black last night but now no clouds at all except on the horizon, and having dolphins for breakfast — yeah, there are a whole bunch of dolphins playing around the boat, which is very fun, doing their little jumps and stuff and it's pretty cool. We were hoping to get some news. We put in some pretty big shifts last night . . . ha ha ha, these dolphins are so close to Jamie's oars, instead of catching a crab I'm scared he's going to catch a dolphin, they're everywhere out here! We did a little bit of surfing this morning too so I am very interested to see what our mileage is compared to the Dark Side. Give us a call! Bye.

I am in the cabin getting ready to come out for my shift when Jamie drawls, 'Looks like we've got company.'

I put my head outside and see a shape flash through the water and fly into the air. Dolphins! And others over there. I grab the camera. The dolphins are just hanging out, like we are a fun thing. They are doing somersaults and jumps. Maybe they want to see what we look like upside down?

Until now the ocean has felt strangely barren and inorganic. It may be full of life but we certainly aren't seeing it lined up in neat packages. It's fun to have something else to interact with, something that shows curiosity, even if the interaction just involves shouting, 'Look! Dolphins!' Then with one last flash of a glistening flank they are gone.

But Jamie has more than wildlife on his mind. At the end of his shift he says, 'The text will be through by now; let's see how much arse we kicked last night.'

He emerges stony-faced from the cabin a few minutes later.

'It says they gained six miles on us last night.'

'Six miles! In 12 hours! Are you joking?'

'I wish.'

There is a long silence. Jamie finally breaks it.

'We need to row some more overlapping shifts.'

'Yeah. You're not wrong.'

Bugger. So they are coming after us. Well, they are going to have to come and prise the lead from our cold, dead hands.

It's just after seven o'clock at the end of our first Friday at sea. I have just had a wash, which is a really nice change from being salty and dirty. We only have an hour off between sessions now, so I only have 20 minutes before I am back on again. I think I am losing a lot of weight because I am not eating so well — I'm not quite sure why. But the good thing about today is that it has been an absolutely fantastic day — just beautiful, gentle rolling seas, and not too hot. We've just been toiling along going at 3 knots, three and a bit knots. My hands are in pretty good shape — the rest of me is in pretty good shape — so I'd better get a quarter of an hour's sleep before I am back onto my shift again.

So far the story of Jamie's life has got up to his last year at an all-boys school.

'I am in the school play — well, it's a show.'

'Oh — which one?'

'*A Chorus Line.*'

'What were you?'

'I'm one of the dancers.'

'You mean like tippy-toe dancing?'

'Yep, had to wear dancing shoes and everything.'

'You can buy dancing shoes your size?'

'Nup. I had to get them specially made. There's some guy in Nelson who makes them. You just draw an outline of your right foot on a piece of A4 paper and fax it down to him.'

'Hang on . . . How many pieces of paper did it take?'

'Only two.'

'He must have thought you were taking the piss.'

'He did. What about you?'

'Yeah, I was in *The Wizard of Oz*.'

'Who were you?'

'I was a tree.'

'Right . . . How did it go?'

'Good. I gave a wooden performance.'

From about midnight we decide to try to keep on doing one and a half hours on, one hour off, through the night. It's brutal. When the sun finally comes up, I look at it sullenly — I could have used you three hours ago.

October 25 — Day 7, barnacle swim

During the night the sea has calmed down. There is still a little chop but there is no swell — it's like being on Lake Karapiro but the water seems sticky, like treacle. There is little glide with each stroke. Maybe we have run into some little eddy of the northern equatorial current that is heading the wrong way? Maybe there are things growing on the boat? I put my hand over the side and wipe my fingers under the waterline. I feel several warty bumps. Barnacles! And after only a few days! We need a hull-cleaning session, and with the sun grilling our skins the chance to get cool and wet seems a very good idea.

We don't want to let the boat stop for a second longer than we have to, so in our shift breaks we lay out the scouring pads and talk about how we are going to coordinate this — who is going to jump off what side, and how we are going to get back on.

I have only swum in the open ocean once before, as part of a swimming with the dolphins trip off the coast of Kaikoura. Jumping out of a boat miles from land is quite disconcerting. I mean it's deep, the water is well above your head, and you can't help thinking about all manner of unseen slippery fanged nasties lurking in the depths.

And what if the boat slipped away from us? There would be nothing more horrible than seeing the boat drift out of our grip, leaving us flailing after it until our energy had gone. Then bitterly bobbing in the water waiting for the inevitable salty death.

Not that there is much chance of that happening. The seas are too calm. The real concern is sharks.

My bible of all things to do with the high seas — the *Ocean Almanac* — states that there is a far greater likelihood of being hit by lightning than being eaten by a shark. It then comments wryly that most people would prefer to be hit by lightning than be eaten by a shark.

The *Almanac* asserts confidently that most shark attacks take place within 100 metres of the shore. I have no doubt that that is absolutely correct. But it is also true that 99.9999% of swimming takes place within 100 metres of the shore. What I really want to know is what our chances of shark attack are in the open water.

Just after midnight on 30 July 1945, a US cruiser was torpedoed by a Japanese submarine in the Pacific. The boat sank quickly, but there was still time for many of the crew to jump into the water. When dawn broke the next day around 750 people were still alive, either floating in the water or on rafts. Shortly after, though, the sharks arrived, and they continued to take the survivors until rescue came three and a half days later. By that time the marauding schools of sharks had taken an incredible 430 of the survivors.

Sharks are exceptionally well designed for killing, and they seem to like their work. Bull sharks are so tenacious that they have been known to pursue their victims onto land (presumably they then get jobs in the short-term finance industry). Sharks show no sense of pain, and keep on biting and attacking even if they are disembowelled. Grey nurse sharks are the only animals that eat one another while still inside the mother — the first two sharks to hatch eat all the other egg capsules.

Sharks are all about teeth. A shark has an endless supply of teeth set in layered rows in its gums. A shark may shed as many as 50,000 teeth in its lifetime. That part of the shark which is not jaw and fang is nose. A shark can detect one part of blood in 100 million parts of water; a third of its bodyweight is used for smelling. But sharks also have excellent underwater eyesight and can see in colour. But they don't just have human senses, they are also extraordinarily adept at sensing vibrations. A fish struggling on the surface hundreds of metres away can set a shark salivating. Sharks can even detect the very faint electromagnetic signals from muscle contractions — the same system also enables some sharks to navigate using the Earth's magnetic field.

So how do we rate on the shark attractiveness front? Our oars had been pricking the sea for nearly a week now. And those splashes would have sounded like a constant dinner gong to any shark within a dozen miles. We have also jettisoned all manner of food particles overboard — soggy gingernuts, bad chocolate, and freeze-dried pot scrapings. We have been leaving a trail of burley hundreds of miles long.

Jamie is being uncharacteristically dubious about going into the water. 'It's the pee,' he says; 'pee is like catnip to a shark. A shark will swim past a hundred people to bite the person who has peed.' And we have been dumping great dollops of delicious urine into the water at regular intervals.

So before we go into the water there is much close scrutiny of the water around the boat for any menacing black triangles.

'Let's listen,' I suggest.

'Mate, I don't think you can hear sharks.'

'No, but we might be able to hear a double bass. You know, "Baah dom, Baah dom".'

With an ungainly cartwheeling leap Jamie crashes into the water. Now the sharks are distracted I adopt a more conservative approach and lower myself in the other side. I have our only pair of goggles, so while Jamie does the sides I swim under the boat and wipe the keel.

The water is very clear. Shafts of golden light penetrate down into the indigo abyss below. I want to drop something to see how far I could see it fall. You have to take your hat off to those freakish freedivers who ride weighted sleds down into that blackness.

I need to kick to stay in place, and it's wonderful to move my legs around in all directions. It feels like a stretch after a long back-seat car trip. After about fifteen minutes we are back on board and rowing again, and drying quickly in the sun. I feel totally refreshed.

'Man! We have to do that again!'

I manage to convince Jamie that we need to have at least three shifts of one and a half hours for sleep at night. Only having hour-long naps, which are more like 45 minutes once you have done the obligatories, is craziness. Jamie agrees, provided we row harder during the first part of the night. So as the sun goes down at around 6pm we start rowing two hours on, one hour off shifts, which gives us a whole hour overlap.

So this means rowing together, which means we have plenty of time to kill together.

I ask Jamie, 'Do you know any songs we can sing? How about U2?'

'Sure, what albums?'

'*Boy*? *Under a Blood Red Sky*?'

'Nup.'

'How about The Beatles?'

'Which one?'

'*Yellow Submarine*?'

'Do you know any songs about being above the water?'

'Hmm. What about show tunes?'

'I know *A Chorus Line*.'

'Yeah, no. How about *Les Mis*?'

'Nup.'

'How about "Tomorrow" from *Annie*?'

'Yep.'

'Great! Let's go then.'

We give a hearty rendition.

'We must sound completely homo,' says Jamie.

We sing it again anyway.

It's been a tough day, but it's been worth it. The GPS says we have rowed a solid 72 nautical miles in the last 24 hours. That should stick it to them. I turn on the satellite phone and with a beep a text arrives:

25/10 20:00 HS 62NM LAST 24 HRS, DS 69NM
YOUR LEAD NOW 6 NM

But we rowed 72 nautical miles! If we are only showing 62 nautical miles closer to the finish then it must mean we are being penalised for the more southerly course the isochrones require from us. There is nothing to do but persevere.

My favourite way into the cabin is to sit on the hatch facing outwards, then duck my head and fall back onto the mat. Once most of me is inside I can then bring my legs up to my chest and spin around. Then it is just a matter of rolling onto my front and sprawling.

Today I am having trouble with everything except the falling backwards part. The fatigue is so bad that once I'm in the cabin it's all I can do to roll onto my front.

After the squalls, the sun sets, and as it gets dark it becomes very,

very still again. The oars chop into the water, and with every stroke the boat reluctantly moves another six inches further forward.

October 26 — Day 8, Daytona Doldrums

The sun doesn't so much come up as the horizon expands and expands. I am finishing off the last night shift, and feeling very light-headed.

There is no wind at all. Nothing. The ocean is a flawless blue skin. It's so still I can see the reflections of the first wisps of clouds in the water. I am rowing on a giant blue mirror. There is a large swell, but the crests are several football fields apart. They are coming at a slight angle to the stern, so that when they arrive the boat tilts slightly and slowly rises, and I can look out down a long, curved wave face. It is like being on the banked corner of the Daytona 500. On the very top of the swell there is just a tiny breeze, a minute puff of tantalising coolness before the long descent into the hot, airless trough.

I yank at the oars but the water is nasty and slow, and I am struggling to do even 2 lousy knots. My back aches, my arms are rubbery. It's going to be a bloody long day.

Sweat is running down my face, sluicing white trails of bitter, stinging sunscreen into my eyes and mouth. I look up to see if there are any clouds that will give us respite. There are none.

But then the clock ticks over and my shift is done. Now I have to move fast because time is short. With a quick jerk I pull in my oars their whole length, until the handles are tucked in under the gunnels and the blades are flat against the side of the boat. I pull off the Velcro straps keeping my feet in the shoes, and pivot around so that I am in a press-up position with my toes in the shoe heels. Now I can arch my back like the figurehead on the prow of a boat and decompress those poor discs. I look out over the bow of the boat to the horizon. There is no land there — it is hard to believe that there ever will be. Each stroke barely moves us half a boat length. We are going as slow as a slow walk.

I turn around and step over Jamie's swinging oars and into the footwell. Inside the starboard deck-locker is the bucket of recovery powder; I scoop some of it into a wide-mouthed water container, add fresh water from the pump, and shake it up to make a hot, sweet, gooey milkshake.

Now it's time to peel off my bike shorts. I clip them under a bungy cord on the deck. My shirt, which is ringed like a coffee cup with sweat and dirt, soon follows. Precious things like my sunglasses and hat go inside, into a container bolted to the bulkhead inside the cabin. I look at the skin of my hands for signs of deterioration. None. Good.

I pump out some fresh water onto a sponge and wipe off the greasy coating of grime, sweat and sunscreen. Feeling new and pink and clean I grab a soft pack of tuna from the port locker, and a handful of crackers, before I slide into the back cabin. Careful not to get any crackers in the bed!

Inside it is at least shady, and with the back hatch open there are a few cooling wafts of breeze. It is all the more enjoyable as I lie there knowing that just a few inches from my nose there are thousands of watts of UV rays smacking into the boat. I have found a better pillow than the slippery orange survival suit. Now I dig out from one of the side bungy pouches my most recent and precious find — a polyprop top. I forgot we had it on board until I found it by accident the other day. Now I carefully spread it under my head and enjoy its softness, its cleanness and its fresh laundry smell. If I place my head right I can get both the draught and the shade. Beside me on the cabin floor a slim parallelogram of sizzling sunlight searches back and forth without finding me in the shadows.

Now I have 44 or 45 minutes before I have to get up. But until then, with a brain fogged from fatigue and the sugars silting into my bloodstream, I can ride the waves of sheer exquisite ecstasy at not having to move my muscles. I am exhausted but I don't want to sleep. Is it too much to ask to be able to enjoy a few precious moments when I am not uncomfortable, to enjoy time passing without having to make any effort? I know that as soon as I close my eyes the next thing I will hear will be Jamie bellowing 'Six minutes!'

'SIX MINUTES!'

How did that happen? Shit, I must have fallen asleep. Don't think. Whatever you do, don't think. It only makes it worse. If you start thinking, this is going to hurt. Just get up — OK?

You're thinking.

No I'm not.

Yes you are, shaddup.

OhmanthishurtsIneedmoresleepIcan'tbelieveIhavetogooutthere Ineedmoresleep . . .

'FIVE MINUTES!'

Damn, I have to get up. I flick the hatch door with my toe. But not too far, because then it gets in the way of Jamie's hands as they come forward on the stroke.

Maybe there is just time to put my head down for another couple of seconds?

Are you still thinking?

Who asked you anyway?

I try moving and my body resists. Oh man, I am really stuffed.

OK, I'll give you the list. Here it is:

- You know you always feel crap for the first 15 minutes.

- This is as bad as it gets.

- This isn't forever. Only another 200 times.

- Just do it.

- Stop thinking.

OK, just let me lie here until I hear the four-minute call.

'THREE MINUTES!'

'Three minutes? What happened to four minutes?'

'Sorry.'

I hide the polyprop deep in the mesh stowage bag and spin myself around, putting my legs into the footwell. I reach out and grab my bike shorts. They feel hot and crisp. I am trying to alternate wearing them the right way and inside out, but after a few seconds of getting myself confused I just put them on. Now standing in the footwell, I reach into the utility box for the sunscreen. I put plenty on my face and the tops of my legs and the backs of my hands. Then the wraparound sunglasses. Then hat. Then iPod

'You got one minute.'

I ask Jamie, 'How's it been?' and he says, 'Pretty good,' which is what he would say whether it was mirror calm or the boat was inverted.

Then, as I fill up my water bottles from the pump, I ask casually, 'So how are the numbers?' By that I mean — how fast have you been rowing?

'Low twos mostly — 2.4 for a lot of the time.'

Meaning that he wants me to believe he has been rowing at between 2 and 3 knots. Meaning that's what I have to do if I want to keep my self-respect.

Then comes the trickiest part — timing the step over Jamie's scything oars with the rocking of the boat. Steady? Go! I take two tottering steps and lurch towards the bow. It helps if I grab a big chunk of his shirt or use his head as a hold as I go by. I'm not fooled by the strength of his swearing. I know he likes having his hat pushed down over his eyes.

So now I am at my seat. I sit down carefully. The last thing we need now is for another seat to pop, and the rubber is black and hot.

Then I must stow the water bottles and tie my feet into the rowing shoes bolted into the footplate. I pick up the oars and fall in behind Jamie. For the first few minutes I work on technique, trying to make the catch smooth, making sure my back is straight. It never starts well — my muscles are tired and sore, I feel clumsy. But quite quickly it sorts itself out. Soon I am in the zone again, and even my bum stops aching as the seat moulds itself to my bottom, and I fall into the clockwork rhythm of the rowing action.

The clock on the GPS ticks over and Jamie pulls in his blades and undoes his shoes.

The shock comes on the oars as I try to keep up the speed. Jamie shakes himself a recovery drink, strips off, and his naked, hairy arse disappears into the hatch along with a pile of crackers and tuna and a bag of crisps.

'What time do you want?' I shout out as the main hatch door is pulled mostly shut.

'Six minutes is fine.'

Then I see the back hatch pop up and I know that Jamie is lying in the coolness.

I try very hard to keep up 2.4 knots on the GPS before I realise it's impossible and that Jamie is pulling my leg. Just like he did yesterday and the day before. It has worked though. Now there is only 53 minutes left, or about 48 minutes until Jamie reappears and time starts to move normally again. I look at the clock. Still 48 minutes. I look away and look back. Still 48 minutes. Boy, it must have just clicked over 48 minutes when I first looked. Still 48 minutes. Maybe it's broken. No, there it goes . . . 47 minutes . . . still 47 minutes.

It's time to start the iPod, which swings in a pouch over my shoulder. Today I am feeling lucky so I put it on random play. One day maybe, just maybe, it might be Christopher Cross, which is my fantasy. To be out on the billowing indigo ocean on a sunny day, with a puff of breeze in the air, and unexpectedly hear the warm, rich, swelling tones that are the first bars of 'Sailing' — then for 4 minutes and 14 seconds everything would be OK. But a new song starts and it isn't Christopher Cross. Another few minutes and I'll get another chance. Only 10 more minutes and I can have a drink.

Today the clouds are fat and fluffy. If that one over there just moves fractionally further to the left there is a good chance that I might get some shade. Here it comes. Here it comes.

Can you believe that it went right around it? Damn. Thirty-eight minutes to go.

Another cloud comes. Now I have shade. But the watermaker growling away underneath me reminds me that it is sucking five precious amps while it is working; I want the solar cells to be charging the battery as well, because the battery voltage has been dipping alarmingly at night.

Waves roll by, clouds build, melt and re-form, songs play. My legs push, my arms pull, my stomach contracts and relaxes, I blow out air that is only slightly cooler than the air I am sucking in. Sweat rolls down my face. Time passes.

But now it's eight minutes to go, so in two minutes I will need to call Jamie out. But I know that he was late coming out last time, so maybe I will call him with seven minutes to go. No, let him sleep.

'Six minutes!'

An enormous toe flicks the door open. The rectangular opening of the hatch is like a TV. Today is a repeat of *Jamie Puts on his Trousers*. Jamie recently came to the conclusion that the shape of his shorts has been irritating his nether regions, so he has cut the crotch out of them. He writhes around before putting both legs into one side, then cursing. At last, successful, he stops with his bum up in the air but his head still down on the pillow, trying to milk the last few seconds of sleep.

'Three minutes!' I shout.

Jamie stirs again then comes out feet first. He stands in the footwell, his bollocks waving in the breeze, scowling at the horizon. He puts sunscreen on, but not that thoroughly, though he spends a lot of time putting it on his nether regions.

'Two minutes, by the way.'

He reaches into the cabin and pulls out the iPod in its yellow waterproof pouch.

'What kind of numbers have you been doing?'

'Mid twos. Sat at 2.6 for a while.'

'Really?'

'Yeah.'

Jamie sits down gently in his seat, adjusts his iPod, picks up the oar handles from the deck and pushes them out. He takes a stroke and immediately the load on my oars decreases. In just 29 minutes my next break will start. I look at the GPS clock — 29 minutes to go. I look away at the ocean. I look back. Still 29 . . .

Listening to audiobooks is one of the few ways to make time pass more quickly. I have just started a new one called *In the Heart of the Sea*. It is such a spectacularly bad choice of a book to listen to on the ocean that it is hypnotically compelling. It's the story of the whaling ship *Essex*, which left Nantucket in 1819 on a two-year expedition to hunt sperm whales. Up until then whales had been pretty good sports about their steady decline to near extinction. Once shot with a harpoon or two they would struggle just enough to make it interesting, then lie there peacefully on the surface and wait to be turned into corsets, scrimshaw, soap, combs, lamp oil and other essentials of Victorian society.

Fifteen months into the voyage, deep in the Pacific, the *Essex* came across an old sperm whale that didn't stick to the script and charged the ship, giving it an enormous blow below the waterline. Although the whale seemed stunned by the blow, it eventually came to its senses and charged again, this time stoving in the wood under the waterline. If this sounds familiar, that's because it's the true story that *Moby Dick* was based on.

Before you could say 'Thar she blows!' Moby had managed to turn the boat into matchsticks. The crew of 20 had to abandon ship and take to the three whaleboats which, by strange coincidence, were not dissimilar in size to our own boat.

Other Atlantic rowboats had reported that whales had paid them a lot of attention, bumping and nudging them. Not to mention Simon Chalk being flipped upside down by a whale off Australia. There's something about rowboats that makes a whale frisky.

Jamie's shout wakes me in the afternoon.

'Hey Kev, we've got more company!'

'Mermaids?'

'Nup. Take a look out the back.'

I put my head out the back hatch and see one, then two large, triangular fins sliding through the water a dozen metres behind the back of the boat. Sharks! But those fins don't look quite right. Could they be whales? I watch them as they surge rhythmically to the surface. They are either air-breathing sharks — or whales.

It's hard to make out what type they are. Could they be the great-great-grandchildren of the one that developed a taste for wood and squealing rowers back in 1820? They come up alongside the boat, still a few metres away. They don't look that big — maybe 3 to 4 metres long. Maybe pilot whales?

Then I remember about whale poo. For some strange reason the manufacturers of the watermaker had specifically mentioned that whale poo was very bad for the filter. It would be just our luck to come across an amorous whale that had had plenty of bran for breakfast, and wants to give us a naughty cuddle before taking a dump.

Maybe we can just keep to ourselves and slowly veer away.

'Shall we throw it some tuna?' says Jamie. 'We might be able to get them to come closer!'

What? I realise that I haven't told Jamie anything about rowboats and whales. I try to respond casually.

'Oh no, better not, eh?'

It's well after sunset, so time to turn on the sat phone and hear from Rob how we are doing. It's a little difficult to tell, because the Dark Side have started to poll out of sync, sending in their position more than two hours earlier. But it appears that there has been an astonishing reversal in our positions. Last night at 8pm we were 6 nautical miles in front. Tonight at 8pm we are about 14 miles behind. They have caught up 20 miles in 24 hours. It's scarcely believable. The only clue is that during a radio interview Goodman has said they were surfing in big swells. Yet that seems extraordinary when it is so flat here, and they are only about 20 miles away from us as the crow flies.

Anyway, there isn't much we can do about it. We have had our few days of glory and now our gallant gallop is over. By the looks of it we are strong contenders for second, and second is very creditable, given the circumstances. After all, it's only our first attempt at the race. It's a shame our lead only lasted a week, but at least we gave them the willies for a little while. Maybe they will have some respect for us now — actually, that's probably a bad thing. They won't stop doing whatever they are doing until they are a long way ahead.

Without the excitement of being in front it's going to be a hell of a long couple of months out on the ocean . . . hang on! That *is* a long time. That's a lot of time for something to go wrong. Anything could happen. Our job now must be to stay as close as possible behind them and take advantage when it does. Just because they have had a couple of good days, we don't need to roll over and show our tummies! We haven't lost yet!

I call Hot Polish Girl, who is down in Dunedin cramming for the first part of her surgical exams. Her small voice sounds brittle and stressed. The exams are horrible. The amount she has to learn is overwhelming including, among other things, the name and location of every nerve, muscle, organ and artery in the body. Her texts are as big as the Auckland phone book. She has been studying from seven in the morning until ten at night, with only short breaks to go to lectures. It's three weeks since she went down there, and she has another three weeks to go. I try to say the right things. Then the call ends and I'm suddenly snapped back to the boat. Thank goodness I only have to row across the Atlantic.

><

October 27 — Day 9, Terminator Doldrums

It's Day 9. I come out to an extraordinary morning. We are sitting on a puddle of mercury — grey, shiny and featureless. The same consistency as the robot from Terminator. *There is not the smallest air movement — it's completely calm, just the squeak of the rowlocks, and the growl of the watermaker. We are rising and falling slowly from a swell from the northeast, which we are greatly encouraged by, as we are hoping that the wind will pick up from there.*

The morning text arrives from Rob. The Dark Side have pulled away another four miles during the night. I pull short, violent strokes on the oars, fed up with the lack of progress.

We decide to go for another barnacle-scraping session. Some of the clumps are almost the width of my little finger. We have become part of the biosystem without knowing it. The reason the log hasn't been working lately is because the propeller is completely jammed up with a barnacle. There is even a fish sucking onto the side of the boat as well! Well that's fine, as long as he flaps. But we clearly can't afford to wait a week between hull-cleaning sessions — we have to do it every third day.

Now the heat comes on. There is nothing but a few sparse, trembling oxygen and nitrogen atoms of atmosphere between us and a 100 trillion tonnes of fusing helium nuclei. It's time for the weed-sprayer.

The weed-sprayer cooling system is Shamus's brainchild, and one of the more cunning things on the boat. It consists of a regular garden 10-litre pump sprayer, and a solenoid with a timer. When filled with water and pumped up, the spray wand will puff a fine mist of fresh water into the air in front of us, for about three seconds every 30 seconds.

While I row Jamie gets it out, pumps it up and adjusts the spray wand in its mount.

'Are you ready?'

'You bet!'

The first puff of mist comes out and wafts over me. I can almost hear the hiss as the sizzle comes off my skin. The evaporating water feels delicious, like a refreshing shower. By the time the next puff comes out I am almost dry and ready for my next spritzing. A big smile spreads over my face. It works!

Two hours later, I am wondering how much of Jamie I could fit into our little pot. I have just finished listening to the final part of the story of the whaling ship. Once the crew were in the whaleboats their situation was grim. They had only a little hard tack to eat, and less water. They were about twenty days away from Tahiti, given the prevailing winds, but they believed that the islands were largely populated with savage cannibals, so they decided to head to South America, two months away.

Over the next few weeks they suffered terribly from the relentless sun, from attacks by sharks and killer whales, from lack of food, but most of all from the shortage of water. 'The violence of thirst has no parallel in the catalogue of human calamitie,' wrote the first mate, who slept with his arm over the chest that held the last of the provisions and a loaded pistol by his side. The boats became separated and two of them were lost at sea.

Eventually the sailors started to die. Being practical folk, their crewmates ate them. Then they weren't dying fast enough, and they had to draw straws to see who would be sacrificed. Eventually there were only two of the original sailors left. Three months after they had gone into the boats a passing ship saw the small whaling boat in the distance and sailed over to investigate. They found two men, not much more than skeletons themselves, and almost indifferent to being rescued. Instead they were intent on sucking on the bones of their dead crewmates, '. . . which they were loathe to part with'.

As soon as my shift is over I reach into the boat, unscrew the cover to the wooden ballast tank, dip my finger into the water and taste it. Bugger, it's mank — tainted with that solvent like substance. I thought I had flushed that out. Maybe the heat is making the solvent sweat or something. I talk it over with Jamie and we decide that first thing tomorrow morning, if the weather is fine, we will flush it out.

Late in the afternoon the majestic mountains of mashed potato above us start to release their load. We row through a vast corridor, with dark curtains of rain passing us on either side. Somehow we are missed.

Eventually there is shade. The sun dips lower in the sky and starts to intersect with the rows of marching clouds. The colours deepen, the shadows grow. I sigh and pull off my hat, and throw it on the deck. Next stroke I can drop my sunglasses inside it. The stroke after that I can wipe my sleeve across my forehead. Now life becomes worth living again.

Jamie is in the footwell having a wash. 'Hey, have you heard of *Puppetry of the Penis?*'

'Yeah, why?'

'Check this out . . . it's called "Hung Chicken".'

'How about that!'

'Tomorrow I'll show you "Flies' Eyes".'

Tonight there is no apprehension about surviving the darkness. The ocean is benign as a suburban swimming pool. But that doesn't stop us scattering the petrels with a rousing chorus of 'Tomorrow'.

'So what are you doing for money while you're at uni?'

'Well, I had the fencing business, and I do a bit of home-kill as well.'

'What's Home Kill? Is that like a pest extermination business . . . like Rentokil? Or would I call you when I want to have a family member knocked off?'

'Nup. It's when a farmer wants one of his cows killed. So we go out there, cull it, and break it up into whatever the farmer wants.'

'So what part of the cow is the sausage?'

'You're joking, aren't you?'

'Of course I am — everyone knows sausages come from sheep.'

'Mate, you're a worry.'

I think for a minute.

'So when you were growing up on the farm did you have a pet pig, like *Charlotte's Web?*'

'Nup, I had a lamb.'

'What did you call it? Ripper? Rambo? No — Lambo?'

'Nup. Blossom.'

'Blossom! What happened to Blossom?'

Silence.

'You turned her into sausages, didn't you?'

When the phone call from Rob comes the news is much better. We have rowed 11 miles further than the previous day, even though the conditions have been very similar. The barnacles must have been slowing us down far more than we thought.

216

When I come out for the next shift it is night. The sky has magically melted away to reveal that there is nothing between us and the aching void of space. The stars are so numerous and dense they drift over like a bright fog. The air is so still that the reflecting sea is grey too. My swinging oar leaves a shadow on the water. We are rowing among the stars, not under them.

It's astonishingly calm. I could easily light a candle. We don't have any candles but we do have Pringles. I could light a trail of flaming Pringles behind us.

After my shift, I can watch the sky as I lie in the cabin. Jamie is a dark silhouette against the white and grey backdrop. Life is strange. Here I am perched over one abyss and looking out into another.

CHAPTER NINETEEN

About the wind coming

October 28 — Day 10

It is dark. It has always been dark. Light is a memory. A day would be a miracle. Could the Earth have stopped spinning?

Finally, the faintest pale glow rings the horizon and the night lifts like the lid slowly coming off a pot.

When I come out for my next shift Jamie is frowning and complaining that the water is very 'jobbly'. There are odd, disturbing puffs of wind from the south, and an easterly swell is starting to roll in.

I have been a bit quiet the last couple of days, as time is beginning to stretch out. I'm starting to feel a little overtrained, my resting heart rate is much higher than normal. But I am eating much better. Nothing like Jamie though. Jamie is eating everything in sight. He'll finish off a packet of nuts, stuff in a choc bar, and eat half a packet of crackers while he's waiting for his pasta to cook. It's unbelievable how much he gets through.

But I had a happy moment today when I was making lunch. It felt like being on a camping trip, then I thought, ten days is quite a long camping trip! We have achieved a lot already. I find myself wondering what it will be like to finish at Barbados. I shouldn't think about it. This is where I am supposed to be at this moment.

We are just hanging out to get to the 20% mark, which will be some time tonight.

We had packed some hard jubes to celebrate getting to 20%. On my next break I look for them in the locker.

'Jamie, where are the hard jubes?'

'Ahh . . . you might need to speak to Rob about that. I think he, ahh . . . unpacked them.'

At my next break I turn on the sat phone and call Rob.

'Rob. There seems to be some food missing from the boat. Do you know anything about it?'

'Oh yeah, I took it off — the night before the race.'

'You did what? How much?'

'I don't know. Quite a lot actually . . . cereals, biscuits, chips, sweets. You had way too much.'

'But I knew every calorie we were taking. It's all on the spread-sheet.'

'But I'm right though, aren't I? You'd have just been throwing it out by now.'

He's right.

'OK, but if I go hungry you're bloody buying me a lobster dinner in Barbados.'

'You're on.'

So some time tonight we are going to pass the 20% mark. I try to think of different ways to talk it up. It's a fifth of the way. Twice 10%. Four times 5%. Almost a quarter, and once we reach a quarter we will be halfway to halfway. Then at halfway we will be over the hump and it will all be downhill.

Nup. Nothing works. There is still a bloody long way to go. How on earth did Rob and Phil do it in 42 days? It looks like it's going to take us 50!

All day the weather has been deteriorating. The wind has picked up to a very fresh breeze, and large waves are starting to knock the boat around. There will be no lighting Pringles tonight. If I emptied a can of Pringles upside down now they would be over the side before they hit the deck.

I check the ballast tank. This morning we drained the contaminated water out and swapped the outlet of the watermaker over from the day tank to start refilling the wooden ballast tank. It has been growling away for hours. Through the hatch I can see the fresh water slopping around inside, but it isn't even half full. Now the sun is setting and our puny battery can't work the watermaker for very long without sun. I don't know how stable the boat is going to be with the ballast tank half full, but my clenching stomach tells me that it certainly isn't going to be more stable than usual. Which means that unfortunately we need to top up the tank with seawater and try again when we look like having two calm days in a row.

The racing, thickening clouds are rushing us into darkness. Jamie gets out the safety harnesses and we put them on and hook on to the line that runs down the deck. The lines are fine except that I have to disconnect myself to get from the bow seat to the footwell. So for the most precarious part of moving around the boat they don't work.

We are rowing the hour and a half on, hour off shifts, but we have little enthusiasm for talking. We are working too hard to stay coordinated in the heaving seas. When I am rowing by myself I have to concentrate; it's not possible to tune out and let time go by. Some time in the early morning we start the Sleep Shifts — an hour and a half each, with no overlap. I move to the stern seat, the one closest to the cabin, to try to get a little more protection from the elements.

The sky is black, there is no light at all. Unseen water roars as it rushes past — it's like navigating rapids in a steep gorge in the dark. The only glimpse of light is the ghostly amber rectangle of the GPS, which illuminates itself and nothing else. There is no horizon at all. The rectangle bobs and weaves like a boxer's chin, jumping from left to right and occasionally jerking into the air. My stomach is starting to jump as well.

Tonight I am listening to *Toujours Provence* on the iPod, a gentle, summery read by a Brit who moves to the south of France, where he has a series of long lunches with local characters and tries to find the perfect truffle. His vivid word-pictures are the perfect escapism and provide a strange kind of comfort. I can't be swept off the deck of a boat to drown in the gulping blackness when I am sprinkling pepper on my snails in a sunny cafe out of Nice.

I just wish I hadn't put the poo bucket so close. I feel myself starting to descend through the symptoms of impending nausea — tender stomach, dry mouth, watery mouth. The light is stitching a mad path left and right. Then the author describes a bad lunch. I join him in his disgust.

><

October 29 — Day 11, Jesus-through-the-feet day

When the sun finally arrives it lifts up the grey lid of cloud, gives us a quick wink, then leaves us to it. The waves are bigger today, 2–3 metres, and coming from the northeast when they aren't coming from everywhere else. The wind is very strong, maybe up to 20–30 knots. It's coming from the east, which is not ideal, but it will do. It's pretty much one permanent Ovahk.

'So do you think we can get a surf on?' suggests Jamie. I'm not sure. The waves are coming from different directions, sometimes reinforcing each other and sometimes cancelling each other out. Just as a tottering wave is about to drop onto the boat one going the other way will suck it down flat. Then the reverse happens — in a few seconds a flat piece of water will rise up and dump on the boat. We each try to spot one of the sturdier waves coming.

'Not this one, the one after the next one.'

'You mean the blue one?'

'Well, I suppose it's blue.'

'I can't see it.'

'That's because it's behind this one — you'll see when it goes.'

'Oh, you mean that one.'

'OK, here we go — yes yes yes!'

'Yep.'

Then six quick strong strokes. When we get it right the boat surges along for a few metres. Most of the time we agree, but then comes the inevitable.

'Yes yes yes!'

'Yes, NO NO NO!'

The large wave that we were about to surf has just aggregated into a behemoth. The back of the boat lifts up and up. The seats slide to the bow, a water bottle tumbles out of the hatch. Jamie is now silhouetted against the sky. We're going to pitch pole.

But we don't. The wave disappears and we drop back level, breathing hard.

'Whoa, that was close! I think I could see Jesus through my feet,' Jamie says, shaking his head.

We decide not to row any more overlapping shifts until the sea calms down.

The light starts to leach from the sky. I feel a level of dread that increases in direct proportion to the fading of the light. Even the clouds aren't hanging around, they are scudding away to the horizon. My guts turn as watery as the ocean around me. Even *Annie* can't help us tonight.

It gets dark. Then it gets darker. It's even darker than the previous night, as we have to turn off the GPS to stop the battery diving into a voltage so low it won't recover. We have only the anaemic compass light to give comfort.

But the wind and the waves are mostly heading the right way, and there's a lot of both. Even with my syncopated thrashings the boat is going around 3–3.5 knots. We are being swept along to the finish — at least the boat is. I just have to stay inside it.

It feels like I am rowing in air as much as water. On one stroke the port oar is waving in space while the other oar is buried shaft-deep into the shoulder of a wave. Then another wave knocks the boat violently, almost putting the gunnel into the water and tipping me off my seat. Then a wave breasts the boat from the other side and dumps fully on the deck. I shout gargled expletives while the boat does its best imitation of a bucking bronco.

There is no chance of coordinated, rhythmic action — each stroke is a conscious struggling creation. The oar handles are continually being driven into my knees and slammed into my thighs. The boat waits until I am at my most unbalanced, then it snaps the other way, sending me, oars abandoned, clinging to the rail. If you could watch me with a thermal imaging camera, it would look as if I was doing eighties nightclub moves, or crap kung fu played backwards.

October 30 — Day 12, surfing day

By the time morning comes the steady wind has finally begun to marshal the waves into slightly more organised ranks, and I start trying to get a surf up. The waves are deceptive. Regardless of how large they look, most of them slide underneath the boat, making no contribution to our progress. I learn that I need not only a large one but a steep one, with a fist of curling white water on top. Ideally there will be two large waves one after the other, so that I can get some speed up on the first one then really get going on the second.

Just before the wave arrives I make some deep, rapid strokes, then I lean back with my legs extended to try and get some weight forward. The stern of the boat picks up and we start sliding down the mountain. All the frustrations of trying to get the boat going over the last weeks are suddenly reversed as it starts to build momentum.

Water squirts in through the scuppers — the plastic flaps we screwed over them are useless for keeping the water out. After only a few seconds the angle of the boat flattens as the wave passes underneath, then after a brief pause there is another strange surge as the back of the wave sucks the boat. This is when the real speed is felt, and without a wall of water about to break over me I feel much better about it. Then the boat returns to its glum bovine waddle, and with my heart pounding I look to the horizon for the next one.

The sky is mostly clear today, and as the sun rises and the heat builds the waves produce another problem. Without the back hatch open there is no airflow through the cabin, which quickly becomes stifling. But to leave the back hatch open is to risk a rude, moist awakening as a large slop of water from some tottering wave is dumped inside the cabin to land on your face. Then many precious minutes of sleep are wasted as you spend them bailing and mopping.

I lie under the back hatch sucking on the air, with my hand hanging limply above me on the handle.

'Jamie, can you let me know if there's a wave coming?'

'I can see one now. What do you want me to do?'

'Call out something.'

'Like what?'

'How about, "Hey there's a wave coming — shut the hatch!"'

Which quickly becomes 'HATCH!'

Sometimes it works, and then it is very satisfying to hear the gurgling thump of water as it hits the back while I remain smugly, if blearily, dry. But it does require a lot of attention and judgement on the part of the person rowing. You don't want to call too many red herrings, but it's much worse if you miss one. But often the waves look as if they are about to drop on the boat, then they retreat at the very last second . . . or not.

A gust of wind blows my hat off and it lands in the water beside the boat. I leap after it, forgetting that my feet are tied into shoes that are screwed into the boat. My leap is abruptly curtailed, with me half out of the boat and the hat sliding past my fingers. It disappears into the swells surprisingly quickly.

It's not the loss of the hat that bothers me; I have a spare. I am alarmed by my sudden urge to fling myself into the sea. What exactly had been the plan of my subconscious mind? Get the hat then walk back to the boat?

Tonight we are hearing Jamie's dating stories from the time when he'd just left school. I am transported as Jamie walks into a bar in Tauranga.

'So you didn't expect to see her there! What did you do? . . . You didn't! . . . What did she say? . . . But how did she find out about her? . . . What are the chances of that! Then what did she do? . . . A whole jug? . . . But then you left? No! . . . Her friend? . . . She didn't mind the beer? . . . Ahh, Waikato Draught. I see!'

Getting through the nights is becoming harder, not easier. From 3am to dawn my brain is checking out. At the end of one shift I am sitting in the hatch trying to take off my shorts when I fall backwards into the cabin. I try to bring my legs in. They won't move. This is it. I am spent. I have hit the wall. This is how they will find me — legs dangling out of the cabin.

I really need to get my legs in. But at some point down my spine the neural messengers peter out, lose interest, mill around and then go get a cappuccino. My legs are not made of lead. They are made of

224

that super-dense material that forms when stars collapse. One teaspoon weighs a tonne. With wings of lead I could fly through the stuff my legs are made of.

I try again to lift them. Nothing. I start with my toes — they can still wiggle. Good. Now heave.

It didn't take as much effort as this to build the pyramids. To raise the Great Wall of China. To crack the human genome. This is The Great Movement of Legs into the Cabin. The old people will tell tales about this feat, legends will be sung by the fire.

I'm in.

Now all I need to do is roll over.

'SIX MINUTES!'

'You're kidding, right?'

'Actually, it's more like five minutes.'

I am still lying on my back. I haven't even turned off the cabin light. How could an hour and a half go by so quickly? How much crappier can I possibly feel?

✕

October 31 — Day 13, we run out of Rohos

There is a chink of paleness on the horizon — after the night, it's a crowbar under my leaden spirits. The gentle new light is softened by a gauze of clouds. Everything is golden. For the next half hour the light illuminates without scarring. I think of a paragraph from Jim Shekdar's book about rowing the Pacific, where he said that occasionally the elements conspire to create a vista and experience that transcends everything — you are transported in rapture, and for a few moments you are the luckiest person on Earth. But it only lasts for fifteen minutes, and it only happens once a month. The rest of the time you are on the rack being lashed.

For once the boats have polled at the same time. We are now about 47 nautical miles behind. Over the last four days the Dark Side have extended their lead at the rate of about eight miles per day. The windier conditions seem to suit them.

During one of my Sleep Shifts I come out of the cabin to find Jamie rowing on my seat.

'What happened?'

'My Roho shat itself.'

'Shit!' That was our spare. Now we are down to one.

'Yeah.'

We aren't going to be overlapping at night anyway. But it does make our changeovers a few seconds slower, as now Jamie has to get out of the seat while I slip in. Jamie suggests we put a nudge on to compensate.

Tonight I have no problem staying awake — how are we going to find the holes in the Roho? If we can't fix them the rowing is going to get medieval on our arses.

November 1 — Day 14, first time fixing the Roho

As soon as the sun is up, Jamie takes the seat into the cabin to try and find the holes. I see him scowling as he turns the rubber over in his hands, running down the lines of rubber eggs.

'Can you see anything?'

'Nah.'

If this was a bicycle tyre we could put it in a bucket of water to see where the bubbles were coming out, but the only bucket we have is the poo bucket. Gross.

Jamie looks up. 'I suppose we could flood the footwell.'

Genius! So then all we have to do is get the auto-steering going, get me into the bow steering position, pull the life raft out, clear two weeks' worth of boat gunk out of the footwell, and finally pull the bung and let the sea bubble in. Then Jamie blows up the cushion and pushes it under the water. From the bow seat I can't see what he is doing.

'How's it going?'

'Hang on. Yeah, found them.'

One cushion has two holes, while the other, which had popped early on, has one. But by now Jamie has eaten through a huge chunk of his break, so we agree that I will take over after my shift. In the meantime the cushions can dry in the sun.

I find the patch kit in the repair box and read the instructions very carefully. I have to swab the puncture area with a tiny little alcohol-soaked tissue, which is included in a little sealed patch, then peel the backing off a rubber patch and press it on.

The problem is that we only have a small square of the patch material not much bigger than a large postage stamp. I'll have to cut a piece off. But if I make it too small it will be useless and I will have to start again. On the other hand, if I use too much there might not be enough to fix the three holes we have now, or for the next time it punctures — and there will certainly be a next time.

The worst hole is right at the base of one of the rubber eggs, so I cut a little strip and carefully apply it, pinching it on until my fingers are numb. I slowly release it. It seems OK. I do the same to the other holes, and when I am done the cushions inflate beautifully.

I am inspired. We can look after ourselves. We can make things better.

It's beautiful outside — we have a half-moon now and a reasonably calm sea, just a little top, and perhaps the odd swell that goes by and rocks us a bit. Mostly it's very peaceful and I can hear the sound of laughing or something coming from Jamie's headset. The moonlight on the water is very lovely, a bit of high cloud tonight. I was rowing for the first time without a shirt tonight because it is so hot out there. I guess we can expect that as we get closer to the equator.

So today marks two weeks of being at sea. This is going to be an interesting month. It's going to be a month spent entirely at sea. It doesn't seem like there is ever going to be an end.

It's the best part of the voyage in a way because right now what we are doing seems so friggin' enormous and futile — later on, when we are near the end, we will look back on this time and feel good that we persevered even when it seemed impossible.

The late-night position update tells us that we are holding our own. They haven't put any more miles on us in the last 24 hours. That's encouraging — our messing about with the seats hasn't slowed us down.

November 2 — Day 15

This morning there are some strange half-digested pieces of tiny fish in the boat. I have no idea how they got there. Maybe we are looking scrawny enough to bring out the motherly regurgitation instincts in passing seagulls. Or maybe there is some Gollum-like creature on the boat who scoops them out of the sea in the middle of the night and snacks on them. I run my tongue over my teeth checking for bones.

CHAPTER TWENTY

Grinding it out

Your Atlantic Cruise Activities!

Hello passengers, and welcome to another fabulous day at sea on your Atlantic cruise! We have another action-packed day for you.

First, a bit of housekeeping. Please do not feed the whales! Also, make sure the watermaker is off when you empty the poo bucket!

For those of you wanting to take part in the Open Ocean Swim Experience, please meet by the starboard side of the ship at 9am — scouring pads will be provided. If you do not have your own shark-repellent please nominate someone in the group to have a full bladder.

A smorgasbord luncheon will be available all day on the main deck. Today's speciality is sushi (freshly brought in [and up!] by seagull).

For exercise there will be some light rowing, followed by a brief break and some medium rowing, followed by rowing.

All-day sunbathing is available on our clothing-optional upper deck.

You are invited to take part in the boat's condensed production of *Annie*. No ability to sing, knowledge of the lyrics or red afro wigs are required. The performance will take place tonight, outside under the stars if it is fine, or outside in the rain under the clouds if it isn't.

The weather for the last few days has been benign and stable. The seas have become variations on small to regular. The winds are fair. Each day the dawn light brings us back from the undead. There is a brief pause, then the pale sun swells until it explodes with searing light. It crawls over the widest part of the sky miserably slowly, with only the shadows from the indifferent clouds providing a brief hint of shelter. Then it sets, and we breathe again, before descending into the endless starry night.

Life on the boat is becoming normal. It no longer occurs to me that the only thing stopping me from sinking through several miles of water to the ocean floor is 9 mm of plywood.

We are becoming more confident. We know exactly how much we need to flick the oars to send them gliding under the rails. We know how much water to add to our Backcountry freeze-dry to get the perfect consistency. We have learnt to ban our pongy clothes from the cabin, and during the day we let them disinfect in the UV rays until they are crisp. I have located the North Star, and I now use it, and other stars closer to the horizon, to steer a course more effectively than the compass when we aren't using the autohelm at night.

I am eating as much as I can, but it isn't enough. Fat is melting away from my gut; my arms are becoming sinewy. My back feels like you could break bricks on it. But my eyes are more sunken. My thoughts are more sluggish and speech comes more slowly.

Sometimes in the afternoons, as a treat, we call friends and family. The calls are planned and savoured, because we have only a very limited number of minutes and sleep is so precious. First, hands have to be dried, then the satellite phone is carefully taken out of its waterproof box and the aerial is screwed in. It's funny how you don't realise how tired you are until you start trying to make complete sentences. That's why the afternoon is best. It's strange calling people, though — for a while you are in their world. Like today I am in a shopping mall in Singapore eating ice-cream and looking for jeans. It's clean, ordered, safe and interesting. Then I hang up and I'm flung back into the middle of the ocean, with a strange feeling of dislocation.

Every time I wake up I remind myself that the ocean isn't infinite. Provided we are going at a fixed speed we will get there eventually. It's mathematically impossible not to. It's impossible not to. It's impossible not to.

The best rowing time is in the evening. As the stifling heat evaporates our mood lifts. Every sunset we sing 'The sun will come out tomorrow'. Then we start what we have come to call the 'Big Session', where we use the long overlapping evening shifts to really focus on getting the most speed out of the boat.

The yarns we tell to pass the nights are getting longer and more elaborate, and more unhurried.

'So I walked into this bar with some mates . . .'

'Hang on, paint the picture. What are you wearing?'

'Jandals, jeans, and a jersey.'

'Bought or hand-knitted?'

'Hand-knitted. My grandmother knitted it for me actually.'

'Oh, does she knit, your grandma?'

And so on.

One morning Jamie comes out from the cabin, looks at me and frowns.

'Wot izt zis! You rowing like unt vomin! Eine veak Vomin! Schnell! Schnell!'

What's he talking about? Oh, that's right. Today is Gay German day — we're spending the morning speaking like Hans the Happy Hairdresser from Hamburg.

Jamie is rummaging through the lunch locker.

'Vo est die schnitzel? Have you heedden ze schnitzel?'

'Ya! Voz me! So schpank me!'

Most days there is a milestone of some sort to celebrate. There are the decile percentages — 20%, 40%, etc. — and the fractions — 25%, 33%. Then there are the absolute distances, which can be distances rowed, and also distances left to go.

On the days with no milestones there is Halloween and Guy Fawkes, a couple of fake birthdays, then national holidays. For Jamaica Day I am planning to stick a cocktail umbrella in the recovery drink and call it a piña colada. Then there are other random days, like tomorrow, which is pencilled in for David Hasselhoff Adulation day. We will celebrate by having a short presentation on 'How the Hoff Brought the End of Communism', and a debate entitled 'The Hoff's Greatest Legacy: *Knight Rider* or *Bay Watch*?'

Jamie is checking the text messages on the sat phone.

'Oh, Rocokoko says hi.'

'Who's Rocokoko?'

'He's a goat.'

'Where does Rocokoko live?'

'In Whiritoa — it's the beach up from Waihi Beach. Mum has a bach there, and my sister Bridget has a house.'

'Sounds great! What's it like?'

'Whiri? It's pretty good. The diving's awesome. We've got a little boat we take off the beach. At night we fry up the scallops and sit round the fire. No, it's pretty good.'

'Is the house close to the beach?'

'Yeah, it's pretty close — you just walk across a little reserve.'

'Sounds great!'

'You should come down when we get back. I'll show you how to pull a cray out.'

'You're on!'

Finding ways to make the time pass is still a priority. 'I spy' was not a success, so I suggest another game idea.

'OK, so I'll tell you three things, and then you have to guess which of the three things are true.'

'OK.'

'I've swum in a piranha-infested river. I've been in a plane crash. I've felt the warmth of Michael J. Fox's bottom.'

'I'm going to say the one about piranhas is true, because the one about Michael J. Fox better not be.'

'Actually, they're all true.'

'You want to do some talking?'

'Yeah, I went into a restaurant in Wellington a few years ago, and when I sat down at a table everyone was looking at me. And then the waitress came over and said that Michael J. Fox had just been sitting there. And you know what? The seat was still warm.'

'OK, I'll go. I have worked as an undertaker, as a chicken sexer, or as a florist.'

'Tell me you were an undertaker.'

'Nup, I'm a florist.'

'You sing show tunes, ballet dance and arrange flowers?'

'Be afraid.'

'I suppose it ties in well with the Home Kill doesn't it? You can knock off the sheep and then leave a nice wreath by the graveside.'

It's night, but I wake up with a bright light in my eyes. It's the full moon coming in through the open hatch. It's so bright it feels hot. Can you get moon-burn?

I move my head so I can look up at it. This is what I have come to see — the full moon out in the middle of the Atlantic.

Then a tiny dark blemish mars the moon's crisp outline. It's like a cloud, but there are no clouds. It's like the shadow of a cloud, but that can't be right. The darkness grows larger and larger — the moon is disappearing right before my eyes.

An eclipse! What are the chances of that? Over the next few hours the interplanetary drama plays out above us. The huge orbs wheel and spin, shadows are cast into space and caught by satellites, and we have a grandstand view. Eventually the moon is completely in the shadows, but then it glows with a faint coppery colour.

I feel very privileged, like I have just been given a present. I've got what I came for. Now I can go home. Pity about the 1300 miles to go.

We have taken to wearing a head-lamp when we get up for our night shifts. The extra light allows us to get into our rowing positions, then we can turn it off and allow our eyes to adjust. Tonight I have the light on for a bit longer because it is so dark. WHAP! I have just been slapped on the side of my head. Ouch. I look down, and there is a wriggling, twitching fish about the size of my hand with a pair of gauzy wings incongruously coming out of its flanks. A flying fish! How weird is that? You don't see flippers on a mouse, why should you see wings on a fish? A couple of powerful twitches and it disappears out one of the scuppers.

A few minutes later I am looking forward when hundreds of flashing silver shapes streak in front of me. It feels like I am being strafed with machine-gun fire. Then they are gone and somehow I have emerged unscathed. I decide to turn the light off.

The arm-wrestle with the Dark Side has reached an uneasy truce. We remain about 50 nautical miles behind. Some days we are a mile or two closer, some days a few miles further away. At least they aren't racing away from us anymore. They are no doubt happy with their lead. That's about two-thirds of a normal day's rowing. They don't have to have the pedal down anymore. If they see us making a spurt they have plenty of time to apply pressure of their own.

Sometimes it feels as if a mile or two gain by us one day will be matched by them the next day — as if they are signalling us not to challenge the status quo, not to try anything. If everyone just keeps their heads we can all enjoy a nice ride to the finish. We are running out of ocean. Soon it will be too late to try anything.

We may not be a problem for DS, but *Rowing Home* are turning into a problem for us. On November 8, a day on which we did a respectable 75 nautical miles, the race website recorded that they rowed an incredible 123 miles. Lin had spoken to them on the phone and reported they were even catching fish as well! They are about 260 miles behind us, but if they pull a few more big days like that it is going to be a very close finish between the three boats.

Lin also told us that *Bright Spark*'s watermaker had broken down, and that the support yacht is having to ferry fresh water to them. *Pura Vida* is having trouble with its watermaker too. This news makes us all the more aware that we are sitting on a water problem of our own. It is now clear that our one good solar panel is working hard to provide the power needed to make the water we drink each day, charge the electronics, and charge the battery to get us through the night. Even on good days there aren't enough sunshine hours left to make significant surplus water. So refilling the ballast tank with fresh water would take days, which just isn't practical now the seas are regularly flexing their muscles.

If the watermaker breaks down having fresh water in the ballast tank won't help us — we'll be out of the race. The key thing is to have enough water to last until the support yacht arrives, and for that we have the day tank and 50 litres of water in plastic containers. We should be all right.

November 10, 10pm — over the hump

A day before the start, in La Gomera, we had met a Spanish crew from the previous race. They told us that when they reached halfway they had a party that lasted for six hours, complete with sangria and paella.

Back at the start our GPS had showed an incomprehensible 2587 nautical miles to Barbados. Now I have just finished a shift and I stay up to watch the large LCD digits count down to 1293 nautical miles to go. I blow a party tooter.

'Halfway then.'

'Yep.'

'So . . . does it feel like we're going downhill?'

'Nup.'

'Row harder then.'

I stand in the footwell looking out at the sun setting into the sea. There is still a lot of sea. I don't know how to feel. I can be proud because I have rowed halfway across an ocean. I can despair because I have half an ocean to row. As painful and uncomfortable as the last few weeks have been, it all has to happen again. It's best not to think at all.

Jamie also seems preoccupied. We spend a lot more time on the Big Session, keeping the pace up. Around 2am it's time for him to go into the first Sleep Shift. As he gets up out of his seat, he says, 'I want you to think about the effort we are going to have to put in if we want to win this race.'

I'm glad he can't see the look on my face. I try to disentangle what I'm feeling. Dismay, because of how frickin' ridiculous it is to expect us to go any faster; horror, at the thought of what would happen if we tried to; and indignation because *he* is asking *me* — I thought I was the Hard Man of the boat. Now he's trying to out-staunch me.

If we want to go faster we either have to row harder or we have to row longer. Harder isn't possible, so it has to be longer. That means less sleep.

But we aren't getting enough sleep at the moment. My face, particularly just before the sun comes up, is like plasticine — I can push a finger into it and the dent stays there for seconds. I seem to remember reading somewhere if you don't get enough sleep you start hallucinating and then you die. We aren't getting nearly enough REM sleep, so we must be near hallucinating.

Physically there is just nothing left to give. If I had more to give I would have given it. I'm feeling worse every day. I'm just trying to manage the deterioration in my condition so that I don't collapse before the end.

So we are second. What's wrong with second? Why can't we just keep on doing what we are doing and maybe the Dark Side will be …uh…abducted by aliens. OK, it's not much of a plan. But it has the big advantage that it doesn't hurt so much and we could still look good. We could stroll up to the finish all relaxed and casual.

When Jamie comes back out we talk about all this. I tell him about the conversation I had during my first meeting with Westlake. We had talked about how the Belgian team had only just beaten the Telecom women's team to fourth place, how Westlake had scoffed about how they were so buggered at the end they could barely walk and had to be helped off the boat.

'So what?' is Jamie's response.

'What do you mean?'

'Would you rather win and be buggered for a few days, or take it easy and drop a place?'

'Yeah, but what's our chance of winning? We're going to munt ourselves for nothing.'

'Mate, unless we try we aren't ever going to know. Do you want to spend the rest of your life guessing?'

Of course he's right. I know he's right. I just wanted to hear him say it.

If nothing else, the extraordinary daily mileage *Rowing Home* has been doing recently means that our grip on second place is looking less and less certain. We have to find another gear.

We talk that night about what it means to us to win. I don't ask about Jamie's motivation; I just have to think about all the sacrifices I have made to be here. All the times I dragged myself out of bed in the dark to go training. All those times that I doubted I was ever going to get there, and the whole thing seemed like pointless vanity. Now I am here.

I am sitting at the top of a mountain of effort. In the context of the last two years of days and nights, the effort to finish the race is trivial. We are out in the middle of the ocean in a rowboat. We might as well row — we have the rest of our lives to sleep. And I think of The Don's advice, of all the people who have ever doubted or insulted me. Maybe it's not the most positive source of motivation, but it's a very effective one.

If there is any time it has to be now — the sooner the better. Our average daily mileage now is around 70–75 nautical miles. If we keep up this pace the race is going to be over in about two and a half weeks. To make up 50 nautical miles in that time means we have to catch up, on average, three to four nautical miles a day. That's a big ask. Even if the Dark Side let us, which would be uncharacteristically charitable of them. Still, as Jamie says, we aren't going to know unless we try.

'Mate, can we really win this?'

'Of course we can.'

'What makes you so sure?'

'Because we only have one Aucklander on our boat; they have two on theirs.'

So it is decided. We will leave everything on the water. We will row our guts out until the finish. If we win that's great. If we come second then we will come so close behind that they won't have had a chance to have a shower. And if we don't do that we will come second but be under the old world record.

'So I expect we are going to have to row a bit longer then?' I suggest.

'Yep.'

'So what's the plan, Shiftmeister?'

'As soon as it starts to get cooler, late in the afternoon, we'll start to row hour and a half on, with half-hour off shifts. That gives us an hour overlap. So we'll do that four times. And then some time after midnight we'll still do our three hour-and-a-half Sleep Shifts, one after another. Then when the sun comes up we'll do hour and a half on, hour off, so we'll have half an hour overlap, and we will do that all day until the afternoon again.'

'Oh yeah, no worries,' I say, once again thankful that Jamie can't see my face, which is mouthing 'What? Are you crazy?' to his back. Half an hour off at night? It's almost not worth getting changed. It's almost not worth getting out of the seat.

'OK, I was thinking of going a bit harder than that, but why don't we start there?' Take that, tough guy!

So it is agreed. This will be our Last Stand, our Big Push. It's time to get a little monkey out here. We are going to row so hard we will decapitate the waves. We will row so fast our rowlocks will glow incandescent. The back swings of our oars will bat seagulls into Venezuela. We will treat the ocean like a big bowl of egg whites and our whirring blades will beat it into fluffy meringue peaks.

We will row until we see Barbados on the horizon. Then we will row faster until we plough up the beach and grind to a halt in a shower of splinters in the carpark of the beach bar. We will row our shattered oar stumps until someone comes out and says, 'Welcome to Barbados!' and offers us a rum punch. Then we will stop. And not before.

We will start tomorrow night. In the morning when the sun comes up we will get everything in order — we will check the equipment, we will make sure the seats are in good condition. And like the three hundred Spartans the night before the battle at Thermopylae, we will wash our hair, sharpen our swords, make peace with the gods and prepare either for the final battle to death — or something that is going to feel similar.

CHAPTER TWENTY ONE

The big push

November 11 — Day 24, the day the rudder breaks

The waves are building again, a little lumpy and disorganised, but still they are waves with a purpose. Late in the afternoon I am on the oars by myself and steering manually to save power, tweaking my heel as required to keep the boat on course.

I move my foot — the stern of the boat doesn't move. I twist my foot the other way — nothing happens. It feels a little loose. I twist my foot again, because I am clearly imagining things. It often appears that things have gone wrong when they haven't — I am often pleasantly surprised. There is no reason why the steering, which has worked so well for the last ten thousand seconds, should choose this second not to work.

I make increasingly large swings with my heel. Nothing happens. Now I feel the cold fingers in my guts. The boat is skewing alarmingly away from its course.

I pull vigorously with my left hand to keep the stern into the waves.

What has happened? Did we hit something? Has the rudder broken off? Keep cool, the rudder is designed to break away. What about the English west–east trans-Atlantic attempt that came unstuck after they lost their rudder. Could we row the rest of the way with no rudder?

With my eyes I trace the cords as they leave the footplate. First they go through a series of pulleys, then they join up with a stainless-steel cable that disappears into a plastic tube mounted through the cabin bulkhead, on the way to the rudder. On one side the normally tight lines are quite slack. The rudder lines have broken.

'Jamie!' I bellow. 'No steering! Check the rudder.'

I see the back hatch pop open and Jamie's mop of hair come out.

'F--k!'

'What?'

'The wire's broken!'

'What do you mean it's broken? It's stainless steel!'

'It's parted down by the pulley.'

'Can we fix it?'

'I don't know.'

Damn. There is no plan for this.

'Let me have a look. Take over the oars for a minute.'

We swap places, then I go into the cabin and stick my head out of the back hatch. On the starboard side, as the steel cable leaves its sheath it goes around a pulley. It is on this pulley that it has frayed to breaking point. Worse, the end has disappeared up the tube that goes into the cabin. And if the end is anything like as frayed as the end that is left hanging off the rudder, then it is going to be impossible to push it back up the tube.

We have to try. I come out of the cabin onto the deck and try to work the cable into the tube. It's useless, like trying to shove a bottlebrush up a pipe with a piece of cooked spaghetti. What now?

I look at Jamie rowing.

'How's the steering going?'

'All right. What do we do now?'

'We're going to have to cut the tube in the cabin.'

'Well, you'd better get on it.'

I go through the toolkit to find the pliers. I hold them up in dismay. They are a true expression of our desire to save weight, and three weeks in the salty environment hasn't improved them any. I'm sure they would be quite good for cutting all sorts of things, like cheese and soggy gingernuts, but not bits of plastic or steel.

In the cabin, a few pinches of the plastic tube reveal that the cable has retreated back to about 60 cm from the transom of the boat. I put the cutting part of the pliers' jaws just in front of the end of the cable. Here goes. No! If I cut here I will be just as badly off. I have to cut behind the cable end. I work away at the plastic until it finally gives way and the frayed end pops out, with all its nasty spiky filaments splayed like a weird gothic hairdo. So now it's simple. Cut the cable to make a neat end and feed it back up the tube out from the transom.

I try the pliers on the cable, squeezing the handles together until they leave big depressions in my hand. Nothing. There is barely a dent on the steel strands. I go outside again to recheck the toolbox. Race rules require us to carry a pretty comprehensive toolkit. I have everything I need to plumb a toilet, or build a house. But there is nothing more potent for cutting steel than what I have in my hand.

Plan B. I am going to have to give the cable end a haircut, trimming the filaments one at a time. I choose a single thin filament and squeeze the jaws of the pliers around it. Nothing. I squeeze harder and work the wire back and forth until the pliers finally gnaw through the steel with a satisfying click. One down, onto the next. I need to be careful to trim the wires into a cone shape to ensure they can be threaded into the plastic tube.

Finally it is done, and I'm ready to try it out. But first I need some slack, so it's out to the deck again to disconnect the cable end from the steering system. Back inside the cabin I tentatively squeeze the cable into the tube. It works! Soon it's out the back of the boat. Now the two ends of the stainless steel cable are dangling next to each other. All I have to do is tie them together in such a way as to make sure the knot doesn't hit the pulley.

But the cable is refusing to be tied. It's slippery and slightly springy, and it's determined to be straight. I am lacerating myself on the spiky ends. To tie this stuff together I need a metre of cable, and if I had that much I could just forget about tying a knot and connect it directly to the rudder.

While I am hanging out the back hatch the stern is surging up and down in the lumpy waves. I am starting to feel queasy. I am also very aware that my wet and greasy hands hold the only tool that can do the job. If I drop the pliers I will have to go in after them. I look out at the swells as I wait for my stomach to settle. There *has* to be a way.

'What's going on down there?' Jamie shouts.

'I can't tie the cable ends together!'

'Why not?'

'The cable's too springy — it won't tie.'

'That shouldn't be a problem.'

'Mate, if you were here you wouldn't be saying that.'

'Mate, if I was there I'd be tying one of my fencing knots.'

Of course, Jamie is a fencer. How could I forget!

'Mate, it's all yours!'

I wriggle back out to the deck and swap places with Jamie.

Ten minutes later: 'Done!'

Jamie comes out looking chuffed with himself.

'Well, I guess that makes you the boat bitch for the rest of the day!'

'Would you just Schnut up and Schnell?'

But I am very pleased. I go back to the oars while Jamie finishes his break. As I come off the adrenaline I am left with a nauseous anxiety. What if this had happened in the middle of the night? What if it had been during a storm? What about the cable on the other side — is that about to go?

This shouldn't have happened — the cable is 6 mm stainless steel going around a fat pulley. Why did it break? What else is going to happen next? Worse, we have lost about an hour of useful rowing — that's maybe two or three miles.

But in the end we got it going again, and when my break comes round I lie down and sleep hits me like an avalanche. I can barely keep my eyes open, and I have to do a shift in a few minutes' time.

When I come out it's getting dark.

'Still ready for the Big Push?'

'I'm feeling a bit flat actually,' says Jamie.

'Oh, what's the matter?'

'No, I mean the seat's gone down.'

'What about the spare?'

'I tried, it's stuffed as well.'

And now it's too dark to fix it. It will have to wait until tomorrow. No Big Push tonight.

The position text comes through — the Dark Side have extended their lead another three miles. I guess there is some encouragement to be taken from this. If it hadn't been for the steering breaking we would have pulled the same distance.

⤬

November 12 — Day 25, Big Push take 2

My trembling hands place another sliver of rubber over a tiny fissure and the inflated seat holds.

Our rowing efforts are being curiously unrewarded, despite the pressure coming from the building seas and fair winds. The boat seems strangely sluggish. Despite having cleaned it only three days ago we must have barnacles the size of sausages down there, or else we are rowing through a patch of treacle.

A barnacle swim is booked for midday. But this will be a different kind of swim than the one in the doldrums, when the boat was dead in the water. Now, with the strong wind and big waves, the boat will happily gallop off without us.

Jamie looks out at the water going past us. 'Should we do it one at a time?'

'Nuh, let's just hit it quick.'

With a quick and completely ineffectual scan for dorsal fins we lower ourselves overboard and clip our safety harnesses onto the grab line. Underwater the boat is an ugly sight. When I wipe my hand over the hull there is no space bigger than a playing card that is free of growths. The boat is kicking and bucking in the waves and as Jamie and I work opposite each other one person's yank is another's hoist.

I am still scrubbing long after the novelty of holding my breath, diving down and clinging onto the keel in the shadow of the boat has well and truly worn off. Despite frequent glances into the blue opaqueness, there is an increasingly nagging awareness that the longer we flap about in the water the more we are testing our luck against whatever lurking sea beastie is certainly down there. It takes us nearly a frustrating hour to clear the boat completely. But now the hull is clean, the seats are plump. We are in good shape. Tonight, the Big Push.

At 10pm boat time I come out for my shift and push the GPS

button that drops an electronic waypoint at our location. The Big Push has officially started. Now let's see how much we can do in 24 hours.

During the Big Session Jamie comes up with a new game.

'OK, so guess my middle name.'

'Arnold.'

'No.'

'Sebastian.'

'No.'

'Humphrey?'

'No.'

'Gwendoline.'

'Isn't that a girl's name?'

'Fine. Gwendolino.'

'Do you want a clue?'

'No, I think I'm nearly there. Michel.'

'Michelle is a girl's name.'

'I meant Michel — you might be French.'

'Fitzgerald is Irish.'

'Mick? Paddy? Sean?'

'No. Are you sure you don't want a clue.'

'No, what's the rush? Bob? Bruce? Barry?'

'No. No. No.'

It's amazing how the hours fly past.

But the half-hour breaks are absurd. With the best will in the world it is still five minutes into the break before I can shut my eyes. And then I have to be awake at least six minutes before my shift. We have cut all the corners we can, but we can't get it down to less than six minutes. That means a maximum nap of 19 minutes. I do sleep. Soundly. For the first few times the novelty of waking up after such a short break is enough to distract me from the discomfort. Then it becomes brutal. My subconscious produces the sneaky, evil thought that maybe we are doing permanent damage to ourselves. I try to ignore it.

Staying awake isn't a problem when we are both rowing. It isn't even too bad when you only have half an hour by yourself. By the time Jamie goes in and comes back out again it's only 20 minutes. And you can count them down if you have to. I have to. I turn the iPod up loud and play some Van Halen, or I listen to comedy like Ali G's interview with Posh and Becks, and I can get through the 20 minutes.

The problem comes when we start our Sleep Shifts of an hour and a half each. By now it's 2 or 3am, and as soon as Jamie disappears into the cabin I can feel my thoughts starting to wander and my movements become uncoordinated. I have my drink bottle next to me filled with water. I try pouring it over my head. Ahh, that's better. Hmm, no it isn't. I was dry and sleepy. Now I am wet and sleepy. I need to think of some other way.

When the neoprene started coming off the oar handles a few days ago we clamped it back on with a cable tie. After clipping off the tail there is a rough plastic bump which I normally try to place in between my fingers. Now I move my fingers slightly until the middle finger is on top of the rough tag. I tighten my grip until it starts to bite into the skin. Not bad, not bad, it is quite pleasantly painful. I see how far I can pull in until I wimp out. I try sawing it from side to side. The pain is quite distracting, good. One hour 19 minutes to go.

November 13 — Day 26

It's early in the day. The sun has just turned me from a clenched huddle back into a human. The seas are very large, looming around and over the boat. It is morbidly fascinating to see the big swells play with us. Some of them are so big I want to wake Jamie up and point them out. It's only fair that he should see the wave that snuffs us. But just as we are about to be buried we reach the base of the cliff, the stern of the boat tilts up and we slowly waft up and over.

There are still those little birds around the boat and sitting on the water. What can they live on out here? There's another one.

WHUMPF.

My face is wet and stinging and I'm spitting out salt water. I open my eyes to see water pouring out of the scuppers. The bilge pump in the footwell is regurgitating water out the side. A wave must have toppled directly onto the back of the cabin. Oh no, the back hatch is up. What's happened to Jamie?

Jamie kicks open the hatch and water pours out.

'Shit . . . sorry mate, did it get ya?'

Jamie laughs. 'Mate! You think so?'

Jamie spends the rest of his break bailing and mopping the back. Even the high-mounted fuse panel got wet, so we turn off all the electrics to let them dry out. Jamie starts pulling other stuff out to dry on the deck. Out comes a sopping black polyprop.

'Hey, that's my polyprop.'

'No, that's mine.'

'Yeah, no, really. I've been using it as a pillow.'

'Yeah? Me too!'

The weather has veered around slightly to the east, so we are rowing at an angle to the waves. The boat develops a nasty rolling action and rowing becomes difficult. We try different angles, and find that by putting slightly more beam-side into the wind, and positioning a couple of water containers off-centre, the boat becomes a lot more stable. We are going more south than we strictly should, but the isochrones tell us that the increase in speed is worth it. Now, when we are rowing together, we are managing to steam along at 4 knots, sometimes more, for several hours.

It's late at night and we are both watching the GPS as it counts up the last few seconds to 10pm. I am feeling confident that we have done a solid distance; last night we were rowing together strongly, and again this evening. Things may have got a bit ropey in the small hours, but today has been a sound effort, mostly 3 knots and above. The clock displays 10pm, Jamie flicks back his oars, detaches himself from the boat, and gets up to bring the GPS to the distance screen — 81 nautical miles. Not bad. Not bad at all.

But how did the Dark Side do? We have to wait for the website to update. Before his next shift Jamie sits in the hatchway, jabbing at the sat phone, dialling the number that prompts the text messages to come through. I'm impatient.

'Come on! What does it say?'

'Hang on. Here it is: "13/11 LAST 24HRS TO 10PM, DS 80NM".'

They did 80 miles? You're kidding me. You are absolutely kidding me. All that work has been for nothing. Damn. It's hopeless. I knew it was hopeless.

'Well . . . I've heard better news,' I say.

Jamie doesn't say anything. He gets up, pours some muesli into a bowl, adds water and sits in the hatch, chewing.

'I think it's pretty good news.'

Like how? I think. But instead I say, 'Well, it's good to be going faster, but it isn't much of a gain.'

'Look at it like this — is 80 miles a big day or a normal day?'

'It's a big day.'

'OK, so chances are, for whatever reason, they're putting on a push of their own.'

'OK.'

'So they busted a gut and we still went further than them. I think that's pretty good news.'

Damn, he's right! Well maybe, but if I have a choice I might as well believe in something that is going to motivate rather than demotivate me.

In the early hours we again swap to the hour-and-a-half Sleep Shifts. The cheer that came from the laughter and camaraderie evaporates almost immediately. The comforting, vigorous clockwork rowing action is replaced by custom hacking. But the moon is up and I am mesmerised by the magical sparkling trail that we leave in the sea as we rise and fall on the backs of giant silvery swells. I'm having trouble keeping my eyes open. I could do with a coffee; I could do with immersing my head in a bucket of tepid long black. But there is no coffee on the boat.

My eyes feel as if they are firmly and persistently being poked into the back of my head. I have lost control of them anyway — they feel like they are pointing in different directions. I once read a *National Geographic* article about the Wodaabe tribe of Africa, who consider it very attractive to be able to roll your eyes independently. Right now the Wodaabes would treat me like royalty. I could be King Kevin, Wuler of the Wodaabes. And it doesn't matter what way you come at me I can see you coming.

There is a lightness behind the back of my throat. Like my head is being disconnected.

Hmm, nice and warm, soft things . . . YOU'RE FALLING ASLEEP. What! What! Oh yeah. Shit. Shit. Keep the speed up. Give me ten good ones. Let's get back to 3 knots.

This is nuts. I need to raise the bar here. Let's try something different. I wait until I start to get that warm dreamy feeling and feel the weightlessness come up from my toes. This time at the end of the stroke I briefly drop the right oar and swing a flat hand at my face.

WAP!

Ow! That stung. But am I more awake? Hmm, yes a little. More startled then anything else. Still, it's better than nothing.

Oh, here comes the feeling again. Right. I'm going to really let myself have it. Here goes.

WAP!

That one made me blink. Ouch. Ouch. That was a good one, my right cheek is quite numb. I make chewing motions to bring it back to life. Awake now! All right! I think this is going to work.

Woosh. Damn, I flinched.

Well it's hard not to. I know it's coming, it's hard to surprise myself. Well I'm just going to have to harden up. Just you wait, brother. Just you wait.

This is a war of my conscious against my subconscious. My mind craves sleep, and it is taking some pretty desperate measures to get it. It's like my subconscious has been locked in a room. It isn't allowed to barge out the Door of Apathy, so it has to float out the Window of Distraction.

It starts with an innocent thought that sets my mind wandering until the associations get freer and freer, down a path into unconsciousness, until by chance I happen to think of something that references the boat again and mental alarms go off, the shuffling neurons snap back into a march, my head jerks up and I look at the GPS.

But now I'm feeling OK. Hey, this is good music — didn't I hear that at that wedding? They had really good sausages at the reception. It would be nice to have a sausage now . . . hmm, yes . . . sausages . . . plenty of gravy from the gravy boat. Boat? WAKE UP!

Damn. OK then, this time you've earned it. And this time keep your head still, will you? And really put your back into that slap. I want to see stars.

WAP!

The hatch door flicks open.

'What's going on out there?'

'I'm beating myself up.'

'Well give yourself one for me.'

'Will do.'

'You might want to try using the pot.'

'Ta.'

The only good thing about the seat puncturing again is that I don't have to slap myself anymore to stay awake. I don't bother changing to our one good cushion. I can use the sensation of my buttock rocking on the carbon fibre to help me stay awake.

November 14 — Day 27, consolidation day

As soon as the sun comes up we start repairs. Jamie finds the holes, and I choose the one that we are going to put the last molecules of the patch on. Now we are down to just two working cushions. Any more punctures and we are on our arses, at least part of the time, unless we can think of some other seat idea.

It's another scorching day. Sheltering from the sun in the back cabin I plot our position on the isochrone chart. According to it, we just reached the line in the ocean that indicates we are 16 days away from the end.

I really like 16 as a number. The figure 6 has a big tummy on it, so it reminds me of a fat, jovial person. Like Friar Tuck or something. So 16 is like a monk standing next to a lamp-post. There's a pleasing symmetry about 16. I mean, four fours are sixteen. And two twos are four. It's certainly one better than 17, which is a loner. But in our current situation 16 is not quite as good as 15. With 15 days to go you can tell yourself that it's only two weeks, whereas 16 is two weeks plus two, so it's a bit cheeky to call it two weeks.

Two weeks, 14 days. Then after that we would be in the second to last week. Then at the end of each day that week we could tell ourselves that we only have to do that weekday one more time. Then it would be the last week. Then it will be over.

I need to change direction so I twist my foot — only the shoe breaks completely free from the foot-stretcher. It's not completely unusable, but it is now difficult to use the foot steering from the bow position. I am turning into the official Boat Rhino. What's next to break?

The sun is setting and the endless night stretches out in front of me. It's time for some fun.

Me in my best cheesy, eager, earnest Broadway stage voice: 'Oh boy, Jim! Isn't it getting dark outside?'

'Nup. Looks good to me.'

'Look harder, Jim; that night sure is getting powerful dark!'

Jamie sighs. 'It sure is, Kev!'

'Don't it feel like your insides are shrivelling up sometimes and you can't go on?'

'It sure does, Kev.'

'You know what I think at times like this, Jim?'

'What, Kev?'

'The sun will come out tomorrow! Betcha bottom dollar that tomorrow . . .'

Jamie joins in and we bellow together. A pair of dismayed petrels fly away grumpily.

'There. Don't you feel better now?'

'Jeepers you're a worry.'

I'm worried that we are going to go cuckoo in the Sleep Shifts again. At the moment we are both putting in a huge amount of rowing from well before sunset to the small hours of the morning, with only half-hour breaks. Then we are expecting ourselves to stay awake alone for an hour and a half, in the most metabolically challenged part of the night. So I suggest that we start with one-hour shifts to get us ready for the hour and a half alone on the oars.

It seems to work. I am listening to a Howard Hughes biography which is fantastic, and I am still pretty with it by the time Jamie comes out for his shift.

Next time I come out Jamie says it looks like there is a bit of a storm brewing. So I look, and there is a huge squall covering half the horizon.

I am hoping it is going to miss us, but it is much bigger than that. It starts to bucket with rain, so I spend a miserable first half-hour with the boat canted over to one side, pulling hard just to stay warm. Which is such a shame because during the day we are hanging out for rain, and then we get it when we least want it!

Then the wind starts blowing from different directions. At one stage it is howling in our faces and pushing us along at 5 knots, and another time it's right in the middle of my back and I really hope that it is just a squall passing over and not a front harbouring a wind change. Then the wind drops until there is no wind at all, and now we are just ticking along on eerily still seas.

Normally with the starlight you can make out something of the seascape, but now it is quiet and eerily calm. Maybe there is a fog out there? It's spooky.

CHAPTER TWENTY TWO

'Excuse me, have you seen Jamie?'

We are 1000 miles out of Barbados when the fatigue poisons really start to kick in.

Maybe it is the nervous tension decompressing from the squall, but this time unconsciousness doesn't sneak up on me, it pounces. This is a shame because I have to get the paint, and the paint is in the fishing village just off the starboard side where the range of thickly wooded hills falls steeply into the sea. Next to the Japanese fishing village I can see the graceful sampans in the harbour; the village itself is mostly in the dark, but I can make out some of the roofs and see the lanterns burning in the windows. Now I wonder where they put that paint. I twitch my foot to head over to it. We need the paint. To paint the boat. Boat?

DAMN! DAMN! DAMN! I steer back on course and am so angry with myself I stay alert through the rest of the shift.

But then Jamie doesn't respond to the six-minute call. I leave it for a minute, then I start banging on the hatch with the spare oar. He sticks out his head, looking very confused, then says, 'What flavour do you want?' I decide to play along, saying, 'What have you got?' He doesn't say anything — he just passes me the survival suit and says, 'Strawberry,' still looking confused.

When he eventually comes out I tell him about what has just happened. He says, 'You're making that bullshit up!'

Then it happens again at the next changeover. This time, when he opens the hatch he says, 'Do you want fondue or lobster hotpot?'

'Fondue! When are you going to start rowing?'

I figure I will just slip into the cabin and have my kip for an hour, then I will either come out and find him normal or he will be squatting on the rail flapping his elbows and clucking. I pitch forward into the blackness of the cabin.

><

November 15 — Day 28

The autohelm is mounted close to one of the scuppers. I've noticed that each time we get a good surge on going down a wave it gets a dose of corrosive seawater all over it. Electronics and salt water have always had an uneasy relationship, and now the inevitable has happened. In a dying spasm the autohelm extends right to the end of its metal arm, gives an R2D2-like squawk, then refuses to move. We are left lolling broadside onto the sea so it is a few seconds later, after I have done a high-speed replumbing of the steering lines, that I am back in my seat and feeling its loss. The autohelm has been incredibly helpful during the day — now we are going to have to steer manually. The only consolation is that as the seas have become bigger we have been using it less and less.

So what's going to be next to break?

In the morning the text message comes through:

15/11 10AM YOU 54 BEHIND. ROWING HOME 267 BEHIND
YOU

Shit! On the first day of the Big Push we were 51 miles behind. Now we are 54. We have gone backwards. We are as far behind as we have ever been. Our Big Push has laid a rotten egg. It's been one bloody thing after another — the rudder, the seats, the foot-stretcher, the autohelm.

During the Big Session there is a long discussion about how we are going. Averagely, it has to be said. But this is about pride now. It doesn't matter how crap we are doing, we have to give it everything. The aim is still to leave it all on the water. As Jamie says, 'If we row our guts out we might still be able to catch them.'

'Tell me about the weekend we're going to have in Whiritoa.'
　　'Well, first we'll arrive, then we'll unpack the cars.'
　　'What day is it?'
　　'It's a Saturday.'
　　'Can I come down on a Friday night?'
　　'Sure. We'll have a few quiets on the deck.'
　　'What's the weather like?'
　　'Sunny. It's always sunny.'
　　'Sunny, but not hot though, eh?'
　　'Oh no, sunny and cool.'
　　'Then what?'
　　'Then we hit the sack, ready for the dive the next day.'
　　'Right. Tell me about the diving.'
　　'Mate, you drop off the boat, it's a 100-foot vis, you go down to the bottom, open up your dive bag and stand back to let the crays walk into it.'
　　'Yeah? You know, I met a guy once who told me you can balance a crayfish on its nose.'
　　'Crayfish don't have noses — are you thinking of a mouse?'
　　'Balance a crayfish on a mouse? That's one clever mouse!'
　　'Could kick Mickey's arse.'
　　'For sure.'

I don't know where I am.
　　I'm standing, naked. I am at peace, not concerned, just a little perplexed. Lights are flashing. I can't make it out, but there's a form.

254

There is mostly darkness, but in the middle a bright white light. I'm here for a purpose, I don't know what.

'What do I do now?' I ask.

'Put on your pants,' says the voice.

So I do. I am still unclear. 'Now what?'

'Sit down.'

I sit, though my seat is uncomfortable. I can't see well, but I can feel hard things in my hands. What are these for? I gently move them, my body hurts. This can't be right.

'What do I do now?'

'Oh, for f--k's sake! Row, ya bastard!'

November 16 — Day 29, the Big Push finally pays off

In the morning I pull out the satellite phone and put the aerial on. As I wait for it to start up I'm thinking about what to expect. We rowed well last night, at least in the early part. There were no major malfunctions. Maybe high 70s?

'What does it say?' asks Jamie.

'They reckon we did 72 to 10am this morning.'

'Is that all?'

'Yep.'

'What about the Dark Side?'

'63.'

'How many?'

'63.'

'How many?'

'Six three.'

'What do you reckon?'

'It's a mistake.'

'Yeah, it must be.'

But what if it's true? It's a bit weird. For the last two days they have been rowing low 80s and high 70s, and now they suddenly drop into the 60s. Either someone has entered a dodgy number into the website or they have suffered some misfortune. Still, as far as news goes, it's better than a piece of regurgitated fish. As Jamie says, 'If we row our guts out we might just be able to catch them.'

That afternoon the Big Session goes well. It isn't until early in the morning when we start the Sleep Shifts that things get mysterious. Jamie goes in first, but just ten minutes later he reappears and stands in the footwell trying to untangle the headphone cord from his neck, as if he is getting ready to start rowing again. I decide to have him on.

'So how come you are so late for your shift?'

He mumbles something and sits down in his rowing seat. Oh, he really is messed up.

'Jamie, go back to bed — you've got another hour of your break.'

It takes a few seconds for it to sink in. Then he looks at his watch, shouts, 'Oh f--k!' and leaps into the cabin.

I have been getting a strange feeling at night, as if there is someone else on the boat. Me, Jamie and another. Maybe I'm counting myself twice?

But sure enough, when I next come out for my shift there is someone I don't recognise sitting at the oars. I can't make him out in the shadows. I watch him for a while. He pays me no attention. But I feel like I have to know.

'Excuse me, have you seen Jamie?' I ask politely.

'Oh mate, you're going to have to give yourself another slap!'

I have been out here for a hundred years. It's going to be great to get my sleep.

'Six minutes!' I bellow.

Jamie kicks open the hatch. Great, he's awake.

'Mate?'

'Yes?'

'What time did you start your shift?'

'Ahh, 3am.'

'And what time is it now?'

I peer at the LCD digits. They are swimming around. Then they clarify. Whoops.

'Umm, 3:10. Sorry, it felt a bit later. See you at 4:30.'

'No problem.'

When I come out for the last Sleep Shift Jamie has half a cushion under each cheek. One side of his has sprung a leak, so he's blown up one side of one of the others that only has a slow leak. So now, from the three Rohos we only have half of one side that stays up and half of another side that has a slow leak.

Now there is a new routine. It's the role of the person moving into the seat to try and get a grip on the slick greasy rubber, wipe the other person's sweat off the valve as best they can, put the metal valve into their mouth and blow a few quick puffs in. The valve has to be screwed shut while the air pressure is going in. That means trying to spin it closed while it's still in your mouth. I will be very happy when we don't have to do this anymore. What are we going to use as another seat cushion?

><

November 17 — Day 30

As the sun comes up I think I have a solution. We are going to have to use the Thermarest. The floor of the cabin is insulated anyway. And even if it was strewn with hot coals we would sleep on it.

On the next shift I concertina up the Thermarest and let most of the air out, then I place it on top of the Throne. It feels like I am sitting on top of a basketball on top of a seesaw. I have to do the hula just to stay upright. My abs are getting a pretty good workout. Actually, I'm not sure that that's a bad thing — Hot Polish Girl might appreciate them. It isn't great, but it works.

This afternoon we are booked in for another barnacle swim. But with the seas the way they are it isn't going to be relaxing. Even with neither of us rowing, just peering nervously over the side, the boat is surging forward on the wave traffic.

Jamie puts on his safety harness, clips the end onto the grab rope and slides into the water. Somehow he loses his grip on the boat and floats away very quickly for the two metres before his safety harness yanks tight. We look at each other.

I let myself over the other side, with more care now I can see how fast the boat is going. I am so concerned about holding on that I don't put on my goggles, which are just sitting around my head. As my head bobs under they come away. I flail around trying to find them but they have been swept away. Bugger.

I can't stop thinking about the horror of being separated from the boat. And with the boat skidding and sliding toward South America with every wave, it's only a thin piece of rope that stops it from being a certainty. Morbidly, I let the safety line play out until it is tight, to feel the next surge pull me along. The things you do when you don't have SKY.

Jamie shouts from the other side of the boat. 'Bloody hell!'

'What?'

'I've been stung!'

'By what?'

'It's one of those little blue jellyfish.'

'A bluebottle?'

'Yeah, I think so.'

'How bad is it?'

'Yeah, not too bad. Come on, let's get it done.'

The hull is in pretty good condition so we don't need to hang around. The thought of stinging jellyfish in the water adds even more vigour to my scrubbing, and it's a relief to be back on deck. Jamie shows me the back of his hand — it looks a little puffy. He can still grip though, and he doesn't think it's going to slow him down.

This time it's Jamie's turn to get the text.

'We only did 73.'

'Only 73?'

'Well, that's not too bad.'

Jamie pushes the buttons and I see a look of surprise on his face. He nods, looking satisfied. Then he turns off the phone, takes off the aerial, pulls in his legs and shuts the hatch.

I'm not going to ask. I'm not going to ask. I'm not going to ask. Me not asking. Ask me no. No ask. Ask.

'Bastard! OK, OK, you can tell me!'

He opens the hatch and gives me a cheeky grin.

'67!'

'Well if we row our guts out we might still be able to catch them.'
'Yep!'

Whatever is happening with them, it's still happening. Or maybe we are just rowing harder than they are?

The Big Session is going well and the boat is humming along, stable as a billiard table. Our oars swing in time, with a sturdy clockwork thunk. I have an idea.

'Hey, how about we think up some army chants? You know, when the platoon is out running together and they're all singing?'

'What have you got?'

'I'll have a think . . . OK try this. You have to repeat each line after me.'

> I want to be an Atlantic Man
> Shave myself with a Pringles can
> I want to see that Atlantic scenery
> Fish for sharks with a bucket of pee.

'Ha! Yeah, not bad. Hang on . . . OK OK, I got one!'

> Little waves, big waves, we don't stop
> We don't care if there's snow on top.
> Who said that rowing isn't fun?
> I'm growing boils on my bum.

'Good one. So when are we going to hear the twins story?'

'When it gets really shitty.'

'It might be soon.'

During the day I have started to be very strict about getting sleep, horrified at what the late-night shifts might bring. At the end of each shift I jump from my seat to the sanctuary of the back cabin as if propelled by a giant spring. Jamie is spending more time cleaning up and working around the boat. The result is that he is starting to look very weary at night. This evening I have an idea.

'You know, I reckon Holiday Shoppe would fly us back Business Class if we won. At least once we're on Qantas.'

'Do you reckon?'

'Yep!'

'What's it like? Are the seats any better?'

'Mate, it starts before you even get on the plane! You want to hear about Business Class?'

'Sure.'

'You know when you walk into the airport to catch a flight and there's a huge line?'

'Yeah.'

'Well, when you're in Business Class you walk right up to your own counter. Qantas in Auckland even have their own hall. It's where all the movie stars go. So even if you have to wait in line behind one person you don't mind because it's Angelina Jolie.'

'Keep talking.'

'Yep. And then when you get on board they offer you a drink straightaway — champagne, whiskey, anything.'

'Waikato Draught?'

'From the tap, in iced glasses.'

'Archibald?'

'What?'

'Your middle name.'

'Look. I'll give you a clue — it starts with B.'

'Bruce? Benjamin?'

'Think of Switzerland.'

'Bocholate? Bondue? Billiam Bell? Beidi?'

'Think of brandy.'

'Napoleon!'

'No, I'll give it to you. It's Bernard.'

'Bernard? What's that got to do with brandy and Switzerland?'

'You know, that dog that rescues people in the snow, with a barrel tied to its head.'

At the shift change after the first hour I take over from Jamie and he goes into the cabin. A few minutes later his head suddenly appears like a jack-in-the-box, saying that he wants to have an eight-minute wake-up call, because he wants to make a meal before the next shift.

So at eight minutes to go I started calling him. Nothing. At five minutes to go he finally opens the hatch. He has his bum up in the air with his head down on the floor. Snoring. I say, 'Three minutes to go!' and he says, 'Yep. Three minutes.' And he turns and shuts the hatch!

This is strange, so at two minutes I say, 'Two minutes!' and I hear, 'Yeah, yeah, two minutes to go — yeah, yeah.' And finally, on the hour, the hatch door springs open but he still has his bum in the air and his snout in the pillow. I say, 'Well that's time then,' and he goes, 'Yeah, yeah.' And I say, 'So that would be time for you to start rowing.' Then something finally seems to click, because he looks up in surprise and says, 'It would be nice to have some warning! What happened to the calls before that?'

Unknown to us, back in New Zealand reporters at TVNZ and TV3 have arrived at work to find they have received a curious email headed 'There's no honour without integrity'. The email states that the speed at which *Holiday Shoppe* is catching *CRC* is too fast to be credible — that we are up to something.

Teresa also receives the email. She tells Lin out on the support yacht, who starts heading toward us to investigate.

CHAPTER TWENTY THREE

The one about the argument

November 18 — Day 31

Another really hot day today. We see the bridge of a ship on the horizon. It seems to be a few hundred yards long, so maybe it's an oil tanker. We try to raise it on the VHF but there is no reply. I'm glad we aren't trying to call it from a life raft.

18.11 10AM DS 67. HS 78. 688 TO GO. GO BOYS GO!

Why are the Dark Side going so slow? Who cares! Now we are only 27 nautical miles behind. But we are running out of water. It looks like the race is going to be over in less than ten days. Which means if we can keep our speed up and don't get any bad headwinds just before the end, like they did in 2001, we might just sneak under the world record!

We call up Lin on the Challenge yacht for news of the fleet. The last boat is the French one, *Madine Meuse Lorraine*, with their impromptu rower. Lin says the support yacht has recently gone past *Rowing Home*, and she is very impressed with their rowing technique and ability to catch waves. More ominously, she warns that the weather is going to turn bad. Strong winds are predicted from the southwest or south. Of the Dark Side there is no news. Although if there was bad news Lin isn't really in a position to tell us.

We started the Big Session as normal at eight o'clock, doing the one and a half hour on, half hour off. Unfortunately the good weather and conditions have gone and we are running through a piece of very bad water. It's very strange, as the water and the weather look exactly the same as they did 24 hours ago and yet we are going noticeably slower for the same amount of output, which is very, very frustrating. It may be strange, but it's not unfamiliar. Something like this happened just before the weather went bad on Day 2, when it felt like the advancing wind was shovelling up the water.

I was worried that there were going to be some thunderstorms at night, because it has been such a hot day with such big, fat clouds. But nothing eventuates. I spoke to Rob at midnight and we talked about the wind, which has started to swing around to the east, and whether this marks the front that is coming. Rob convinced me that it would be a good idea to head a degree or two further south, so that the coming southerly will put us back on track. So now we are heading further south, even though it is taking about half a knot off us.

But as I nod off just after making this tape I realise that the rowing noises are sounding strange. I look out and Jamie is rowing, kind of, but mostly weaving from side to side with his eyes closed. It looks like he is doing a Stevie Wonder impersonation.

'Hey mate, are you awake?'

'Yeah, yeah!'

I try to go to sleep but it still isn't right, and when I look back he is still doing it.

'Are you sure you're all right?'

'Yep.'

'Coz you look like you're going to fall off your seat.'

'I don't need you to check up on me!' Maybe he is awake.

'I thought you were asleep!'

'I'm doing 2 knots!'

'It's not how fast you're going, it's how fast *they* are going.'

'Don't tell *me* about rowing fast!'

He hasn't said much to me since. So I suppose he really must have been awake.

November 19 — Day 32

The text the next morning tells a grim story. We only managed 29 nautical miles overnight, compared with 40 miles the previous night. The Dark Side haven't polled, so we can't check how badly we are doing against them. We can only hope that this weather is affecting them as much as it is us.

It is heavily overcast. The sun rises up behind the clouds and the temperature remains blessedly cool.

I finished my last Sleep Shift at around 7am, and when I came out the ocean had lost its beautiful freshly ploughed look. Now it's like we are in a bathtub with a three-year-old. Waves are coming from all over the compass. The wind has swung around and established itself from the south. So far it isn't too strong but it is slowing us down. We're slow, but it's no Day 2. It's going to be a long two or three days until this passes. I suppose it was expecting too much to have the good weather hold out until we got to the finish, so it looks like we won't get under the record now. Neither will the Dark Side.

My shoulder started to hurt today. In a way it's a blessing that the wind is tending to roll us over, because it means I don't have to use my arm so much on that side. Rowing on the Thermarest is murder on my stomach.

Jamie hasn't really talked to me today other than a few lines at the last shift. He seems to be a bit surly. I don't know quite how to approach him. I guess we will talk tonight.

It's a strange day without the usual banter, each of us lost in our own world between the headphones, steaming under the sun. Maybe he has taken offence at what I said.

It's late afternoon when the sting has gone out of the heat and muscles start to unclench that I try to break the silence. It helps that we aren't looking at each other.

'So, Jamie, what's on your mind, mate?'

There's a long pause. I start to think that he hasn't heard me.

Finally he says, 'You know when Rob first called me over to his house to tell me I was in the team?'

'Yeah?'

'Well, he and I had a pretty honest chat.'

'Yeah?'

'He told me he was worried that I was too young to deal with what this race was all about. I've never used my age as an excuse for a poor performance, and to hear him say that, well, it just pushed my button. I was fuming, and I told myself that I would prove him wrong. Now, here we are, and I'm dropping my game. But I'm not going to let it happen again. So, sorry mate, for being a bit quiet.'

At first I feel sympathetic to his outburst of honesty, then I'm bewildered that it has taken this long for the guy to show a few cracks.

'Mate, don't worry about it,' I say. 'We just have to work out ways to stay awake.'

So we agree to try and tweak the shifts again, to ease into the full-on Sleep Shifts. And that we aren't to let a brother come out to the oars sleepwalking, and we give ourselves permission to grill each other until we are satisfied we are OK.

Afterwards I feel relieved, grateful that the air has been cleared.

'Tell me some more about Business Class,' Jamie asks.

'Mate, you want to know a tip?'

'What?'

'Ask the hostie for a survey form when you sit down.'

'Why?'

'Because then you get the extra-special service. You get a *lot* of personal attention.'

'What kind of attention?'

'Well, that depends on who you are flying with.'

'How about Thai?'

'Free foot massage.'

'True!'

'Yep. Well, maybe just one of your feet. They haven't got all day.'

November 20 — Day 33, the storm cometh

20/11 10AM. YOU 22NM BEHIND

Which means for the last 36 hours the two boats have been going about the same speed. They are holding us off. That's all they need to do for the next week.

Since yesterday the wind has been from the south so somewhat on our beam, but it has been manageable — we have still been able to make progress at between 2 and 3 knots. But now when I look over my shoulder there is no mistaking the fact that something is coming. On the horizon there is a line of massed cloud, impenetrable and purple with energy. The sea has turned a jade green underneath it. The wind is getting stronger and the ridges of the waves are lined with white. It's so striking that I take a photo. It's the kind of science fiction-looking cloud that heralds the arrival of an alien spaceship. If we are going to be munted by a storm it might as well be a freaky-looking one. If only I was looking at it in a *National Geographic*.

The wind is now more or less from the south-southwest. It is a flawless wall. It is an invisible, perfectly repulsing force, like when you try to push the same poles of two magnets together.

The churning green seas start knocking us back. We struggle as the boat pitches up and down. It's Day 2 all over again. Except then we were as strong as oxes, and now we are little lambs. We are both rowing together and making little headway. Logic soon starts to poison my thoughts. *This isn't right, we don't need to do this. We are putting too much strain on ourselves. They'll have their sea anchor out. If we both have a short break we will be much fresher, and then we can go faster.*

My body desperately wants me to listen, but I am deeply suspicious. I know how my brain works. It will put forward all kinds of reasonable ideas about why I should stop. But then Jamie's shoe breaks off the stern foot-stretcher and we can't row together anymore. We need both of us rowing to make any progress, so now we have to put out the sea anchor.

Once again I am kneeling on the bow pulling out the metres and metres of nylon fabric and feeding it into the water. It opens out and the line goes taut.

Jamie starts to work on the shoe. I sit in my seat, my head hanging down, too tired to move. There is a painful ache behind my eyes. My arms don't work. I feel utter and complete fatigue. I am flatlined. Spent.

I feel a drop of liquid fall on my knee — is it going to rain as well? No, it is saliva drooling from my open mouth. This is bleak. We have dug so deep for so long. There is nothing left. There was nothing left a week ago, and now I feel far worse. But this lack of movement feels horribly wrong. I don't know what to do — I have to make choices, but I don't know what to do.

The GPS shows us sliding up to the north. My voice is a hoarse croak: 'Mate, we can't stop rowing.'

'Why?'

'Because they think we are still rowing. They'll remember what happened on Day 2. So they aren't going to stop.'

'Yeah.'

'So we can't stop. Can you pass out the isochrones?'

I stare at the curves, trying to make my brain work. My attention is flitting all around. The bucking and heaving boat isn't helping any. But it looks to me that we need to go west — we could even go northwest. It is the westerly component of our course that we are most in need of — we don't need to take the wind head-on. Any progress west will get us closer to the finish.

Jamie finishes making emergency repairs to the foot-stretcher. I kneel on the heaving deck while he rows, trying to take the pressure off the line as I haul in the sea anchor.

We push off again, this time more to the west. The deviation allows us to make some progress, even if it is very ragged and most of the time the GPS is baffled and uncertain. I still feel lousy, but a much, much better class of lousy. We are out here to row. At least now we are rowing. Fortunately conditions don't get any worse, nor does it rain. Just a steady wind from the south-southwest.

The sun is setting when we get a text from my brother Grant:

YOU ARE 12 MI. BEHIND DARK SIDE. THEY HAVE BEEN
BLOWN NORTH OVER THE LAST 12 HOURS THEY HAVE ONLY

We call Rob, who fills us in. Over the last 12 hours we have rowed only 23 nautical miles toward the finish. It has been our worst progress since Day 2. But the Dark Side have rowed only 16 nautical miles, and not toward Barbados, so at the end of the day they are only 12 miles closer. We are now only about 11 miles behind! Their lead has been halved in one day!

There is plenty for Jamie and me to talk about now as we row together, as our fatigue-stupid brains sift through the implications. The Dark Side must have put out their sea anchor and stayed on it. They must have. Which is strange, because they know when they did that on Day 2 they gave us a huge lead. And they know that we know that. But they *still* put out their sea anchor, and sat on it for hours. There can only be one conclusion. They're stuffed. Now I can pull a bit harder on the oars. Now every bit counts.

There is one other bit of good news. By mutual agreement it's time for the twins story.

'So there I am at the bar, watching a footie game with my mates, and these two really hot girls walk in, and they start chatting to us.'

'Of course!'

'After a while we notice that they look pretty similar. So I say to them, "Are you twins?"'

'And what do they say?'

'They say, "Yep." But then they start having me on about drinking. So I say to one of them, "I bet you couldn't scull a jug of Draught."'

'And then what?'

'Well, then she did!'

'And then?'

'And so did the other one!'

'And then what?'

'I went back to talking to my mates.'

'And then?'

'Waikato won the game.'

[Long pause.] 'Um . . . is that a drinking story?'

'It sure isn't a fishing story. Why?'

'No reason.'

I rowed flat out tonight trying to stay awake, pressing the cold flannel against my head occasionally. If I stopped for just a few seconds I would nearly fall asleep and fall off my seat. So then I'd row hard some more, and then I'd almost fall asleep.

November 21 — Day 34

YOU ARE THREE NAUTICAL MILES BEHIND AT 10 AM. DARK
SIDE HAVE DONE 14 NAUTICAL MILES IN LAST 12 HOURS
YOU HAVE DONE 22 NAUTICAL MILES. THEY ARE FURTHER
NORTH. WIND SHOULD BECOME EASTERLY LATE TODAY.
A SEVEN-DAY RACE TO BARBADOS! GRANT

I'm absolutely baffled.

'I don't get it. Has something happened to them? We make our worst 12 hours ever and we still go past them? Why is this headwind slowing them down so much?'

'I don't believe it either, it isn't right. I wonder if they are calling in their position wrong to try and get us to ease off?'

'No. But it might be a mistake on the website.'

'Yeah. Don't worry, mate, if we row our guts out we might just be able to catch them.'

But what if the news is true? It means that by now we are very close to each other on the water — the same distance from Barbados, but just a few miles away from each other. I look at every whitecap, every little fleck of white in the distance to see if it is their silver-sided boat.

And I do more thinking. They are probably getting the position reports like we do. That means they would have known some time last night that we had caught up 11 nautical miles on them. Wouldn't they have leapt out of bed, pulled in their sea anchor and started rowing? But they can't have. Did they hear the news and do nothing about it? Because in the next 12-hour period, still rowing into headwinds, we gain another eight miles on them. If that's true, then they really are knackered. Or maybe they only get updates once a day? In which case they would have got a nasty shock this morning. In one 24-hour period we have gained nearly 20 miles on them.

So the race starts from here. I guess we're kind of excited. But so many things can go wrong that I don't like to think about it. So we are just going to keep our heads down, take things as they come and get to the end. And although I know in practical terms it's going to be seven or eight days away, psychologically it still seems a long, long way away. A day still seems like a very long time. Knowing that we're going to finish soon doesn't make any hour any easier. I can't wait to lose this headwind, but as long as it hangs around we seem to be charging past the Dark Side.

Unknown to us, back in New Zealand, Anna turns up to work at Holiday Shoppe to find a letter on her desk. It is headed 'And Still There's No Honour Without Integrity', and in angry, sarcastic tones it sets out a theory to explain how we must be sailing to have caught up with *CRC*.

The letter is unsigned.

We start the big overlapping shifts as soon as it begins to get a little less blazing hot, around 4pm. As the sun sets we get the next position update.

21/11 LAST 12 HOURS HS 27 DS 26 U 1NM BEHIND.
U ROLLING THEM! ROB

So now it looks like the Dark Side are back at the oars. If they were stuffed, they aren't stuffed anymore. Now it is a sprint to the finish, just 485 nautical miles away. That's almost 900 kilometres — just the better part of the length of New Zealand to row.

I have this horrible vision of us in sight of each other, rowing down the coast of Barbados, giving it everything we have only to be pipped at the finish. Then spending the rest of my life remembering every tiny pause I have taken at the oars and wondering if that was the one that cost me the race. It's too awful. I would much rather get out in front as soon as we can.

Jamie isn't feeling so good in his stomach. He doesn't even want to sing 'Tomorrow'. But he has a lot to say in the Big Session about the difference between good teams and great teams. Good teams catch up to the leader then fade away; great teams keep the pressure up and the leaders crack.

Tonight we try a couple of half-hour on, half-hour off shifts just before the Sleep Shifts to try and perk ourselves up for the hour and a half alone at the oars. My half-hour isn't very good. I am constantly nodding off, having to dig my finger hard into the cable tie and whack myself frequently.

Then Jamie comes out for his first shift, and just in case there is a sleep malfunction I set an alarm on my watch to wake me up for my shift. The alarm wakes me up. I look out. Jamie is doing Stevie Wonder. I scramble onto the oars.

So during the Sleep Shifts I set my alarm clock every 20 minutes so that I wake up to see how he is doing. I hear the alarm, listen for the rowing. If I don't hear anything, I call out until I do. Then I go back to sleep.

In the last shift I set my watch alarms for every 10 minutes.

I don't know how long I can last on such short naps. It seems a shame that we are so close to finishing and doing so well that all we have to do to get the prize is stay awake.

I put my head onto the survival suit with the polyprop on top, and tonight, by some fluke of chemistry, they smell of macaroni cheese and pineapple — that reminds me of Mum cooking lunches for us on cold, rainy winter days, and I fall asleep smiling.

November 22 — Day 35

22/11 10AM HS 30.1 DS 29.8 BOTH BOATS HAVE 455NM
TO GO. YOU'VE GOT THEM. ROB

Neck and neck! With less than a week to go. The good news is that we haven't been penalised for having a pretty ordinary night; the bad news is that we aren't pulling away. Rob says we are less than 7 nautical miles away from each other on the water.

Now the headwind has gone, replaced by a very light wind blowing onto the stern — just enough to hold the mask of sweat on our faces on this incredibly hot, calm day.

There are no clouds on the horizon, so it takes a long time for the sun to go down, and the sweat is still raining off us well into the dusk.

The news media in New Zealand have sensed an upset, and we are booked to do some radio interviews. We speak to Murray Deaker and Peter Montgomery, and phone in to Jon Ackland's radio show. We try to split the interviews between us so we can share the burden of sleep sacrifice. I'm not sure that I make a lot of sense, but I listen keenly to Jon's advice that when someone has caught up to the leader after a long chase it is very rare for the leader to then pull away. So we are looking good.

> *Everyone is telling us to giddy up. But if we could go any faster we would be! Jamie is grumpy about the time we are spending talking and not sleeping. We get a lot of motivation from plugging back into the New Zealand vibe, and we get to name-drop the sponsors, but we don't want to lose the race because we spent so much time talking about it. We agree that we won't do any more interviews until the end.*

November 23 — Day 36, the day of the Big Wet

We didn't poll in last night, and as soon as it's decent we call up Lin on the yacht to make sure she has our position, and that it goes up on the web.

> *Spoke to Grant as well this morning. All we knew about the position last night was that it had not been updated. But today we got the information that [long pause, sound of snoring] . . . getting close enough now that we can really start to taste it. I think that is what I was saying before when I faded away. That's right, we hadn't been*

272

updated. Which is a bit of a shame because we are very keen to let the
Dark Side know that we are still here and not going away.

In the early morning we turn on the phone. There is a surprise text. For some reason both boats polled at about 7am.

23/11 U 11NM IN FRONT, 379 NM TO GO! YEE HA!

Jamie is quiet for a long time.

'Do you really believe that?'

'It does seem a bit too good to be true.'

'Yeah. What if they called in their position to make us think they're behind, so we would ease off?'

'What are you saying?'

'I say if we row our guts out we might be able to catch them.'

Another stinking hot day. We are a piece of cheese under the grill, on the top rack, oven door closed. But coming up behind the stern of the boat is a mob of plump grey clouds dragging gauzy skirts of rain underneath them.

First the squall blocks out the sun, then the wind picks up, then I hear the hiss as the rain rakes the water. Then the squall hits and it's like we are under a waterfall. Each drop is large and juicy, like a hurled water-bomb. Half-eaten gingernuts, old crackers and pieces of flying fish are being flushed out the scuppers. The bilge pump coughs into life as the footwell starts to fill up.

Soon the deluge is sluicing the sunscreen off my face, and there is a feeling of swelling up, relaxing, unshrivelling — I am a raisin becoming a grape. I put my head back and open my mouth so I can drink from the sky.

The squall is flattening the waves and the wind has picked up to a fresh breeze. My arms dimple with goose bumps. The wind is dragging us along with it — I can do nearly 4 knots rowing by myself, in mostly smooth, rolling seas. I start whooping and hollering.

Jamie cracks open the hatch and shouts over the roar: 'How is it?'

'Awesome! You might want to bring out the raincoat though!'

With Jamie rowing as well we are now doing at least 4, sometimes 5 knots. Eventually the squall passes, but with scarcely a break it is replaced by another and then another. We are in a squall alley.

We are giddy with our change of fortune. Jamie has an idea: 'Let's just row together until night-time!' It's tempting, but we would be complete toast at night.

The GPS screen flicks up some new numbers: 99 hours. Then they disappear, then in the next surge they come back again.

'Hey Jamie, the GPS is telling us how many hours we have to go!'

Holy cow! The Atlantic isn't infinite after all. There is going to be a time when this is all over. Those images of the beach bar start to become a little bit more real, and my tugs on the oars become a little bit more urgent. I look over my shoulder to see if there is anything out there. Of course there isn't. Let's not get carried away.

Over the next few hours the 'time to go' reading starts to stabilise. We now know roughly when we are going to finish — some time in the morning in four days, touch plywood.

Later that afternoon the squalls finally leave us, and as the adrenaline drains out of my system I am left feeling desperately tired and empty. And now the night is going to start. If I feel this wobbly now, how am I going to feel in the middle of the night?

Late at night we are looking forward to finding out how we are doing. The Dark Side polled in with 361 miles to go. Nothing from us. Sometimes the boats' Inmarsat units don't poll in, for no obvious reason. It's very frustrating. We have had an excellent day and we want the Dark Side to know how well we are doing. In the end we phone the support yacht so Lin can relay our position to the website.

I try another game.

'Have you heard of the Keep Asking Questions game?'

'What's that?'

'Do you know *Whose Line Is It Anyway?*'

'Is that the one with Ryan Stiles?'

'So you have heard of it?'

'What's your point?'

'Did you know that it's one of the games they play on that show?'

'Why wouldn't I know that?'

'Because ... oh damn, you got me!'

I can hear a toilet flushing, quite clearly. And giggling. Now tooth-brushing. That's a lot of rinsing.

Before the race I asked my friends to make tapes for me to listen to during the row. I have been hoarding them as a secret weapon against the night zombie. So tonight, when every blink risks turning into an impromptu nap, I get out the first one.

Some friends in Singapore have taped their daily routine. I have been shopping, hanging out by the pool, and now we are all going to bed. I have just listened to their going-to-bed routine, including teeth-brushing. It's fabulous drama — I'm riveted.

Others have sent me music compilations. 'Six Months in a Leaky Boat' is popular. Ha, ha. Others are reading out inspirational or funny stories and poems. Before I left, one friend had been insistent that I take the CD case on the boat as well as the CD. Now I'm listening to her explain why: 'If you look inside the album cover you'll see a little present that I left for you and Jamie. I think you'll enjoy Miss October.' But a CD case weighs 5 g, so it had been left behind . . .

The tapes are magic, but I don't have enough of them to listen to all night. When I am not listening to them I quickly descend into the Twilight Zone. As soon as Jamie closes the cabin door for the first half-hour pre-Sleep Shift I start hallucinating. I see him fiddling with the GPS, or fixing something, and I have to stop rowing so I can watch what he is doing. Then I wake up and start rowing again, angry with myself.

Jamie doesn't have any tapes. So I set my alarms again during his shifts and put my head out and have a word or two if he's looking wobbly. I try to keep it positive and just bring some enthusiasm, saying how wonderful it's going to be to win, and that we have done so much and now all we have to do is stay awake and we'll get there.

Again a very strong recollection of three people on the boat. I think that at one point I came out and saw Elvis, or Jamie dressed as Elvis. Or at least he had an Elvis wig on. It's possible that there is a wig on the boat, but I've never seen it before or after.

The sun comes up and my face feels as if I am wearing a heavy mask of clay. My head either lolls forward or tilts to one side. My lips are as big as bananas and my mouth won't close.

November 24 — Day 37

24/11 10AM. U 13NM IN FRONT. ROB

'Sounds like "Row harder" to me,' says Jamie.

Jamie is looking thoughtful.

'Mate?'

'Yep.'

'Tell me some more about Business Class.'

'Mate, the hosties are all outstanding. They only take former beauty contestants. And they all love fishing.'

'Rock or surfcasting?'

'Both. And they love diving for crays. And they can shuck a bucketful of oysters in 10 minutes with one hand while they tap a keg of Waikato Draught with the other.'

'True?'

'Yep. We just have to hold it together for four more days, then you'll see.'

November 25 — Day 38, the support yacht goes past

AT 11AM U HAVE 245NM TO GO. U R 22NM AHEAD OF CRC. LESS THAN 4 DAYS TO GO. THE PAIN IS TEMPORARY!

'Well, it's not impossible . . .'

'Yep. Something might still go wrong with them.'

'So it's still worth a nudge.'

'Yep. If we row our guts out we can still catch them.'

I rowed hard last night and now I'm feeling very disconnected and almost dizzy. My skull is an aquarium; my brain has been replaced with a clear fluid. If you look at my eyes you can see goldfish swimming inside. It's not unpleasant but it's disconcerting, in a muffled kind of way. Even the thought that we are going to meet up with the support yacht today doesn't get much of an internal response.

Sometimes when I sleep I get very unlucky and dream about rowing. Today, for some reason, I have the 45-minute nap from heaven. I wake up feeling like I've had eight hours' sleep. I am transformed.

I need it. It's another frigging scorcher. A fair and gentle wind, with chubby clouds trotting in from the northeast. When a cloud passes overhead I row harder to try and prolong the relief. Then the heat comes back on, and all thoughts are short and brutal.

It has been over five weeks since we have seen anything man-made. So when the mast and sail of the support yacht appears over the swells, it is very strange, very Other. It's like seeing a spaceship.

Then the hull comes into view. Lin is aft at the wheel, and the crew are all on deck waving at us. There seem to be a number of girls in hotpants and bikini tops strewn about the boat.

The yacht is now alongside and on a slightly converging course. When we are a few metres away Jamie stands up and gives a salute, shouting 'Permission to come aboard!' The inevitable lurch comes exactly then and he has to sit down very quickly. The sudden movement is more than the top he has roughly tied around his waist can take, and he reveals a generous slice of 'Startled Chicken'. This makes the girls laugh.

For the better part of an hour we have a shouted conversation across the swells while we row alongside them. The yacht draws up along one side of us, and then along the other. Some of the crew are taking photos and videos, while others are answering our questions about the other crews. Conditions are perfect for rowing, and inspired by the audience we are doing nearly 5 knots.

Then they tweak the throttle, slide off to the southwest and are soon lost to the waves. That must be a nice way to travel.

Later that day Lin emails a report from the boat back to Teresa.

Hi all
Busy day on the water with vis on CRC and Holiday Shoppe,
both rowing two-up at speeds of 4–4.8 knots. Wind light but

more in rain squalls. Holiday Shoppe have more wind and swell than CRC enabling them to surf a little faster.

NONE OF BELOW FOR WEB SITE
Flat enough to get v close and chat to both pairs . . . Holiday Shoppe . . . are putting themselves through one hell of a pace rowing two-up for a large percentage of the time. As a pair they were rowing more efficiently and faster than CRC today. Looking at them and hearing their routine I am not surprised that they are doing so well. We have lots of video footage of both boats.

CRC have tried rowing two-up for 18–20 hours but find that they are too tired, Holiday Shoppe putting up with being tired but 'seeing things' in dark . . . Will talk more in Barbados but no worries about cheating at all . . .

ONLY CRC UPDATED AT 10PM. THEY HAVE DONE ABOUT 32NM IN 12HRS. 238NM TO GO FOR THEM. THEIR BEST RUN FOR A FEW DAYS SO THEY ARE PUSHING. GRANT

But we have had a good day ourselves. Seeing the yacht has only reinforced how close we are to the finish, and this has lifted our spirits. Just two more nights to go.

I look up at a particularly starry night sky and see that we are about to be overtaken by an enormous cloud. It is shaped like an arc — at its middle it must be as high as a 200-storey building, with a symmetrical tapering arm coming out each side. It looks like we are going to be attacked by a giant croissant. It blocks out the stars as it comes. As it passes overhead it becomes very windy, then it moves on and it becomes eerily calm.

There is a new moon. We have been out here a long time, seeing the moon go through its phases. Now they are starting to repeat.

CHAPTER TWENTY FOUR

A little too close to the bottom of the Atlantic

November 26 — Day 39

The wind and waves have got the idea now — a nice fresh wind on the stern and big, curvy rollers to shove us towards Barbados. At this rate, some time in the morning on the day after tomorrow, we'll arrive. That's a timeframe that's almost conceivable. It's looking like we might finish under the world record of 41 days, 2 hours and 55 minutes.

> AT 1.15PM TODAY YOU ARE 34NM IN FRONT OF DARK SIDE. 157NM TO GO. LESS THAN 48HRS TO ROW AT THIS RATE. SEE YOU ON FRIDAY! CHEERS, GRANT.

'That's very strange, but I'm not going to argue,' I suggest.

'You don't believe it, do you?'

'You don't really think they have figured out a way to make themselves appear somewhere they aren't?'

'Maybe it's a mistake — maybe someone typed it in wrong to the website. How bad would you feel if we got to the end and found out we were second?'

'Maybe if we row harder we can still catch them?'

'You don't think I'm going to be the first one to stop talking in questions do you?'

'Why would I think that?'

'Because . . . you got me again!'

Now the seas have reached the critical volume and velocity where we are able to surf-surge again. Imagine if we had got these waves in our first couple of days — we would have shat ourselves. But there have been a few waves under the keel since then. Come on wave 12,432, you're not as scary as you look . . . Hang on, maybe you are . . . Here we go . . . The swelling wave picks us up and thrusts us forward at 6 knots, then 7 knots, then . . . rolls away. I think in my next break I might dig the safety harnesses out.

We still want to row overlapping shifts as much as possible. The hottest part of the day is only just over when we drop our breaks down to half an hour. Now it's nearly dark and I am starting to feel very light-headed.

Finally it's time to wake Jamie. I call out 'Six minutes!' a couple of times. The hatch flicks open its couple of inches, and bang on five minutes later he comes out.

'How's it been?' he asks.

'Yeah, not too bad. Mostly above 3 knots. That's 30 seconds to go, by the way.'

We swap places and I roll forward into the footwell where I can stand up gingerly, letting the blood flow slowly into my internal organs. I chug a recovery drink and put on the pot for the freeze-dry.

It's going to be dark soon, and I pull out one of the head-lamps to show Jamie how I've fixed it. Then the bow starts to tilt down and down and down . . .

It's deep out in the ocean. I mean it's well over your head. You certainly can't touch the bottom even standing on someone's shoulders. Actually, that feels like someone's shoulders underneath me.

I am swimming overarm even before I reach the surface. I have to get to the boat. There's a picture in my mind of the safety line snapping tight when Jamie jumped in for a barnacle swim a few days ago. I reach the top ready for a swim to the death. But the boat is right there. Stopped dead in front of me, like a recalcitrant pony standing guiltily over its freshly bucked rider. And it has snapped upright, just like it is supposed to. Oh thank you, God. I lunge for the grab line at the beam. Oh, f--k, where's Jamie?

'Jamie!' I bellow.

'Yep.'

His voice comes from the other side of the boat. I can't see him.

'All right?' I ask.

'Yeah.'

Oh thank God. I hear Jamie laughing. 'Shall we clean the barnacles off now we're here?'

You are an utter nutcase.

I wish I could share his enthusiasm, but I can see what Jamie can't. 'Mate, it's not good! Everything has been thrown out. Get in and sort the steering out before another wave comes. I'll throw stuff up.'

Jamie pulls himself on board and looks out over my side.

'F--k!'

The throne bobs past my nose.

'Take this!'

A water container. A Roho. A packet of gingernuts.

The boat lifts up, white water surges past and I have to hang on tight to the grab lines. Jamie nearly falls over.

'Quick, get the oars sorted out and keep the stern into the waves.'

I am still trying to find stuff in the water in the dark. I see the Thermarest uncoiled and floating, and throw it on the boat.

'I can't see the other seat. Can you see it?'

Another wave surges us along. Jamie is grunting at the oars. 'Nup. Hey, we really need those steering lines working, eh.'

I pull myself on board. Shit, the life raft should be here too! I stare out helplessly into the blue-black murk, seeing less and less in the twilight. We're being swept along by the waves now and trying to go back would be hopeless, not to mention dangerous.

The stern steering position is absolutely munted. Jamie has taken one of the shoes with him when he abandoned ship. We have to get the bow steering going, but we haven't used it since the steering on the foot-stretcher cracked. It's still broken, but at least it's usable.

It's too dark now to see the steering lines. We need some light. I pull open the hatch and peer into the darkness. I hear slopping sounds. I put my hand in and find that water has pushed into the cabin and flooded it right up to the lip of the hatch. I reach into the container mounted high on the inside of the port bulkhead. Bugger, it's full of water too. The iPod and the minidisc were both out of their dry bags, now they are ruined. I can't find the head-lamp. Oh shit, that's right, I had it in my hand when we went over.

But there is a faint glow in the cabin, coming from *under* the water. I reach down and pull it out. It's a tiny keyring torch. I had unsuccessfully tried to break into it before the race, to get its LED bulb for the compass light. Now it has somehow got itself pinched in the turmoil and turned on, and it is still working underwater. It's a little miracle.

We use the light to find the steering lines and reconnect them. Now that one person can row and steer our situation is at least stable. I take out the safety harnesses from the back cabin, put one on and throw the other to Jamie.

The GPS screen is blank, it must have gone underwater, but the compass light still works. What's next? Sort out the back cabin. I need to get the water out but I can't see our bucket anywhere. I empty the chips out of a Pringles container and start scooping. Several times I have to hang on again as water tumbles and roars past outside, and my heart races. *Is it going to happen again?* The Pelican box with our essentials in it is still intact and the contents are dry. So is everything else that is in dry bags. I try and tell myself it could have been a lot worse.

'Six minutes!' roars Jamie. Now it's my turn on the oars. That has to be the worst Sleep Shift ever.

Once I'm at the oars I can start to slow down and breathe through my nose. That was close. That could have gone real bad. But at least we are alive. No big GPS, no stove, no pot, no life raft, no music. We've been rinsed back to the Stone Age. But that's the least of our worries. Our biggest problem is that we have lost our other seat. Now we can only row one at a time.

What idiots we were not to have been clipped on! And our seats too — they were supposed to have been restrained, except we unclipped them weeks ago to get into the lockers underneath. All that confidence that had been building up about being able to handle ourselves out here has been left bobbing in the ocean. We have been out for so long we have started to believe that the Atlantic is a toothless old family Labrador, when really it is a cunning pit bull, waiting for us to let our guard down so it can take us. What if it had happened half an hour later, in the dark? The Atlantic can take us any time it wants to.

And now our speed — have we blown it? Before our swim we were rowing 4 knots together. We still have a hand-held GPS, and it tells us we are now only doing 3. If the Dark Side are 35 miles behind it might take them 35 hours to catch up. So we have to get to the end before they get us. But we can't finish in 35 hours — it will take us well over 40. So they could row quite a bit less than 4 knots and still take us. Shit, have we thrown it away? Is it going to be a sprint finish? The thought of rowing neck and neck down the coast of Barbados is just too agonising to consider. I yank away at the oars in the darkness.

'Hey Jamie, better give Rob a call. Someone needs to know where we are exactly, in case it happens again.'

'Yeah, all right.'

Rob's journal

N13.39.81 W57.45.69

Just back from BBQ where I received a call from Jamie telling me they had capsized. We didn't talk long — they were trying to organise the boat. Really worried about their safety and race position. I won't write about this on the web site as we don't want to give DS a sniff of the chance that beckons.

We agreed he would call again at 5am. Five came and went without a call; 5:30 past and then 5:45. I was getting really worried about them not meeting the sched. The seas were obviously getting up and they could easily have capsized again. Finally Kevin called just before 6am. What a relief!

It's my break. I'm sprawled on the floor of the cabin. How far we've come! At the start of the race I was a fleshy, plump creature of comfort who needed to be tucked into bed with a hot-water bottle and a blankie. Now I am naked and lanky, lying sprawled on the floor of the cabin, using an unfolded laminated map on a blanket to stop the breeze cramping my twitching muscles. When I turn on the camera to film a diary entry I see that my face is gaunt, my cheeks are hollow, my eyes racoonish.

I am finding it hard to sleep, knowing that I might wake upside down and underwater. It isn't a nightmare anymore, it's a memory. Just one more day and one more night to go.

Ironically, we get more sleep that night than we have for a long time. We are rowing one up, hour on, hour off. So in every two-hour period we sleep for about 45 minutes. For once when I am rowing at night it isn't hard to stay awake, for I'm thinking about the Dark Side churning out of the darkness towards us.

What can we make a seat out of?

><

November 27 — Day 40, the day after the capsize

I come out for the first morning shift.

'Hey, have you seen the poo bucket?'

'No, it must have gone over. Try the Pringles container.'

'Ta!'

The sun comes up on our last full day, and the weather has been custom-designed by an ocean rower. There is a high white cloud that takes the sting out of the sun without making the day grey. The swells are large and purposeful, and the wind more or less on our stern. We're going to make it.

Rob has already contacted Lin and now we call her with an update. She is very concerned about us, and asks us to phone in regularly. She also promises not to let the Dark Side know that we are wounded in the water.

We work up a seat idea. We can take a hatch cover out of the back cabin. It's wider than the rails so we can just sit it on top of them. It won't slide back and forth like it should, but with the Thermarest concertinaed on top at least it's the right height.

We check the phone again and again until the position report comes in.

27/11 U R STILL ABOUT 30 MILES AHEAD OF DARK SIDE.
HOLD IT TOGETHER!

So we are losing ground. One day to go. It's going to be tight.

Only one day to go. But knowing that doesn't make any stroke any easier. In fact, it's harder. In my head I am already at the finish line, in a cold spa pool full of champagne and fruit salad, then I open my eyes and I am back on the endless ocean.

I look up and see a shape high in the twilight sky. It's a plane. So there *is* another world out there. We must be close.

One last call from Rob, who is now in Barbados waiting for us. He tells us that he has a little surprise in store. Are we still thinking about girls in bikinis? Because he has that all under control. Oh, and Grant, Jamie's girlfriend Kate and his sister Bridget have arrived too, and they will all be out on a boat to see us.

I start the Big Session on the fixed seat. To keep up with Jamie's stroke I have to lean a long way forward and then a long way back. It's weird and unnatural, and not very effective. I look like I'm rowing a whaleboat. After half an hour of telling myself to harden up, I finally relent.

'Hey, I'm crap at this, do you want to have a go?'

'Yeah, give it here. We do a drill like this in rowing training all the time.'

The night is as dark as the inside of a gumboot. And now there's not even the friendly light of the GPS to keep us company. The seas are heaving and waves are tumbling, rushing, crashing around the boat. It's easy to imagine that we are nearing the edge of a flat world where the accelerating ocean will sweep us abruptly into the abyss.

My stomach clenches whenever I hear a whitecap crash, bracing myself for the shove, for the one that is going to pounce on the boat. If we are going to go over again it will be on a night like this.

285

I start the Sleep Shifts, and as soon as Jamie goes into the cabin I am mugged by fatigue. I have no tricks left to keep myself awake, and bloody Jamie keeps crawling out of the cabin, trying to fix something. I have to stop rowing and peer at him very closely to see what he's up to. He seems to be standing on the water painting the side of the boat. Now he is ten feet in the air above the cabin. That's strange.

'Jamie, if you want to come down why don't you use the spiral staircase?' I hear the creature, who once was Kevin, croak.

The hour very slowly passes. At least I think it's an hour, I don't really know when I started. I'll give it a bit longer then call out 'Jamie'. I am relieved when a far more substantial Jamie comes out of the hatch (and not a giant talking chicken). I get into the cabin and I am just closing the door when Jamie yells out, 'Six minutes.'

'It can't be — I've only just got in.'

'No, I've been rowing for an hour.'

'You're kidding! I've still got my hand on the door. What time is it?'

'I don't know.'

'What time did you start?'

'I don't know. Ages ago.'

'We'll split it — give me a half-hour.'

'You owe me one.'

'Likewise.'

He could be right. How should I know? I'm a penguin.

Back at the oars adrenaline and fatigue are battling against each other. Sometimes, when a wave crashes and the roar of the white water in the dark comes closer and closer, adrenaline wins. Most of the time fatigue wins. At other times on my break when I am more coherent I get out the hand-held GPS to make sure our course is still good for the northern tip of the island. This means standing up in the footwell and holding the GPS until it finds the satellites. Finally the position comes through, and then I have to match the position up to the chart — latitude, then longitude. I keep making mistakes and having to go and recheck. Then I have to work out what our heading needs to be, given our actual track across ground, then correct for magnetic deviation, then for the fact that our compass is facing the wrong way.

But it is essential that we know which way we are going. With the wind and the waves shoving us, big last-minute course corrections aren't going to be possible. We are like the space shuttle trying to re-enter the atmosphere. Too far south and we will be shredded on the coral reefs. Too far to the north and we might not be able to swing around into the lee of the island before the wind and currents push us past and we will have to be towed in.

I wonder how close we will be before we see Barbados. How about now? No. How about now? Still no. It is in the deepest, most synaptically sluggish part of the night that I look over my shoulder again and see stars out on the horizon. I look again. They are too bright, and too many different colours. They aren't stars. They are lights. Barbados. Right on schedule. Maybe each light is a house, where people sleep for more than an hour at a time. Dryness. Coolness. Greenness. Stableness. It doesn't look like a tropical island — it looks kind of hilly. I don't know anything about Barbados. What do they do there? Play cricket and make rum?

Jamie comes out for his shift.

'Look! Barbados!'

'Oh bloody good.'

The dawn light, when it arrives, is slightly soggy, filtered dimly through an overcast sky. It calms the waves, soothes the nerves, and begins coaxing my shrivelled pineal gland to start leaking some wake-up juice into my brain.

There's an island on the horizon. We're actually going to do it. We're going to get there.

CHAPTER TWENTY FIVE

She's a man?

November 28 — Day 41, The Finish!

The outline of the island becomes clearer. There are hills, and there seem to be green fields, and grass — it looks vaguely like New Zealand. And there is a wonderful smell of fresh, transpiring greenery.

Now the rigorous shift schedule is completely abandoned. There is no thought of being inside the cabin. One person rows while the other does the chores, cleaning up the boat, having a shave, putting out the sponsors' logos. Jamie is looking for something.

'Hey mate, have you seen my good shorts?'

'Not for a couple of days.'

Jamie looks anguished. 'Oh no! I had them drying on the deck when we went over!'

'No worries, mate — you've always got a Pringles container!'

'Nup, I've got an idea.'

He comes out of the cabin with the thermal top, cuts off the arms and puts his legs through the armholes. A couple of safety pins around the waist and he has a very passable pair of shorts. The zip at what was the collar even makes a passable fly. He looks very silly, and we laugh at what Kate will think when she sees him for the first time in two months.

We watch the distance to the waypoint get smaller and smaller. It gets down to single figures. I show Jamie; we laugh at that too. There seems to be a lot to laugh at today.

We are nearly at the waypoint at the northern tip of the island. Once we cross this longitude we have officially completed a crossing of the Atlantic. As we get closer we can see the Woodvale yacht waiting for us.

The crew shout and wave as we approach. As soon as we get within earshot I call out, 'Have you seen any other boats go by!'

They laugh and say, 'No!'

I'm not sure if I was joking, because it's a huge relief when I hear that. As we pass by they give us a big honk from the airhorn, and three cheers.

'Well done, mate,' I say to Jamie.

'Yeah, same.'

Another boat appears, pounding over the swells. It's another massive launch, and we can see Rob, Grant, Kate and Bridget, plus Emma Keeling from TV3. We wave and shout, but mostly they are too far away to hear and it's too rough for them to pull alongside. The Woodvale yacht drops a little tender with two crew which motors along beside us, and we follow them around the point onto the sheltered western side. Slowly, slowly as we make our way around to the lee of the island the big swells fade away. The Atlantic has had its last chance and we row seven miles down the tranquil west coast to the hotel and marina complex at Port St Charles.

We are collecting a little fleet now. Dozens of small pleasure boats have come out to see us in. It's strange seeing so many people. An enormous jet-black man in a tiny boat stands up and booms, 'Welcome home!' before his friends pull him down, laughing and saying, 'Dey not dem. Dey de udder boys!'

The sun has been up for about five hours before we finally see the entrance to the Port St Charles marina complex. The support yacht motors ahead, with its little tender chasing after. A black stormcloud that has been threatening for the last hour opens up with an astonishingly heavy downpour that sends the rest of the spectator craft scampering for cover, and we are left rowing the last few hundred metres to the entrance by ourselves.

'Don't worry, mate,' Jamie says. 'If we row our guts out we might still be able to catch them.'

The sun comes out as we round the breakwater. The end is easy to see — it's where a hundred people are standing on the wharf smiling and clapping. We glide the last few metres, put out our oars, and strong hands pull us alongside. I'm smiling so much my face is aching.

So at 11:32am *Holiday Shoppe Challenge* pulls up alongside a pier at Port St Charles marina — the 106th boat to have been rowed across an ocean, and the fastest pair to have rowed across the Atlantic. We have set a new world record of 40 days, 5 hours and 31 minutes.

An official-looking man with an open-necked shirt reaches out his hand and says, with a toothy smile, 'Welcome to Barbados!' I clasp his hand and take my first shaky steps on land. It isn't really land, it's a floating dock, but it feels like land. It feels very, very good. I want to lie down and give it a big old hug.

Hands gesture us towards the small customs office a few metres away. There are forms and a little writing, and a white-shirted official asks me if I want a hamburger. A hamburger? Sure. When he comes back with the hamburger I bite into it and exclaim, 'That's the best hamburger I've ever tasted!'

'Of course, mon! Dat New Zealand beef!'

Grant presses a cellphone into my hand. 'It's Mum,' he says.

I can't resist. I have been dying to say these words for so long.

'I told you so!'

Teresa and Lin come up and give us hugs, which is pretty brave given the state we're in. It is a particular delight to see Lin, who has been such a friendly and encouraging voice down the end of the phone.

Customs takes only a few minutes, then we are back out with the crowd and doing interviews from the boat. Then there is a commotion and Rob appears leading an enormously tall woman wearing a tiara and a kind of spangly, silvery dress. She's every bit of 2 metres tall, and is quite a magnificent creature if you overlook the suspiciously large Adam's apple and the enormous hands.

As Jamie and I each give Rob a backslapping embrace she totters onto the boat in her heels. When she has everyone's attention she puts her arm around Jamie and addresses us and the crowd. She welcomes us and says she hopes we enjoy our stay on this beautiful island, then she adds, 'and if there is anything I can do to make your time here more enjoyable, please let me know — especially you with the funny shorts.'

Jamie looks like he has just pulled a 10 kg cray, and happily poses for the cameras while the Diva puts kisses on his cheeks.

I whisper to Rob, 'What is that?'

'Isn't she lovely? We met her at the drag show last night.'

Jamie still has his sea goggles on. Even after we tell him, he takes a bit of convincing. We get him to confess on video, to great hilarity.

After six weeks at sea I arrived in Barbados, and I got told after an hour that I was being kissed by a six foot six woman who was actually a man.

Finally the interviews are done and the spectators melt away, until only family and friends remain.

I call Hot Polish Girl: 'I did it!'

'I knew you would,' she says. But I get a telling-off because she had to hear that we were all right after the capsize from the radio.

We walk up to the little cabana bar at the marina, with its thatched roof. A black man with a gold tooth and a crisp white shirt is ready to serve.

'Are you the guys who just rowed the Atlantic?'

'We sure are.'

'May I offer you a rum punch on the house?'

'You sure can!'

Jamie and I sit out on deckchairs and tell story after story to our family and friends. After a while Teresa and Lin arrive with a clipboard and it becomes a formal debriefing. They want to hear about the weather conditions, about our shifts, what worked and didn't work, and particularly the capsize — exactly how it happened, and what equipment we lost. Lin scolds us for not being clipped on.

Anna from Holiday Shoppe calls up — they are having a conference on the Gold Coast. She puts me on speaker-phone so the conference can hear me.

Jamie is watching me curiously as I hang up the phone.

'Did she happen to mention anything about anything?'

'Congratulations, mate. You've been upgraded! You're flying home Business Class!'

Sitting feels so very good. To be able to lie back and have nothing to do feels very, very good. So does drawing in lungfuls of air and exhaling slowly, just enjoying the easy swing of my diaphragm. To hold something cold and sip it. To be able to look around me at things that aren't blue. To think freely and not to have to shunt gloomy thoughts away. Every other second I realise anew, 'We just rowed the Atlantic!'

I feel proud. I feel vindicated, to have risked so much and to have pulled it off. It seems like just last week I was sitting on the sofa wondering what to do with my life. All those months when I was either miserable because I didn't know that I was going to get to row across the ocean, or I was terrified because I might. It has all paid off, it is all worth it. I feel like I can take on anything. Now I want to circle the globe in a helicopter, now I want to skydive from the stratosphere.

I also feel very, very lucky, and very grateful that we made it. I can see now that this happy ending was never guaranteed. I want to buy a bunch of lottery tickets while it lasts.

Physically I am incinerated. My shoulder muscles have seized up so I can barely lift my arms above my head, and I can walk only in a slow waddle. At the same time I feel energised, like I never need to sleep again.

Grant has organised a little villa for us to stay in, and Jamie is going to stay at a house with Rob, Kate, Bridget and a couple of other friends. As we head off we agree that we will come back to see the Dark Side arrive in a few hours. It's strange to see Jamie go. It's like losing a leg. We have spent so long within arm's length of each other. Who is going to row the next shift?

I walk into the villa. It's also strange being inside a building, it's very quiet. I go into the shower and warm water comes out of the taps. I don't like it. It feels wrong. It feels too . . . comfortable. That's not what it's about. I turn it onto cold, and rinse off six weeks of salt water and grime.

I lie on the soft, clean bed and try to sleep. Now there is another problem. With my eyes closed the bed is at sea. The bed is actually moving, bucking and surging. There is no question that the bed is at sea. I open my eyes — it's not the bed that is at sea, the whole room must be at sea. Have I fallen asleep and woken up on a boat? I must have. There is no doubt that the whole room is bucking and swaying, in the signature unrhythmic beat that only the open ocean produces.

There is only one way to sort this out. I will get up and go to the curtains and pull them apart. Then I will see that the house is on the ocean. I am as sure of it as I am sure of anything. I get up and sway across the room. Before I open the curtains I have a thought. If I am wrong — and there is not sea out there — I am going to be completely freaked out. I pull open the curtains. There is a garden.

That's very, very weird. The garden seems to be moving too. I go back to bed.

The Dark Side arrive after sunset, some nine hours after us. I get to the marina just as they pull up to the wharf. I work my way through the crowd to get to the boat's side. I'm looking forward to seeing them. Like schoolboys after a playground fight, I have more respect for them now. It wouldn't have been the same race without them. They have pushed us right to our limits and beyond. We have both had an amazing adventure, and we have spent the last six weeks within a few miles of each other out on the ocean. They are two of the very few people on the planet who can understand what we have just gone through. I catch their eyes, and shake their hands. They don't look that happy. 'Well done. You were very … quick,' Matt offers, and turns back to the crowd. OK, I guess they are disappointed. Well you would be.

I glance over their boat. They had also started with Roho cushions, but they have been replaced by two jury-rigged foam seats that make me wince when I see them. Those must have hurt. Had they not taken a puncture repair kit?

We have a week before we fly home. My sister Sharon flies in from the UK, and other friends arrive to join the party. We go to the beautiful coves, with palm trees nodding over the water, we jump in the huge pool at Port St Charles and swim up to the bar. At night we go out to the huge open-air clubs to dance.

There is an ergo at the gym at Port St Charles. I try it, and watch the clock continuously as it ticks through ten lousy, painful minutes. I suppose I achieved our goal — psychologically there is nothing left. I don't care if I never row another stroke in my life. I think about the other rowers still at sea, and shudder. I weigh myself on the scales — despite eating as much as I could over the last six weeks I've lost 15 kg. No fat boy anymore. I'm looking pretty lanky.

I have a very uneasy relationship with sleep. I don't ever *feel* like sleeping, there is too much of life to suck up, but then sometimes I open my eyes and time has passed. Sometimes I feel a very sudden and overwhelming fatigue, like profound jet-lag, and then I have to lie down on the floor, coming back to life 45 minutes later.

There are plenty of idle hours too. And I feel strangely edgy. The big driving purpose that has been pulling me forward for the last two years has gone. Now what do I do? I know — have another rum punch and enjoy walking around feeling like the world is a pretty good place. Occasionally we run into the Dark Side at the pool, or talking to Lin. They are guarded. 'Something's up,' says Rob.

The locals are warm, friendly and very courteous. We are at a restaurant one night, and I go into the men's room where I inadvertently push open the door of an occupied stall, hitting an unseen man's massive knees.

'Whoops! Sorry!' I say.

From behind the door comes a deep, dark voice. 'Don't worry, mon — it was my me-e-stake.'

One night we hear about a street where some bars are having a party. The Kiwi posse heads down, and soon we have cold drinks in our hands and are making friends with the locals. The sun sets, a warm, gentle rain starts to fall from the dark Caribbean sky, and everyone spills out into the street to dance in the rain. I am young, alive, with friends, on a Caribbean island and life is very, very good.

CHAPTER TWENTY SIX

Not possible by human effort

Sunday morning, November 30

The phone rings in the villa. It's Teresa.

'Ah, Kevin — I'm afraid to have to tell you that there's been a protest.'

'A protest? Against us? About what? From who?'

'It's been lodged by Mr Goodman and Mr Westlake. Can you come down to the office? I really don't want to say any more on the phone.'

Jamie is out, but I get hold of Rob. We meet down at the Challenge office at Port St Charles. Teresa explains that the Dark Side have accused us of unlocking the solar panel from its restraints and swinging it up to act as a sail. How bloody ridiculous!

'Well there might be an easy way to end this right now. Let's go down to the boat and see if it's even possible.'

'Yes, I think that's best,' Teresa responds. 'That's what I was going to suggest.'

As we walk down to the boat I'm thinking that with any luck

Gordon would have locked off the nuts, or they will have rusted over and corroded in such a way that it is clear they haven't been used in the voyage, or something. But what if that's not the case? How can we prove this is bullshit?

My heart rate jumps when I see the Dark Side by the boat — arms folded, shaking their heads, with stony looks of professional dismay. I don't like the look of this. At least Lin is there to referee.

'Shall we look at the solar panel then?' suggests Teresa. We all lean over to look at the bolts in question, the ones that attach the stubby arms of the supports to the solar panel frame.

'You see! That head's burred!' Westlake says in a voice that proclaims victory.

'No it isn't!' I say, because it isn't. It looks like a normal head.

'. . . and you can see that there's no corrosion!' says Goodman triumphantly.

'Yes there is!' I say, because there is. What's with the Jedi mind-tricks?

I feel myself flushing. I have been so stupidly naive. They aren't here because they have some concerns they want to get answered. This is not an inquiry. This is theatre. They are here to condemn us and convince Teresa their protest is valid, and they aren't going to let any inconvenient facts stand in their way. No Queensberry Rules here, this is a street fight.

Lin is undoing the nuts and bolts that hold on the two little arms that restrain the frame of the panel. Access is awkward from the back hatch. Using only the crappy tools from our toolbox, she perseveres for a few minutes, and after dropping a couple of nuts in the water manages to undo the bolts. Now untethered from the back, the panel could pivot on the bolts at the other end and swing up in the air. It could indeed rotate all the way up.

Goodman and Westlake look away, shaking their heads. Case closed. Oh, the desperate lengths people will go to.

Call me slow, but I don't get it. Of course if you unbolt the restraining struts you can move the solar panel. That's why the struts are there.

Goodman keeps up the theatre: '. . . and you can see the hole that's used to hold the panel in place when it's upright. It's clearly been used — there were no washer marks around it at the start of the race, and now you can clearly see them . . .' He is pointing to a hole near the bottom of the frame. Teresa nods hesitantly.

What? That's absurd! Now they are just making shit up. They might as well say, 'You see that space? That's where the engine went.' Actually, why is that hole there? And why are there washer marks around it? I'll worry about that later.

Rob is faster at figuring out what is going on and is venting his anger. Some terse words are exchanged. I'm losing my cool too. I suggest that we take the restraints off the Dark Side's solar panel and see what happens. Westlake agrees.

We move the circus a few boats down to *CRC* and Lin gets to work. Again it is awkward for her, but eventually she gets the panel free from the restraints and swings the back up. Unfortunately the front of the frame is mounted a little lower on the roof of the cabin than ours, and this stops the panel going higher than about 45 degrees.

'Ha!' I say. But I am not very good at this play-acting nonsense. The idea that they would have used the panel to gain an advantage at sea is pretty far-fetched, and the same is true for us. But Westlake and Goodman are very good at this — making accusations and giving straight-faced testimony. That's their day job. They are changing the rules of the game so now it's played on their terms.

Teresa takes us to one side and tells us that the Dark Side are going to lodge an official protest. We can pick up a copy of it tomorrow. She isn't too sure what the process will be, but there is likely to be a hearing later in the week and before that we will have a chance to put in our own written submission.

At that point Jamie jogs up to the boat, and we debrief him as we walk back to the cars. I'm forcing myself to take slow, even breaths. Rob is shaking his head.

'I can't help but wonder if this isn't as much about getting at me as it is about you guys,' he says.

'What do you mean?'

'We were still going back and forward about things while the race was on.'

'With Westlake and Goodman? On the satellite phone?'

'No, with their lawyer . . .'

'The whole race?'

'No, it ended about the start of November when we agreed to go to arbitration.'

'What's left to be decided?'
'It's still all about splitting up the equipment.'

It's a strange thing being accused of something you didn't do. It doesn't matter if you are as blameless as a smurf, it's very hard to rebut the accusation without sounding guilty. I don't want simply to *declare* we are innocent — that's just another useless declaration. I want to *prove* we are innocent, but that isn't going to be easy. The conversation in my head goes like this:

> Me: That hole on the panel doesn't show anything.
> Accuser: Oh really?
> Me: Yes, it's far too low down to brace the panel.
> Accuser: I see that you've clearly done some thinking about this. So where is the arm you used to brace the panel?
> Me: What arm?
> Accuser: You probably threw it overboard.
> Me: Of course we didn't! That's absurd! What are you talking about? We could have used an engine and thrown it overboard.
> Accuser: An engine? It's worse than I thought! No further questions, Your Honour.

I call up Gordon and ask him what's going on with the mystery hole in the solar-panel framing.

'You remember,' he says. 'When I put it on the first time it was tilting the wrong way for the northern hemisphere. I had the boys unscrew the panel, turn it 180 degrees, drill new holes and mount it the other way.'

Ahh, that's right. And it wouldn't be difficult to prove. The 'mystery' holes are the same diameter and distance in from the ends as the real ones, and the power cable from the panel now comes out the 'wrong' end, the one that's up in the air. It's clearly arse about face. I wish I had remembered that down at the marina — not that it would have made a scrap of difference.

The next day Rob and I go down to the Challenge office at the marina to pick up the protest document. Hang on a minute, it's huge! It's nearly 40 pages long! As well as affidavits from Goodman and Westlake there is some very dense material from a marine engineer about wind resistance and boat speed, and there's even a contribution from Rachel Brown about nutrition. They haven't been doing this from the pool bar at Port St Charles. During how much of the race were they putting it together? When did they give up on rowing? Was some of it even done before the race?

It's like a take-home exam. The hearing is scheduled for Thursday, so we have three days to prepare. The family sit on the porch at the villa and pass around bits of the document until we have read it all.

The main point of the convoluted document seems to be this: '. . . to increase their speed in the manner in which they did after 15 November by human effort alone is impossible.' So the claim is that we unbolted the solar panel and put it upright. They state unequivocally that before the race there weren't any washer-marks around the mystery holes, but at the end of the race there were, indicating that the holes were used during the race to brace the panel upright. They even claimed to have seen a photo of the side of our boat, taken from the support yacht a few days before the end of the race, in which the mystery hole was apparently not visible, leaving them to believe that 'a bolt was left in the hole when the photograph was taken'.

There are two other allegations as well: that we had periodically turned off the Inmarsat D+ unit at night to hide our inhuman speed, and that we hadn't capsized at all, but had thrown our life raft overboard to reduce weight.

Their protest submission ends in a breathtakingly cheeky section entitled 'Credibility'. Here the Dark Side invited the jury to consider our credibility, given that 'a Barbados newspaper' (name and date not supplied) had (mis)reported that after the capsize our boat had been upside down for several minutes, and that we had 'since admitted' to the race organisers that the boat did not capsize but instead had 'broached, causing [us] to go overboard.'

Those are different? Nautical semantics aside, from when we had first spoken to Lin while still at sea, up to the debriefing session at the marina, we had been consistent about what had happened. In any event, I loved the image of them questioning our credibility from the top of a pile of sandbags they had had to barge over the Atlantic as a penalty for being caught trying to sneak an underweight boat up to the start line.

Was there a chance that the people hearing the protest would give any of the accusations any weight? The protest document still managed to look like it had been put together by normal people — the typed pages were mostly in order, and there weren't too many spelling mistakes. Superficially it might look like a pavlova, but would the jurors look underneath the thin layer of icing sugar to find the steaming cowpat below?

It didn't matter that we knew we were innocent — how on earth could we *prove* it?

'Kev, I think you need to look at this,' Grant says.

Grant had arrived in Gomera with a new digital camera, and he had taken lots of photos of the boat before the race and at the start line. One of the photos was taken in the last couple of days before the start, when the boat was moored broadside on to the pier. Down in one corner of the photo is the solar panel. Grant pushes some buttons on the back of the camera and the photo zooms in, then zooms in again, and again. Now the 'mystery' hole is filling the screen, and around it is a halo of scratches. Washer marks. Faint but unmistakable, at the start line. I'll be damned, they *had* made up the stuff about there not being washer marks at the start!

It's a cool picture, and at the very least it reflected poorly on the Dark Side's powers of recollection, but it didn't alter the accusation — the mystery holes might still have been used during the race, or even if not, then some other way was used to go inhumanly fast.

So how fast is inhumanly fast? I look through the protest document carefully. They claim right at the start that '*HSC* dramatically increased their speed from 15th November'. So how fast was that? I check the document carefully. They never work it out. They just say that we did. That's strange. How can they prove we went inhumanly fast without working out how fast that is? I check again. Nope. Oh well, we'll just have to do their work for them.

The one stream of data no one can dispute is the information provided by the locked and sealed D+ units. During the race this information had been put on the official website. The data had even been provided in the Dark Side's submission, conveniently converted into 24-hour distances, daily speeds, and distance to go.

At 10am on November 15 the D+ units on the Dark Side and *Holiday Shoppe* both squawked up their positions. We were as far behind as we had ever been — 54 nautical miles. From then on we started to catch up. Twelve days later at 10am, we were about 30 miles in front. I did the maths — in those 12 days we rowed 822 nautical miles. Is that a lot to row in 12 days? Let's compare it with the 12 days prior to the catch-up.

'Grant, could you work out how far we travelled in the 12 days prior to the 15th?'

'Just a sec.' He taps away on his laptop. '819 nautical miles.'

'Are you sure?'

'Yep.'

I lean back from the computer. So we didn't row any faster! So much for the Big Push! So much for all those extra hours of rowing! But the numbers are clear — all that extra effort we put in was only enough to compensate for our deteriorating physical condition and some average performances in the small hours of the night. All we managed to do in the two weeks we were catching up was to maintain our speed. But if we didn't go any faster, how did we go past them?

'Can you do the same for the Dark Side? What did they do in the twelve days prior to the 15th of November?'

A few minutes later Grant says, '823 nautical miles.'

Yeah, that makes sense. In the first two weeks of November the lead stayed about the same — we rowed 819 nautical miles, and they rowed 823 nautical miles.

'So what distance did the Dark Side row in the twelve days when we were catching up?'

'742 nautical miles.'

'Are you serious?'

'I'll check.' And he did. We all did. We all got the same answer. For the 12 days before November 12 the two boats rowed nearly the same distance. In the next 12 days we continued to row the same speed while the Dark Side rowed some 80 nautical miles less.

They had slowed down.

For the last month we had plugged along at the same average speed, while the Dark Side fell away. We were the tortoise to their hare. Despite their claims to the contrary, there was no inhuman speed.

So why did they slow down?

I did some more numbers about how we overtook them. There was one day, a week before the end of the race, when we made up that enormous 20 miles, nearly half the lead, in just 24 hours. It was day 33, the worst of the days we were rowing into headwinds.

'Are they any clues in their submission about what happened to them on Day 33? Why they went so slow?'

My sister Sharon looks up from her chair. 'It says here that they had their sea anchor out.'

'Really? Where does it say that?'

'Right here.'

She shows me. In Westlake's submission he sets out the five different shift patterns that they rowed. But then he goes on to say, 'Twice during the race, namely days 2 and 32, we spent time on sea anchor due to weather conditions. During this time we were not rowing in any of the above shifts.'

If they were counting days by elapsed time, then day 32 would be our day 33. Surely he doesn't mean they spent all day on the sea anchor? But regardless, while they were resting with their sea anchor out, we kept functioning — we kept rowing into the headwinds, gaining mile after mile. You can't sail into a headwind. We had made by far our biggest gain in conditions when any kind of sail — solar panel or otherwise — would have been useless.

So why hadn't they tried to show that we went faster? It isn't like they didn't have the position data — it's all in their submission. Were they so convinced they didn't slow down that they just assumed we must have been going faster?

No, that can't be the whole story either. They might have been that confident before the strong headwinds arrived on day 33. In fact, that probably explains why they put their sea anchor out for so long on that day — they had convinced themselves that we had been sailing; now, with the headwinds, any sail would be useless, so they could afford to have a rest.

But then the next day they get out of bed, get the position report and find out that their lead has evaporated. They realise that we hadn't been sailing — because while they have been sleeping we have kept on rowing into the headwinds and caught up. It must have been devastating for them.

But then they row to the finish and claim we used a sail anyway.

Why would they do that? Why would they claim that we went faster without even attempting to prove it? Did their mountainous self-belief cloud their judgement or is there some other, darker motive?

The phone at the villa rings. Grant answers, then hands it to me.

'It's Radio Sport — they want to talk to you.'

I am so naive.

Over the next few days Rob, Jamie and I take call after call from radio stations, newspapers and TV, all of them wanting to know what's going on. I don't know what to say, I don't know what we are allowed to say. Are we allowed to discuss the facts of the case in public before the hearing? I try to say that protests are part of boat racing — it's just like the recent Louis Vuitton Cup, when it seemed like half the races ended in the protest room. Protests are just part of boat races. I even believe it. Until it occurs to me that the protests that happen at the end of America's Cup races are nothing like this. This isn't about judging whether or not a boat had right of way — they are saying that we cheated. I am getting sick of saying, 'No, we didn't cheat.' We didn't. We shouldn't have to say it.

I am genuinely surprised that the reporters don't really care about what happened out there. When I try to quote figures and distances they cut me off — it doesn't fit within their sound bites. Their approach is, 'You've been accused of cheating. How do you feel about that? Oh, and by the way — did you cheat?'

Somehow I thought the media was about reporters digging for the truth. But now I find out that, at least in the mainstream daily media, there's no time for that. If someone makes an accusation, that's a story. If it's a really inflammatory accusation and you can get a good emotional response from the other side, then that's a better story. It doesn't matter if the accusation is entirely baseless. If it turns out to be false that will be another story — a much smaller story, because it doesn't sell as many papers.

The irony is that we are being accused of cheating by a team that had been caught trying to sneak an underweight boat into the race. I try and mention that in some of the interviews, but somehow it falls flat. It's like it doesn't address the point. It sounds tit for tat, or as if we are trying to throw people off the scent. Besides, it isn't a good story — it's not 'Mate versus Mate'; it's not 'Victory Snatched!' They want sound bites and emotion. All we can say is that we are looking forward to the protest hearing, and as soon as we get ten minutes in front of the judge all this will be sorted out.

Disturbingly, some of the reporters hint that they have known for a while that a story is brewing. They mention that they received an email in the middle of November. No, they won't tell me who it was from. No, they won't forward it. They are obliged to protect their sources.

Meanwhile, back in New Zealand a battle is being won for hearts and minds and we are losing. Their lawyer/spokesperson Michael Smyth is everywhere — on the radio and TV — pumping out the same message about how fast we caught up, how uncanny it was.

Rob is even angrier than I am. 'This has nothing to do with you and Jamie, this is about them attacking me,' he keeps saying.

I'd much rather not be in the position of having to defend myself, but in a perverse way I am glad to have a driving sense of purpose again — a new race to win.

I arrive late at the team house on the morning of the hearing. Rob is sitting on the porch waiting for me.

'Don't worry about it,' he says. 'It's been postponed.'

'Why?'

'Challenge Business have been running around trying to find some rules to hold the hearing under. It turns out that under international yacht-racing rules all boats have to be in before the protest hearing can take place.'

'But that could be months!'

'Yeah, it will be.'

'Bugger.'

Later in the day we start to get calls from the media asking us which other boats are joining the Dark Side in their protest. We ask them what they are talking about, and one of the reporters forwards a press release the Dark Side have just issued through their lawyer. I read it a dozen times. It's breathtaking. What starts out as spin on the facts ends in a wild skid.

'We are led to believe by race organisers their reason for the postponement is other crews presently racing may wish to lodge a protest against *Holiday Shoppe* . . . we are pleased other crews are lending their support.'

We call up Teresa, who exclaims, 'That's not what I said!' So Rob and I draft our own press release in response, clear it with Teresa, and send it out to the reporters. It takes hours, it's time-consuming and frustrating. When it comes to manipulation of the media we have a lot to learn. I don't have a clue how to fight this dirty.

The only upside of this peculiar little incident is that the Dark Side have lost credibility with Teresa. But they don't need her anymore — the protest has been lodged successfully and the process is now in place.

On the way home we don't actually start flying Qantas until we get to LA. When we board the jumbo the attractive hostess leads us left, up towards the front, then she keeps on walking. It turns out that on that particular flight they also do Business Class service in First Class seats. The look on Jamie's face is like he has just seen a tanker of Waikato Draught break down in front of his house.

We arrive at Auckland airport early in the morning. Anna and the Holiday Shoppe team have taken over the Arrivals area and there is a sea of people cheering and waving in yellow Holiday Shoppe t-shirts. Some of them are making a welcome guard of honour with oars. Friends and family are there. Dad's there. A tearful Mum's there.

When all the hugs have been given and our innocence has been protested once again for TV and radio, I see Hot Polish Girl standing quietly at the back. She has driven up from Tauranga to surprise me. I hold her in my arms for a long time and it is like the rest of the crowd has disappeared. Then I put something in her hand. It's the St Christopher. 'Thanks. It worked,' I tell her.

'Nice abs,' she says.

CHAPTER TWENTY SEVEN
The summer of protest

A friendly journo lets slip that it was Steph Brown who had sent the shrill emails to the media while the race was still on.

When the Dark Side arrive back in Auckland a few days after us the TV3 reporter asks them if they think their actions have taken the shine off our win. Goodman's response is, 'They have done that themselves — we never went public with it . . . we would have thought that you'd keep it out of the media . . . and they went public with it.'

At first I am astonished, then I am laughing. It's hard not to admire their balls. Didn't they go to the media first? Hadn't Emma Keeling told us that she had heard from them the day after we arrived that there was going to be a protest? Not to mention the emails that Steph had sent to radio, TV and newspapers before we had even finished the race. If Emma had been doing the interview at the airport I am sure she would have called them on it, but she was on holiday in the US. Are they very smart or very lucky?

A few days later, as I wait in the green room before doing an interview with SKY Sport, the presenter admits, 'I have to be honest with you. I think they have something. I can't see how you caught up so fast. I don't know how you can convince me.'

I sigh. 'Give me two minutes. I bet I can.'

The Don is agitated. He brushes invisible crumbs off the crisp white tablecloth. We are having lunch so I can tell him the story and ask his advice. But as soon as the plates are taken away he raises a heavily ringed hand to cut me off.

'You overestimate these people and underestimate everyone else. How do you think their actions come across to the public? Of course their protest will be thrown out. But here's the thing. You mustn't stop there. You need to overturn every single one of their accusations, right down to the pettiest. Use their weapon against them — get *them* found guilty of bringing a malicious complaint and wasting everyone's time. For you the race is on again. This time the stakes are even higher.'

So Rob and I start adding to the brief written submission we had put together in Barbados. I am determined not to let it spoil my summer. I have overseas friends to show around New Zealand, Sharon is coming back from the UK to get married, and then I have another wedding to go to, in Pakistan. I call up Jamie.

'I don't think I'm going to be able to make it down to Whiritoa for a while.'

'Don't worry, mate; the crays will just get fatter.'

Jamie has his own problems. He arrived back to find his car had been stolen, and he is now training for the Coast to Coast multisport event. I don't want to drag him into this; it isn't really his fight. He is happy to help out, but this isn't what he signed up for.

So in a chalet in Mt Cook National Park, in a hotel room in Karachi, and in a castle in Dunedin I put together our written response. I check and recheck the numbers. They show that there was nothing unnatural about our speed during the race — not just when we were catching up, but any speed — peak speed, day speed or night speed, or average speed at any time in the race.

Rob is also preparing documents for the final arbitration wrapping up the 2001 dispute.

'How's it going?' I ask one day.

'Slow.'

'Don't worry, mate, you're nearly there. It'll all be over soon.'

We have realised that trying to present our side to the media isn't very effective when they are far more interested in creating a controversy, so we are now declining interviews. The Dark Side are not being so shy. In mid-December there is an article in the *New Zealand Herald* headed 'Money clash lurks behind rowers' feud'. It makes the connection between the 2001 race and the current protest. I am particularly struck by a couple of hypnotically self-assured Westlake quotes:

'The big thing with Matt and I being policemen is that we are professional enough to know we are out there to do the race, and to do it with integrity . . .'

'I know Jamie from New Zealand rowing and I must say I [am] very disappointed.'

It could be worse — we could still be rowing. All through December and into January the boats trickle in. Strong headwinds and currents have meant several were cruelly blown back just as they reached Barbados, and they had to be towed around the north of the island. *Per Ardua*, the RAF boat, is the second to last to arrive, coming in on January 2, after 78 days. Then finally, on January 18, 2004, 94 days after starting out, the French boat *Madine Meuse Lorraine*, with the Challenge crew-member Jeremy Hinton on board, rows in to Port St Charles.

Not long after this Teresa sends me an email saying that the protest hearing will be held in the Woodvale offices in Southampton on January 27. Contrary to the Dark Side's press release, no other crew has expressed any interest in joining the protest. The panel will meet and consider the protest document and our response, and we are to be available by phone. But by happy coincidence Sharon is having an encore wedding reception for English family and friends in London that week, so I decide to go over in person. Soon after I learn that Westlake is going as well.

It's late at night on the day before the written submission is due to be sent in. There is just one thing missing. The Dark Side claim that when the support yacht went past us a few days before the finish a photo was taken that showed the mystery hole in the solar panel frame blocked over, demonstrating that we had carelessly left a restraining bolt in there. They say they found this when they went through the photos with Teresa in Barbados, although they neglected to supply the photo in their submission.

It is such a minor nonsense that I haven't considered it until now. I assumed that if the hole looked blocked it was because the shot was taken too far away, or because of sun glare or something. But to finish off the report I email Teresa and ask her to send the photo over.

Finally, at midnight, the photo comes through. It takes a long time as the file size is very large; Teresa is sending it in full resolution.

The photo comes up on the screen. I look at it. There is the boat, side on, and there is the hole right there where it should be, not filled in at all. Damn, it must be the wrong photo.

I call Teresa.

'I think you've sent me the wrong photo, you can see the hole on this one. Is there another one?'

'Kevin, there are plenty of photos, they looked through all of them, but this is definitely the one. In any case, I've just gone through them all — they all show the hole.'

'Are you sure?'

'I'm sure. This is the photo they saw.'

This photo shows a hole. They say it doesn't. I am getting a cold, prickly feeling again.

Teresa said they looked at all the photographs. Their submission also refers to viewing multiple photos. So even if they had found a photo that didn't show a hole, they have seen other photos that do. But they still say there was no hole. I don't understand.

It bothers me deeply. They have made plenty of other false claims. But the rest of them are slightly more difficult to refute — it takes a few minutes to go through the numbers about the speed claims, so it is just possible that they were lazy and had not done the maths. Maybe they really thought that they hadn't seen washer marks before the race. Maybe they forgot that they had gone to the media first. Maybe Steph didn't tell them she had been pestering the media for weeks. Maybe they thought that, even though we were only a handful of miles away, we didn't have headwinds the day they sat on sea anchor and we gained 20 nautical miles on them. Maybe there is a reasonable explanation for why their boat lost about 5% of its weight on the way over to the start line. Maybe they hadn't been orchestrating a smear campaign against us. Maybe they genuinely believe they are right and are just naturally talkative.

But even wearing my rosiest-coloured glasses, and giving them every possible benefit of the doubt, I can't find a way out for them on this one. They saw there was a hole. They kept seeing photos that showed a hole, then they said they saw a photo that showed there was no hole.

It is now 3am. I call Rob.

'Rob, they're up to something. They're going to pull a stunt at the protest hearing.'

CHAPTER TWENTY EIGHT

The protest hearing

A few days later I walk into the meeting room at the Woodvale building in Southampton. There are five people seated behind a long table. Teresa introduces them: the Chair, Penny Carter, 'a very respected international juror' who has chaired sailing protest hearings 'at the highest level'; Phil Morrison, the boat-builder who actually designed the Atlantic-class rowboats; John Searson, a meteorologist who also competed in the '97 race; Nick Fenner, an around-the-world sailor, solicitor and specialist in marine law; and finally there is Matthew Ratsey, technical director of Challenge Business. Teresa is sitting in as well. Wow, they have all the bases covered.

The format is very simple. There are no lawyers, the jurors have read our written submissions. We are here to make verbal presentations — the Dark Side first, us second. The panel will ask us questions. Jamie and Rob are waiting in Hamilton to take calls if any of the panel want to talk to them. Then the panel will make up their mind, and we will either be vindicated or we will go join the Foreign Legion.

'Any questions?' Penny Carter asks.

I take this opportunity to suggest that the hearing could be a lot shorter if we just look at the original claims that appear in the official protest (that of 'inhuman speed') and not all the lesser distracting claims, which of course we are happy to address. The Chair tells me that we are going to be examining absolutely every claim regardless of when or how it was made, thank you very much Mr Biggar.

Westlake goes first. I hold my breath. This is it. But within a minute or two I am breathing again. He is going to stick to the script and follow their written submission. He even brings up the photo, the one taken from the yacht that is supposed not to show the mystery hole. I suggest that we put it on the screen so the panel can see it for themselves.

Teresa puts it up. They look at the photo, then look at me, baffled. Westlake suggests that it may be the wrong photo. Teresa suggests that it isn't, and that all the other photos also show the hole. The panel look at Westlake, now even more baffled. He continues, however, and after about an hour he finishes.

After a short break it's my turn. In my introduction I tell the panel that we are quickly, fully and comprehensively going to dispatch all of the accusations against us, and then focus on the real issue, which is the Dark Side's malicious hijacking of the protest process by making completely unsubstantiated claims in an attempt to discredit our ... at this point the Chair cuts me off, saying that we certainly won't be doing that as it is outside the scope of this hearing. She suggests that I should confine my commentary to rebutting the specific accusations against us.

So I begin with our defence against the 'inhuman speed' claim. A few minutes into the presentation Westlake's laptop beeps. A few minutes later his phone rings. When the third electronic interruption comes some of the panel are looking amused while others are looking annoyed. I make a quip that if this was Wimbledon it might be grounds for a professional foul. But Westlake could walk around the room dressed as a morris dancer and playing a tuba and it wouldn't change anything. The panel isn't having to concentrate too hard to get this stuff.

I show them a little scale model I have made of the solar panel, and demonstrate how correcting its original mismounting created the mystery hole. I tell them about flushing our ballast tank, about the capsize and losing the life raft. They ask some good questions. After about an hour it's all over. We break for lunch. By the time we come back they are already drafting up their conclusions.

TVNZ's UK correspondent has arrived with a cameraman and I'm chatting with them when we are asked to return to the boardroom for the delivery of the verdict.

The Chair reads it out:

> The evidence does not show that the Holiday Shoppe Challenge used their solar panel for improper purposes.
>
> The accidental loss of the life raft and other fundamental equipment, although demonstrating a serious lack of seamanship, is not in breach of the Class Rules. The loss of the life raft did not afford a sufficiently material advantage over the last two days of the race to affect the result.
>
> With regard to the water ballast there is insufficient evidence that this Class Rule is infringed.
>
> Boat speed — The panel has concluded that the speed differential between the boats towards the end of the Race is consistent with the rest of the Race and therefore can be explained in a number of ways, for example: changes in the rowing pattern, use of the sea anchor, the steering mechanism, success in surfing the waves and the physical and physiological condition of the crews.
>
> The protest is not upheld and the Holiday Shoppe Challenge is confirmed as the winner of the Woodvale Atlantic Rowing Race 2003.

So that's it. We've won. The panel sombrely shake our hands and leave. Westlake and I are left to pack up our documents. There are just the two of us in the room. If I want to say something, now is the time. I say nothing.

Westlake appears on the TV3 news that night and says, 'The only people who really know what happened are Kevin and Jamie, and Rob Hamill, being involved in the team. They've got to look to themselves.'

He tells TVNZ, 'I don't hold anything against them personally

— much the same with people you end up arresting. It's a process you go through, sometimes you win and sometimes you lose.'

Meanwhile the TV crew offer me a lift in their car back to London. By the time we arrive it's night and the adrenaline has worn off. I'm beat. They drop me off somewhere near Earls Court, and I make my own way to Grant's house.

The adventure is finally over. What started two years ago with me sitting on a sofa in Howick watching TV now ends on the other side of the world with a walk through empty streets, my hard soles echoing on the damp cobblestones.

EPILOGUE

Wow, that's a long time on such a little boat!
So what did you do for exercise?'
— comment made to Jamie in a bar

I am living in a leafy cul-de-sac in Howick, a beautiful, sleepy suburb that rolls down to the sparkling waters of the Hauraki Gulf.

Yes, in the end Mum had her own 'I told you so' moment — I am broke, jobless and still living at home with her. But now I have taken down the posters of George Michael and packed away the stuffed toys.

I'm back in my old life, but some things are different. Difficult jobs are still difficult, but that's not an excuse for not doing them anymore. I know now that if I keep chipping away at them I will get there in the end, even if at first it seems hopeless. Even if it is tidying my room. Even if it takes almost twenty minutes.

I start to go running. I'm not very good at first but the runs get longer and longer. Now nothing seems too long. The sound of a storm outside my window makes me smile. I get grumpy less easily.

It takes a long time to get back to normal. It's a long time before day and night start to be different things again and I stop being wide awake in the middle of the night or sleepy in the afternoon. There are some things I don't want to return to normal — I want to keep the feeling of gratitude I now have for the simplest things in life, like dryness, and stability. When I find myself thinking crazy, ambitious ideas now I can't just dismiss them. I have to take myself seriously, and so the world seems to be brimming with possibility.

Soon after arriving back from the Canaries I go down to Tauranga to visit Magda, the Hot Polish Girl. We go to a restaurant and I order a big side of broccoli. I have been craving fresh vegetables since I got back on land. I don't know what they did to that broccoli but it is the most delicious green thing I have ever tasted. Magda laughs at the look of delight on my face. She calls it my Broccoli Face. I'm seeing a lot of Magda at the moment. Magda is seeing a lot of Broccoli Face.

Three days after the protest hearing in the UK Rob received the final ruling from the arbitrator in his own long-running dispute with the Dark Side. The arbitrator decided in favour of Rob in all of the points under dispute. He agrees that the Westlake team have been playing silly buggers with the equipment, saying that they had 'at times, unintentionally or otherwise, misled Mr Hamill as to the whereabouts and nature of disposition of some items'. He orders them to pay for the equipment not returned, and eventually orders them to pay Rob's legal costs.

Jamie, Rob and I finally get the weekend at Whiritoa. As soon as I open the car door and take in a lungful of the tingling sea air I feel like I know the place already. It is just as Jamie described it — a house under the giant pohutukawa trees just back from the beach. We drink around the fire, and swim in the surf, but it's too rough to go diving. The crays are still there getting fatter.

Jamie spends some months working for the University of Waikato, giving speeches at high schools around New Zealand to encourage senior students to mix education with sport. Near the end of the year he gets a place on the National Bank graduate scheme and moves up to Auckland, so we decide to get a flat together. Sometimes, to wake him up in the morning I open his door and shout out 'Six minutes!' Ho ho! Sometimes when we are out of food we open a freeze-dry for old time's sake.

Life moved on for everyone. Rachel Hamill who, unknown to her, was pregnant when she was in the Canaries, came back and had baby Declan. Rob and Rachel moved out of Hamilton onto a little block in the country where Rob can drink unfluoridated water and they can make their own compost, raise hens, and grow organic vegetables and young boys. Rob is now working on a new trans-Tasman rowing race — you can read about it on *www.bridgetobridge.co.nz*.

Back in the Canaries, after years of litigation, Chris finally won his court battle regarding Sky Park. He was last seen in the Mediterranean on a newly bought 18-metre yacht, with Grace and Tayla on board.

Gordon at the boatyard began to focus on making kayaks, with the Barracuda brand, and soon began cranking them out as fast as he could from the old shed in Silverdale. Jon Ackland went on to become the performance coach for the America's Cup challenge.

Our boat, *Holiday Shoppe Challenge*, was repainted and rebranded as *Sun Latte* and sent across the ocean again with another New Zealand crew, Tara Remington and Ian Rudkin. Their passage was difficult and they were hit with a series of storms. After 46 days at sea, during which they were attacked by a shark, and with a leak in the hull, they were capsized by a large wave and finally made the decision to abandon ship for the life raft. The support yacht eventually arrived and they were rescued, but before our boat could be scuttled the yacht was called away.

We all expected the boat to disappear quickly under the waves, but the next day when I logged on to the internet it was still there, its beacon chirping away. I suppose because it knew the way it soon shook off this little setback and started galloping towards the finish line. Each day for some weeks it made around 30 miles to the finish. It started to get so close to the Carribean that Rob and I were talking about hiring a boat to go out and salvage it. But then one morning there was no report, and I figured that at some time in the night our plucky rowboat had finally succumbed to the Atlantic.

Then some time later we received word from the race organisers that the boat had finally made it over to the other side and washed up in Guadeloupe. I like to think that some fisherman got a big surprise when he saw it nosing into the harbour one morning, and it is now his pride and joy.

Jamie calls. He has been asked to give a little talk about the race to a Probus group in Pauanui, but he can't make it. He asks me if I'll speak in his place.

'Sure. What's Probus?'

'It's like Rotary for old people.'

So a few days later the Starlet and I are winding down through the Coromandel Ranges to Pauanui, a little patch of pleasant suburbia by the sea. A little while later I look up from the lectern and see a large room full of grey hair and smiling, wrinkled faces. It occurs to me that I am younger than most of these people by about forty years. I start the talk.

'So my story begins when I was 32 and my life was nearly over, so ...'

I have to stop because a hundred faces have just broken into gales of laughter. Some of them are actually doubled over and gasping for air.

What have I said? Then I realise and, at long last, I can laugh too.

Jamie and I are sitting on the couch at the flat, watching TV.

'You know, mate, we don't want to stop after doing just one thing.'

'What are you thinking?'

'Walking to the South Pole.'

'Yeah? Sounds good. Let's do it!'

ACKNOWLEDGEMENTS

There are many, many people who behind the scenes made a vital contribution to this rowing adventure. They each formed a link in an unbroken chain of hands pulling me off the couch in Howick to pushing off the boat in the Canaries. Every single one of them was essential, from the people whose belief in us led them to provide funding of tens of thousands of dollars, to people who came out and banged away on the boat for a couple of hours. I am indebted to all of them and we would like you to know who they are.

Certainly none of this would have happened if it hadn't been for Rob Hamill — without his utterly groundless belief in my abilities, his endless encouragement, expertise, personal financial contribution and indomitable courage in the face of insurmountable obstacles I would never have made it.

A special thank you to the late Sir Edmund Hillary and Lady June for their patronage of our campaign, generous donations, and wonderful hospitality at some inspirational morning teas. Kaye Parker of Cure Kids, and the Cure Kids kids for keeping all our troubles in perspective. Jon Ackland for his table-thumping coaching sessions. Wheldon Hobson for putting the last piece of the puzzle in place. And of course Mum, for her lifetime of encouragement and unselfishness, and her extraordinary patience.

A big thank you for the energy and enthusiasm of the Holiday Shoppe head office, specifically Digby Lawley, Anna Rennie, Matti Koopman and Natalie Jones, and all the Holiday Shoppe shops for getting in behind with their support — thanks for believing in us! Absolutely pivotal behind the scenes was Mark Jennings from TV3, without whose vision and personal commitment we wouldn't have got there. Thanks to Paul Wilkes, who helped us get the sponsorship deal over the line. Also to Robin Murray and Ken Williamson from Scottwood Group, who provided vital funding support. Also Bryan Gould, Stephen Knightley and Debbie Stevens from the University of Waikato.

Thanks to Scott for being such a big part of the campaign — we went through so much, it's a shame it didn't work out.

A pillar behind the scenes was John Street from Fosters Ship Chandlery — thank you to you and your staff for your amazing generosity and helpfulness.

We also owe a debt to Bill Speedy and Alister Wishart from Ocean Bridge for efficiently organising the transport of our precious cargo, and Bernard Vidal at Marfet, for helping with our freight dilemmas! Thank you to Kelvin Ricketts from Regency Duty Free for being a stalwart supporter again — without his help there would be no record of our adventure.

Ross Munro and Greg Flynn from Line 7 for their fabulous custom-made clothing and wet-weather gear, and their wise advice behind the scenes. Rob McGregor from New World Victoria Park for feeding us at sea. Peter Maire from Navman for their wonderful unit which we watched almost continuously for six weeks.

Accor hotels for generously providing the venue for our Cure Kids fundraiser.

Patrick Geals of NZMP for providing a range of products, especially the extraordinary Endurance Bar, as well as financial assistance.

Ron Brown from Altex, for being our very first sponsor and providing a really sound painting system. Weaver Marine, for the exceptionally watertight hatches that saved us on more than one occasion. Andy O'Sullivan from DME for the Roho seats that really saved our arses!

Chris Needham, John Oates and Richard O'Flaherty at TransCold who went to such great lengths to try to keep us cool.

Shamus and Sue Fairhall from SSC, who came up with the incredible and imaginative boat–body interfaces that played such a vital role in our comfort. If I'm smiling in the photos at the end it's because of them!

Mike Weeks at HCB Technologies for the batteries. Paul Sands at Reid Technology for their solar panel expertise, and Lloyd Klee from Safety at Sea. Roger Tweddell for the antiskid. Terry Hendrickson from Trailcom. Andrew Perring and Johaniek Sulzberger from Tech Rentals (now Bearcom) for the communications solution that gave us a link to the outside world and kept us sane.

John Roberts at RFD for his support with the watermaker. Peter Loeffen at Rowpro for his awesome software, which made the million-metre row work! Gary Reid from Concept2 for lending us the rowing machines for our indoor rowing record attempt. Terry Daniell for keeping the books straight. Dean Geddes for writing a prescription for a pie a day!

The Unitec boat-building class of 2002, ably led by Rob Shaw, Chris Lovegrove and Paul Donahoe, for building such a fast, strong boat! Gordon Robinson, Charles, Steve and Dan from GR8 concepts — thanks for the memories (just kidding — you did an awesome job). Barry Young for his advice about safety on the boat. Geoff Chao for helping with the deck tread.

Chris, Anna, Kiwi Anna, Grace and Tayla, Alfredo, Pedro and all the helpers at Tenerife for your kindness and hospitality.

Drs Geoff Leyland and Andy Philpott from Stochastic Optimization for their cunning and innovative routing advice and exceptional support in crunching the numbers for the protest rebuttal. Robert and Donna Ward from Beacon Hill Villas, Barbados. Debra and David Cossey for their tremendous help in Barbados.

Paul and Sharon Hollis who hosted us at Float, a unique venue at a sensational location. Sue Hamill for her magnetic help. Iain Thain from Phillips Fox. The staff at the Centre for Sport and Exercise Science at the Waikato Institute of Technology for their wisdom and expertise —

especially the round-the-clock supervision of our heat chamber rows — that was above the call of duty, and thanks to Andrea Brakkhuis for coming up and helping with the food packing. Gordon Chesterman and Michael Wall for your advice. Travis Field for his contacts in the business world.

Ross Biggar for all the support and boat-haulage duties at awkward hours. Sally Major at the Auckland office of BCG for her fantastic admin services, and Perry Keenan for his spine-stiffening advice. Joanne Daniell and Richard Swan who put together the logo. Paul Taylor for giving back the rights to my life story, which I lost to him in a poker game all those years ago

John, Sharon, Grant and Alexa, Biddy, Kate and Hamish for making the effort to come out to Barbados — it was much appreciated and made it very special. Charlotte Dawson and the panel of *How's Life* for their shrewd insight into the male mind. Gizzy Girls for their inspirational messages. Grant Biggar for his generosity in Barbados and London. Rachel, Finlay and Declan Hamill for their staunch defence of the campaign. Sir Chay Blyth for creating the world's toughest rowing race. To our parents for letting us go, and all our friends all over New Zealand and around the world who supported us in this incredible journey!

John McCrystal for suggesting I get the book published, and Jenny Hellen, Karen Ferns, Sarah Ell and the rest of the Random House team for making the process so enjoyable.

And, of course, the biggest thanks go to Jamie, who came out of nowhere and ended up being the best possible person to row an ocean with and a top bloke besides. But mate — we can't have just two books on the coffee table. Let's make it three in a row!

For more information, photos and video clips go to
www.kevinbiggar.com